BUSINESS STUDENT GUIDE
How To Make A's In Business Courses

Norma Carr-Ruffino, Ph.D.
San Francisco State University

PEARSON
Custom Publishing

Cover art by Glenn Kremer.

Printed in the United States of America

10 9 8 7 6 5 4 3 2

ISBN 0-536-21243-0

2006160174

CS

Please visit our web site at *www.pearsoncustom.com*

PEARSON CUSTOM PUBLISHING
75 Arlington Street, Suite 300, Boston, MA 02116
A Pearson Education Company

Contents

Alphabetic Index of Symbols Used in Evaluating Papers

~~Word~~ = Delete this

✓ = Good point (relevant, interesting)

word (or cap) = Capitalize

Word (or lc) = Use lower case; don't capitalize

— Use dash properly 6.6.6.2

- Hyphenate, compound adjective 6.2.6.4

Do not hyphenate 6.2.6.4

(Word) (or mis) = misspelled; see Dictionary

acc   Be accurate 6.2.3

Ad hom Personal attack 6.5.6

ag   Need agreement-subject/verb 6.2.5
          Need agreement pronoun/noun 6.2.2.2-3

art   Use correct article (*a,an,the*) 6.2.1.7

Bandw   Bandwagon technique 6.5.5

BegQ   Begs the question, circular reasoning 6.5.8

Bias   Personal bias 6.5.10.

cl   Clarity isneeded here 6.2.3

comp   Use comparatives correctly 6.2.3.5

conc   Be concise 6.2.2

cons   Be consistent here

cons-s/pl Be consistent in singular/plural 6.2.4.3, 6.2.5.1

cons-vo Be consistent in voice (person) 6.3.5.9

contr   Use contractions properly 6.2.4.5

d neg   Double negative 6.3.3.7

dm   Dangling modifier 6.3.3.4

doc-dt Out of date 2.3.2.9

doc-f   Doc. Form incorrect 2.5.7

doc-none Paper lacks doc. 2.5.7

doc-so Weak source(s) 2.3.2

ds   Double space this

exp   Expand on this idea/topic

expl   Explain term/idea 6.4.2.5

FA   False analogy 6.5.4

fig   Use figure form for number 6.7

flow   See *Tr-flow* below

Gen   Hasty generalization 6.5.2

hang   Paper needs to "hang together" 6.4.4

hdg   Use headings 2.5.3

hdg-f   Heading format/level needs work 2.5.3.2.-6

hdg-sp Use specific wording in heading 2.4.1.9

inc   Incomplete info 6.2.3.2

incoh   Incoherent; rewrite; get help

intro   Need introductory paragraph or sentence(s) 6.4.4

intro-hdgs Insert introduction between headings 6.4.4.6

item   Itemize, bullet or number 6.4.3.5.4

jarg   Avoid jargon 6.2.3.5

mis   Misuse of the word 6.2.4, Dictionary

mis-no. Misuse of *number/amount* or *few/less* 6.2.3.7.

mod   Use a better modifier 6.2.3

mod-pl Place modifier by word(s) modified 6.3.3.3

Non seq Non sequitar 6.5.3

obv   Obvious, no need to state

om   Needed word(s) omitted

org   Organization needs work 2.4, 6.4.2

out-f   Outline format needs work 2.4.3

over   Overuse of word 6.2.1.4

pc   Need parallel construction 6.3.6

pc-hdgs Use pc for headings 2.5.3.4.2, 6.3.6.4

pc-items Use pc in bulleted, numbered items 6.3.6.4

P-concl Paragraph needs concluding sentence(s) 6.4.1.3

P-cr   Paragraph too crowded with topics 6.4.1.4

Pers   Personification 6.5.1

P-lg   Paragraph too long 6.4.3.5

P-lim   Limit paragraph to one topic 6.4.1.4

Pol   Polarization 6.5.9

P-org   Reorganize paragraph 6.4.2

pos   Try positive approach 6.3.7.8

poss   Use possessives properly 6.6.5.2

Post hoc Correlation is not cause 6.5.7

prep   Use correct preposition 6.3.2.3

pro-ag Pronouns must agree w/antecedent noun in
          number and gender and be consistent. 6.2.4.3

pro-case Pronoun, use the right case 6.2.4.2

pro-cl Unclear who/what pronoun refers to 6.2.4.1

pro-mis Misuse *that/which/who* 6.2.4.7, 6.3.2.4

pro-poss Incorrect use of possessive pronoun 6.2.2.2.3

pro-self Incorrect use of *self* pronoun 6.2.4.10

pro-sexist Use pronouns in non-sexist way 6.2.4.11

P-top   Paragraph needs topic sentence 6.4.1.1

Pu   Punctuation incorrect 6.6

Quo   Handle quotes properly 2.5.2.5-9, 6.6.4

Quo?   Is this a quote? 2.5.2.5-9, 6.6.4

Ratl   Rationalization 6.5.11

rel   Make this relevant or omit 6.4.3.3

rep   Repetitive or redundant 6.2.3

s/pl   Incorrect use of singular/plural; see Dictionary

sl   Avoid slang 6.2.3.5; see Dictionary

sp o   Spell out this word 6.2.4.3, 6.7

spec   Use specific word(s) 6.2.3.3

ss   Improve sentence structure 6.3

ss-awk Awkward sentence 6.3.5.9

ss-cr   Sentence too crowded w/ideas 6.3.4.7

ss-c/s 2 sentences joined, comma splice 6.3.5.3

ss-fu   2 sentences fused 6.3.5.2

ss-inc Incomplete sentence 6.3.1.1, 6.3.5.5

ss-lg   Too long 6.3.4

s sp   Single space this

ss-ro   Sentence runs on, rambles 6.3.5.4

ss-vary Vary sentence structure 6.3.4.2

Subj   Too subjective 6.5.12

t/g   Use table/graph 2.5.4

t/g-d   Discuss data from *t*/g 2.5.4.8

t/g-i   Introduce *t*/g properly 2.5.4.7

t/g-p   Place *t*/g properly 2.5.4.5-6

tech   Too technical 6.2.3.4, 6.2.4.11

tr-flow Improve transition, flow 6.4.4

tr-P   Need transitional paragraph 6.4.4

tr-sent Need transitional sentence(s) 6.4.4

tr-wd   Need transitional word(s) 6.4.4

v-act   Use active verb(s) 6.2.5.6

v-cons Use consistent tense 6.2.5.3

v-no   Use proper singular/plural 6.2.2.3, 6.2.5.1, Dic.

voice   Use another voice (person) 6.3.5.10

v-spec Use specific verb(s) 6.2.5.5

v-str   Use stronger verb(s) 6.2.5.7

v-t   Use proper verb tense or form 6.2.5.2,see Dic.

wd div Divide word properly, see Dictionary

Symbols to Use in Evaluating Papers

GENERAL

~~Word~~ = Delete this

✓ = Good point

word (or cap) = Capitalize

W̲ord (or *lc*) = Use lower case

(Word) (or *mis*) = misspelled

acc Be accurate 6.2.3
cl Clarity isneeded here 6.2.3
conc Be concise 6.2.2
exp Expand on this idea/topic
expl Explain this 6.4.2.5
inc Incomplete info 6.2.3.2
incoh Incoherent
pos Try positive approach 6.3.7.8
obv Obvious, no need to state
om Needed word(s) omitted
rel Make this relevant or omit 6.4.3.3

DOCUMENTATION

doc-dt Out of date 2.3.2.9
doc-f Form incorrect 2.5.7
doc-none Paper lacks doc. 2.5.7
doc-so Weak source(s) 2.3.2, 2.5.2.5-9, 6.6.4
quo Handle quotes properly 2.5.2.5, 6.6.4
quo? Is this a quote? 2.5.2.5, 6.6.4

GRAMMAR, GENERAL

ag Need agreement-subject/verb 6.2.5
        pronoun/noun 6.2.2.2-3
cons Be consistent here
cons-s/pl Be consistent in use of singular/plural
        6.2.4.3, 6.2.5.1
cons-vo Be consistent in voice (person) 6.3.5.9
d neg Double negative 6.3.3.7
prep Use correct preposition 6.3.2.3
poss See possessives 6.6.5.2
s/pl Incorrect use of singular/plural, see Dictionary
voice Use another voice (person) 6.3.5.10

ORGANIZATION & FORMAT

ds Double space this
hang Paper must "hang together" 6.4.4
hdg Use headings 2.5.3
hdg-f Heading format/level needs work 2.4.1.9
hdg-sp Use specific wording in heading 2.4.1.9
intro-hdgs Insert intro between headings 6.4.4.6
item Itemize, bullet or number 6.4.3.5.4
org Organization needs work 2.4, 6.4.2
out-f Outline format needs work 2.4.3
s sp Single space this
t/g Use table/graph 2.5.4
t/g-d Discuss data from t/g 2.5.4.8
t/g-i Introduce t/g properly 2.5.4.7
t/g-p Place t/g properly 2.5.4.5-6

LOGIC

Ad hom Personal attack 6.5.6
Bandw Bandwagon technique 6.5.5
BegQ Begs the question 6.5.8
Bias Personal bias 6.5.10
FA False analogy 6.5.4
Gen Hasty generalization 6.5.2
Non seq Non sequitar 6.5.3
Pers Personification 6.5.1
Pol Polarization 6.5.9
Post hoc Correlation no cause 6.5.7
Ratl Rationalization 6.5.11
Subj Too subjective 6.5.12.

MODIFIERS

Comp Use comparatives correctly 6.2.3.5
d neg Double negative 6.3.3.7
dm Dangling modifier 6.3.3.4
mod Use a better modifier 6.2.3
mod-pl Place modifier next to word(s) modified
        6.3.3.3

PARAGRAPHS

Item Itemize, bullet or number 6.4.3.5.4
P-concl Need concluding sentence(s) 6.4.1.3
P-cr Too crowded with topics 6.4.1.4
P-lg Paragraph too long 6.4.3.5
P-lim Limit to one topic 6.4.1.4
P-org Reorganize 6.4.2
P-top Need topic sentence 6.4.1.1

PARALLEL CONSTRUCTION (pc)

pc Need parallel construction 6.3.6
pc-items Use pc in bulleted, numbered items
        6.3.6.4
pc-hdgs Use pc for headings 2.5.3.4.2, 6.3.6.4

PRONOUNS

contr Use contraction *it's* properly 6.2.4.4
pro-ag. Pronouns must agree w/antecedent noun in
        number and gender and be consistent. 6.2.4.3
pro-case Use the right case 6.2.4.2
pro-cl Unclear who/what pronoun refers to 6.2.4.1
pro-mis Misuse of *that/which/who* 6.2.4.7, 6.3.2.4
pro-poss Incorrect use of possessive *its* 6.2.4.5
pro-self Incorrect use of *self* pronoun 6.2.4.10
pro-sexist Use pronouns in non-sexist way 6.2.4.11

PUNCTUATION

-- Use dash properly 6.6.6.2
- Hyphenate this compound adjective 6.2.6.5
Do not hyphenate
pu Punctuate this sentence properly 6.5

Symbols to Use in Evaluating Papers

SENTENCE STRUCTURE

ss   Improve sentence structure 6.3
ss-awk   Awkward sentence 6.3.5.9
ss-cr   Too crowded w/ideas 6.3.4.7
ss-c/s   2 sentences, comma splice 6.3.5.3
ss-fu   2 sentences fused 6.3.5.2
ss-inc   Incomplete sentence 6.3.1.1, 6.3.5.5
ss-lg   Too long 6.3.4
ss-ro   Runs on, rambles 6.3.5.4
ss-vary   Vary sentence structure 6.3.1.3

TRANSITION/FLOW

Intro-hdgs Insert intro between headings 6.4.4.6
tr-flow   Improve flow 6.4.
tr-P   Need transitional paragraph 6.4.4
tr-sent Need transitional sentence(s) 6.4.4
tr-wd   Need transitional word(s) 6.4.4

VERBS

v-act   Use active verb(s) 6.2.5.6
v-cons   Use consistent tense 6.2.5.3
v-no   Use proper singular/plural 6.2.5.1, Dictionary
v-spec   Use specific verb(s) 6.2.5.5
v-str   Use stronger verb(s) 6.2.5.7
v-t   Use proper verb tense or form 6.2.6.2, Dic.
v-tr   Use transitive verb properly 6.2.5.7

WORD USE

art   Use correct article (*a,an,the*) 6.2.1.7
conc   Be concise 6.2.2
contr Use contractions properly 6.2.4.5
expl   Explain term/idea 6.4.2.5
fig   Use figure form for number 6.7
inc   Incomplete info 6.2.3.2
jarg   Avoid jargon 6.2.3.5
mis   Misuse of the word 6.2.3, Dictionary
mis-no Misuse of *number/amount, few/less* 6.2.3.7.
over   Overuse of word 6.2.1.6
poss   Use possessives properly 6.6.5.2
rep   Repetitive or redundant 6.2.2
sl   Avoid slang 6.2.3.5. Dictionary
spec Use specific word(s) 6.2.3.3
sp o   Spell out this word 6.2.434, 6.7
tech   Too technical 6.2.1.1, 6.2.3.4
wd div Divide word properly, Dictionary

How This Book Can Help You

The *Business Student's Guide* will help you to do a better job and save time, whether you are a business student or a business instructor.

The Business Student's Guide Helps Students

If you are a business student, using this book will help you to make the best grades possible in business courses, as well as in other courses, by giving you specific information on how to do the assignments typical to most business courses.

Feedback with a Bonus. If your instructor uses the Symbols for Evaluating Papers to mark corrections on your assignment papers, you get a real bonus. When you look up the meaning of the symbols in the table in this preface, you find *both* the meaning of the symbol *and* the paragraph numbers within the Guide that discuss the improvements you need to make.

How to correct, improve—explanations and examples
The guide makes the feedback process very powerful. You are directed to explanations and examples that will allow you to improve virtually any problem that surfaces in your class assignments. to enhance learning through the feedback process.

Skills-Enhancement: Writing, Speaking, Analyzing, Organizing, Researching, Collaborating. You acquire your most important business skills through completing assignments made in your business courses. The Guide helps you to acquire these skills faster and with greater depth of understanding.

The Business Student's Guide Helps Instructors

If you are a business instructor, using this book will help you to guide students toward higher performance levels in completing their assignments—while saving you and them a great deal of time.

Time-Saving. As an instructor, you save precious time you would normally spend in repeating instructions—in your syllabi and in classroom explanations of assignments. You save time in grading assignments—by using the abbreviated "symbols for evaluating papers" rather than writing out long repetitive correcting remarks and feedback. None of the instructors who responded to a survey on this topic said they enjoyed this aspect of teaching. Many said it was a boring, grueling chore, but one they were committed to doing because it helps their students so much. Now you can provide even better help to your students—with the symbol feedback system that is quick and easy.

Research-Based. This book is based upon results of a detailed survey sent to business faculty in over 100 colleges and universities throughout the United States. They responded to detailed questions concerning

- The types of assignments they make for their courses
- The number of assignments made
- Which aspects of each assignment are most important for grading purposes
- Their preferences regarding details of assignments, formats, documentation, writing style

Many professors sent copies of course syllabi and other handouts that described their expectations and gave specific instructions for doing course assignments. In addition, a survey of students revealed the kind of guidance they need for various types of assignments, elements within assignments, and specific questions that arise.

What's Different about Business Assignments?

Business assignments differ from assignments in other disciplines in several ways.

- Finding business facts requires a specific knowledge of the types of business resources that are available.
- Most business instructors expect students to use business writing style, which may differ from the writing style used in other disciplines.
- Business writing is more concise, to-the-point, and practical than many other types of writing.
- Business reports and memos have their own style and format.
- Business terminology is unique. Summaries are often called executive summaries and have their own format. Group assignments are usually called team projects or work team projects. Oral presentations may be called briefings or oral briefings.
- Business assignments focus on clear, concise, cooperative, results-oriented communications and actions.
- The orientation is toward bottom-line results—communicating clear goals, motivating people to carry out plans efficiently and effectively, making the best use of resources, recognizing and capitalizing upon opportunities, anticipating and recognizing problems, getting to the source of problems, developing clear action plans, and achieving high-level performance and productivity.

All the skills learned in general education courses must be translated and transferred into this business orientation. This book can help students to make that transition.

The Students Who Need This Book

This book is designed for all post-secondary business students, including those who:

1. Are in community colleges, 4-year colleges, or universities
2. Are in undergraduate or graduate programs
3. Have chosen business as a major or minor, or take an occasional business course.

Ways Instructors Can Use this Book

Here are typical ways that instructors use this book:

Preparing the Course Syllabus

When preparing course syllabi, refer to the Guide for all specific instructions that parallel your own, rather than repeating the instructions in the syllabus. When students ask questions about routine details that you know are contained in the Guide, ask them to read that part of the *Guide* first. If they need further explanation, you can give it.

Explaining Assignments

When assigning oral presentations, refer students to Exhibit 5.6 Talk Evaluation Checklist. Run off copies of this evaluation sheet, perhaps incorporating some of your own comments and use it to grade student presentations. Each of the five categories can count for 20 percent of the total grade, for example—or you can assign your own weighting system. If you also record the student's grade on a separate class list, you can give the Evaluation form to the student at the end of the class session—for immediate feedback on performance.

"Beefing Up" Assignments

Some instructors report that they now require students to prepare outlines for all their papers and executive summaries of longer papers—based on instructions and formats given in the *Guide*.

Marking Papers

The index of Symbols for Evaluating Papers allows you to streamline and improve the paper correction function. The Alphabetic Index of Symbols allows students to interpret the instructor's feedback and to locate discussions of each writing problem, along with examples and instructions for correcting and improving. When it's time to mark papers, use the Symbols for Evaluating Papers found in the preface. This will save you hours of writing those routine, repetitive feedback comments, allowing you more time for comments on unique, specific issues.

Handling Rewrites

Students can link your feedback symbols to explanations and examples of the assignment issue in question. The Business Students Guide serves as a learning aid for correcting writing errors and problems. Require students to submit the original paper with the rewrite, and your evaluation becomes short and easy. All you must do is check your feedback symbols and see if each problem has been corrected.

I sincerely expect that the use of this book will help the students and instructors who use it as much as it has helped me and my students.

Norma Carr-Ruffino
Professor of Management
San Francisco State University

THIS CHAPTER PRESENTS suggestions for conducting a case analysis in a step-by-step sequence of activities:

1.1 OVERVIEW: CASE STUDY APPROACH TO LEARNING

1.1.1   OPPORTUNITIES TO PRACTICE DECISION MAKING

The case approach to learning offers you the opportunity to practice making business decisions in the relatively risk-free environment of the classroom. When you analyze cases, you get to select and apply various approaches, theories, principles, rules, and analytical tools you have learned in your business courses. You gain practical experience at identifying and solving business problems. And you get invaluable practice at defending your recommendations for actions when the class and instructor evaluate your ideas and debate the merits of your solutions. What's so risk-free about this process? Think about the consequences of making disastrous decisions on the job. Compare that with the consequences of recommending poor decisions in a case analysis. The classroom suddenly seems pretty safe.

1.1.2   SPECIFIC OPPORTUNITIES provided by the case method include:

- trying out your ideas and approaches

- discovering the strengths and weaknesses of your analytical skills

- sharing, making mistakes, and learning with your classmates

- exploring various ways of making decisions in response to business opportunities and problems

- seeing more the big picture of the global marketplace and how various players fit in or not

- learning about the inner workings of companies and how departments interact internally and with external stakeholders

- receiving invaluable coaching from your instructor

- generally sharpening your business skills

1.1.3 **THE END RESULTS ARE PROBLEM ANALYSIS AND RECOMMENDATIONS.** You must analyze, or take apart the case, looking for underlying problems as well as the obvious problems. Then you must develop a set of recommendations for action to resolve the problems. These recommendations may be derived from the case material, material from the environment, and your knowledge of business practice gained from interviews, research, and business courses. The business course in which the case is assigned is most important because the case is designed as an application of theory, concepts, and other information covered in the course. Recommendations may range from modifying mission or purpose, strategies, goals, and policies to rewriting rules, operating procedures and action plans.

1.1.4 **ANALYSIS** means breaking something into parts. Case analysis consists of

- Breaking the case situation into parts

- Determining the facts that are significant to each part of the problem

- Classifying the component problems and facts in some form that leads to a synthesis

- Interpreting the significance of the facts by drawing deductions and inferences

1.1.5 **SYNTHESIS** means putting together. A case syntheses involves

- the creative structuring of the data, problems, and analysis into meaningful comprehensive problems

- the development of goals, strategies, and plans for the company that represent the solutions to the company's underlying problems

1.1.6 **REQUIREMENTS FOR SUCCESSFUL CASE ANALYSIS** are that you

- Know what questions to ask in order to begin the analysis

- Separate your opinions, biases, and beliefs from the facts

- Come up with a preferred course of action, and preferably one or two alternative action plans, with   some prediction of the results that each is likely to bring

1.1.7 **FIND AN ANALYTICAL STYLE** that works best for you. Some suggestions are given in this chapter.

1.1.8 **ACCELERATE YOUR LEARNING CURVE.** The degree of learning you experience from the case process will be in direct proportion to the degree of time, effort, and interest you put into the process. Some suggestions for making the most of these opportunities follow.

1.1.9 **PREPARE.** Use the suggestions given later in this chapter to prepare your case analysis.

- Thoroughly read and understand the case; respond to the case questions.

- Think about unasked questions that may come up in class

- Prepare any further assignments made in connection with the case.

1.1.10 **LISTEN.** Listen carefully to what others in the class have to say about the case, as well as the instructor's comments. Take brief notes on items you're likely to forget, but focus most of your attention on just being there in class and taking in what others are sharing.

1.1.11 **PARTICIPATE.** You have a responsibility to the class to share your ideas. You have a responsibility to yourself to subject your ideas to open debate and evaluation, so that you can identify your problem-solving and decision-making strengths and overcome weaknesses, step by step. You also have a responsibility to yourself to continually improve your skills in verbalizing your ideas to others.

1.1.12 **FOLLOW UP TO COMPLETE THE LEARNING CYCLE.** After each class discussion of a case, take a few minutes to jot down some follow-up notes. These will normally include

- facts you missed

- ideas that are vital to the case

- conclusions that can be made or generalizations that would apply to other, similar situations

1.1.13 **REVIEW.** If cases are included in exams in some way, when you study you can refer to

- The case itself, focusing on your underlined passages and marginal notes

- Your response to the case

- Your after-class follow-up notes

1.2 MAKING AN INITIAL ANALYSIS

1.2.1 **DETERMINE THE TYPE OF CASE** and response needed.

1.2.1.1 SHORT, SIMPLE CASES may require that you simply answer the case questions. In most instances instructors are impressed when you can give examples that relate to the case, either from your personal experience or from an article in the current literature. These types of cases are often given as part of a reading assignment and to prepare students to discuss case applications of the chapter concepts in a class discussion.

1.2.1.2 LONG, COMPLEX CASES may constitute a project to be evaluated and graded by the instructor for a designated percentage of the course grade. You are expected to do more research and an organized, complete written report of your case analysis in this type of assignment.

1.2.2 **GRASP THE KEY FACTORS OF THE CASE.** For some people, underlining or highlighting helps the process. For others, making marginal notes is best. For most, a combination works best—underlining a few key passages and noting brief ideas or drawing diagrams in the margins. If it's a major project, writing a separate summary may be helpful.

1.2.3 **READ LONG COMPLEX CASES** that are a project, read the case at least a week or so before the case analysis is due. Skim some of the details and focus on the particular situation in which events are now taking place and to which the exhibits apply. Skim the exhibits, noting the type. Look for general problems, issues, opportunities, and note key players. After this first overview reading, try to answer these questions.

- What type of case is this (see types that follow) and what type of analytic tools and additional information do you need?

- What is the general nature of the company and its setting?

- What questions have been assigned for you to answer?

- What significant unassigned questions might be raised in class?

- Why was the case assigned now? What is going on in class that relates to this case?

1.3 SELECTING AN ANALYTICAL LEVEL AND APPROACH

1.3.1 **BEFORE MAKING A DETAILED ANALYSIS,** gathering additional information, or working with formulas, models, and other analytic tools, decide on your analytic level and approach, to ensure that you spend your time where it counts most.

1.3.2 **UNDERSTAND VARIOUS LEVELS OF ANALYSIS.** You should ask yourself (and the instructor if necessary) what level of analysis is expected.

(1) **A COMPREHENSIVE IN-DEPTH ANALYSIS** of all key issues, including recommendations for actions along with supporting data?

(2) **A SPECIALIZED IN-DEPTH ANALYSIS** of one particular issue of the case? One that provides much detail on that issue?

(3) **A KEY-ISSUES ANALYSIS** that focuses on identifying the main issues and alternatives? This type of analysis is designed to respond to what you think will be the initial question your instructor will ask. It is designed to generate initial class discussion of the case.

(4) **A SURFACE ANALYSIS** of assigned questions that is designed to provide you with at least a minimal class contribution when for some reason a more detailed analysis cannot be prepared.

(5) **AN EXPANDED ANALYSIS** that that brings in information from other sources, such as current events, company interview or documents, personal experience?

1.3.3 **THE NATURE OF THE CASE** may determine the analytical level. For example, four types of cases that call for various degrees of analysis are:

(1) CASES THAT FOCUS ON APPLYING CONCEPTS. These cases are often used in management and marketing courses, especially introductory courses. They are usually short, highly structured, with little or no superfluous information. You are expected to apply one or more management concepts to the problems within the case situation and to generating solutions or recommendations. A variety of solutions is usually possible, so there is rarely "one right answer." Think of concepts recently presented in your course that could be applied to the case.

(2) CASES THAT FOCUS ON FORMULA APPLICATION. These cases are also short, highly structured, and contain little or no superfluous information. However, a right answer or best solution often exists. You are expected to arrive at the answer by applying formulas or models that have been presented in this or previous courses. If you are told which formulas or models should be used, review them before you read the case in order to identify the data you will need to set up the problem or model. If you do not know which formulas or models should be used, read the case first to determine which of these analytical tools would work best.

(3) CASES THAT FOCUS ON IDENTIFYING PROBLEMS AND OPPORTUNITIES and applying concepts. These cases are usually longer, from 10 to 50 pages, including several exhibits. They are less structured than the shorter cases and may contain irrelevant, excess information that you are expected to weed out. You are also expected to identify the underlying problems and opportunities and to apply concepts, preferred practices, or theory to the solution of the case. One best solution or right answer usually does not exist.

(4) CASES THAT FOCUS ON CREATING NEW CONCEPTS OR APPROACHES.
These cases are usually given to advanced masters or doctoral candidates.

1.3.4   SELECT AN ANALYTICAL FRAMEWORK (an outline) for analysis that suits the particular case. The outline might be based on

- economic objectives

- administrative process

- functional areas of the business

- business systems

- human resources

- deviations from the norm

- description and evaluation of the situation

- combination of these or other approaches

(1) ECONOMIC APPROACH

Analyze basic economic objectives, policies, strategies, plans, and implementation. For a narrower economic focus, you might use an engineering-economic focus, or an accounting focus, or some combination. Some questions for the broad economic approach are:

- What is the company's mission?

- What broad industries should the company belong to?

- What should the product areas be, given the company's competitive edge and its resource capabilities?

- What are the trends of growth, the potentials, for these product areas?

- What major policies identify the firm and guide its operations?

- What should be the competitive strategy of the company? What special opportunities appear to be neglected by competitors?

- What short-range and long-range plans does the company have?

(2) ENGINEERING-ECONOMIC APPROACH

- Apply cost accounting techniques, such as Breakeven Analysis.

- Apply cost/benefit analyses.

- Build a Decision Tree.

(3) ACCOUNTING APPROACH

- Apply financial tests to the organization, such as figuring its current ratio and comparing it with that of competitors.

- Apply turnover ratios for the organization's accounts payable, its inventories, its employees, and other assets.

- Apply measures of profit, such as Return on Investment.

- Derive financial statements, such as Balance Sheets.

(4) ADMINISTRATIVE APPROACH

The focus is on immediate problems and how to dispose of them in terms of the present goals of the firm. Use the following outline to classify problems before tying problems together.

- Analysis of the situation
- Basic objectives
- Plans for action, schedules, and budgets
- Implementation of plans
- Control operations

For each problem cluster or major problems, develop major alternative action plans. In order to integrate the analysis, a summary will be needed to present the recommendations and the arguments in support of them. This is essentially a systems approach and any demands of subsystems must be considered and balanced in the solution.

(5) FUNCTIONAL APPROACH

Analyze the functional area, such as production, marketing, or finance, showing functional relationships. The danger of this method is failing to provide for integration of functional areas in the solution. Problems in the various functional areas must be tied together when they are in fact related. To aid integration, when you outline a problem, list it in its primary classification (such as production) in large letters. Then list the problem in small letters under other functional areas that it spills over into. Identify company objectives and policies in the particular functional area. Evaluate, and where appropriate, reformulate them to guide the development of solutions.

(6) BUSINESS SYSTEMS APPROACH

Use information flow and material flow systems to analysis the situation.

- Evaluate the impact of major factors in the external environment, such as the economy, the competition, new laws, etc.
- Diagram information networks or communication networks, such as management information systems, communication systems, decision processes.
- Apply standards, Management Science, and/or models to problems of work flow, scheduling, inventory control, and similar problems.

(7) BEHAVIORAL OR HUMAN RESOURCES APPROACH

Focus on the key people in the case, taking these kinds of actions:

- Identify or develop organization charts, department boundaries, coordinating relationships; identify other key relationships.
- Identify strong protagonists on each side of the issues. If they are the keys to this case, analyze these people, their backgrounds, success records, and their ideas about the opportunities and management of the company.
- Determine how well the company is using employees from diverse backgrounds, perceptions, values, etc. in work teams to stimulate innovative approaches and creative solutions. Are the doors open to qualified females, people from various ethnic groups, persons with disabilities, gay persons, older persons?

- Determine how well the company is using participative problem-solving, decision-making, and control to meet its goals. To what extent are employees allowed to participate in these functions?

- Explore human resources through job design and redesign, training programs, and analysis of wages and benefits.

- Suggest conflict resolution through creative confrontation, negotiation, intervention, collaboration, team building, and similar methods.

(8) DEVIATION-FROM-NORM APPROACH

Follow this process:

- **Locate deviations from the norm.** What should be occurring in this situation? What is actually occurring? Any deviations from the goals and standards that the firm should be achieving are potential problems.

- **Separate and prioritize deviations.** Try to break up general deviations or problems (morale, for example) into subsets of specific deviations; for example "productivity is off by 10 percent, workers in two departments do not communicate as well as in the past." Then rank the deviations according to their urgency, seriousness, and potential for growing worse.

- **Further define each deviation.** Specify what is and is not a deviation by asking such questions as:

  a) What is/is not a deviation, and what is/is not the thing or object on which the deviation is found?

  b) Where is/is not the deviation on the thing or object, and where are/are not objects with the deviation occurring?

  c) When does/does not the deviation appear on the thing or object, and when are/are not objects with the deviation found?

  d) How large or small are the deviations, and how many objects with or without the deviations exist?

- **Look for distinctions or differences** between things affected by the deviation and things unaffected by it.

- **Look for changes** that have occurred in the problem area. What has changed that might have contributed causes can be deduced from the changes? Look for possible causes for the deviation that underlie the change you have discovered. Then establish one or more statements as to the possible causes, statements that can be tested.

- **Identify the cause** that most precisely explains all the facts that are known about the deviation or problem. That is the most likely cause.

- **Establish specific objectives** (goals) that a good solution must meet. Include criteria (standards) for measuring results. Divide objectives into a) musts, those that are essential to a good solution, and b) wants, those that provide an ideal solution.

- **Rank or weigh the objectives** according to importance. Keep in mind the results that are essential and desirable and the resources that will be available, such as money, staff, technology.

(9) DESCRIPTION-EVALUATION APPROACH

This is a format that may be combined with any of the approaches discussed so far, or with other approaches to a particular case.

- **Necessary Background Information** – past history; future changes, opportunities, threats

- **Present Situation** – description of what's going on and evaluation of what's working and not working

- **Proposed Solution**

  Description of issues to be confronted, changes to be made, new approaches or systems to initiate.

  Evaluation of how proposed changes would improve the situation. These might be improvements in thinking strategically, meeting short-range and long-range goals, productivity, motivation, teamwork, efficiency, cost effectiveness, and similar factors. Present and compare alternatives.

  Implementation of the solution action plan. Consider how to initiate the changes—steps, timing, barriers to overcome, probable reactions, and results.

  Follow-up of the action plan: controls, evaluation, modification process.

1.4 MAKING A DETAILED ANALYSIS

1.4.1   **REREAD THE CASE THOROUGHLY** when you are ready to spend more time working on it. This time make notes according to the type of case, analytical approach and level you have decided to use. Note issues or exhibits that need to be further analyzed. Here are some types of questions to ask:

- What is the company's mission? Strategies? Objectives?

- Who are the key stakeholders?

- What are the most significant actions, attitudes, policies, strategies, symptoms of problems, root problems, and issues—in light of the objectives and content of the course?

- How do these significant factors relate to company mission and objectives?

- Are there any conflicting statements, attitudes, or approaches?

- Are there any statements that appear to be based solely on personal opinion? Separate fact from opinion.

- Are there any conflicts between what people say and what they do?

- What significant matters are not being discussed? Why?

- Which problems indicate that current, potentially effective strategies, objectives, policies, or procedures are not being implemented effectively?

- Which problems indicate the need to change strategies, objectives, policies, or procedures?

1.4.2   **UNDERSTAND EXHIBITS,** their purpose in this case, and their main components. Categorize each exhibit as either

(1) TYPICAL EXHIBIT, the type of exhibit found in many cases, such as organizational charts or financial statements. Note any unusual or uncommon items you find within the ordinary type of exhibits. Such abnormalities may provide a clue to the diagnosis of the case.

(2) UNIQUE EXHIBIT, a exhibit designed solely for this particular case situation.

1.4.3   **SYNTHESIZE** the various issues and problems into coherent, broad problems, if possible.

1.5 GATHERING ADDITIONAL INFORMATION

See the chapter on Finding Business Information for tips on sources of business information—in the library and elsewhere.

1.5.1 **CREATIVE ASSUMPTIONS** about case information may be permissible where certain facts or numbers are not provided and cannot be obtained.

Ask, "What can I reasonably assume from the case information?"

1.5.2 **DETERMINE IF YOU NEED ADDITIONAL INFORMATION** to complete your case analysis. Do you need information about the global market, the economy, the environment, the industry that will provide a setting for the company's situation? Do you need to update the case material because of recent developments?

1.5.3 **PINPOINT THE BEST SOURCES** of the specific information you need.

1.5.4 **CONSIDER DOING AN INDUSTRY AND MARKET ANALYSIS.** Does the case provide enough information about the company's relative position within the industry? Do you need answers to some of the following questions:

- What industry group does the company belong to?

- How do the policies, strategies, and actions of other companies in the industry affect the company you are analyzing?

- How will the company's policies, strategies, and actions affect competitors? The industry in general?

1.5.5 **GATHER INFORMATION** about the potential case situation—as much as your time schedule permits in light of the significance of the assignment. While you must edit the information to fit space and time limits.

1.5.6 **SIFT THROUGH THE CASE INFORMATION** for answers to pertinent questions that may help in formulating solutions. Pertinent questions will vary but might include: How is the problem similar or different from other situations in class discussions, the text, or your personal experience?

1.5.7 **KEEP ASKING QUESTIONS** and gathering information until you have a satisfactory grasp of the situation. In most cases you should focus mainly on the current situation, looking at past history to get the whole story and at future possibilities to complete the picture.

1.6 IDENTIFYING ROOT PROBLEMS, KEY ISSUES, AND OPPORTUNITIES

1.6.1 **STATE SIGNIFICANT PROBLEMS** within each subtopic of the outline, problems evidenced by the data of the case, whether direct or inferred. State why you conclude such a problem exists. This rationale is especially important when you identify problems that are due to trends indicating future probabilities. These will probably be surface problems.

1.6.2 **AVOID FOCUSING ON SURFACE PROBLEMS.** The most common case analysis error is focusing on surface problems or symptoms instead of getting at underlying or root problems. Solutions to surface problems are like band-aids or patches. They temporarily hold together or smooth over the breakdown, but the allow the underlying problem to worsen in the long run. In most cases you must dig deeper to find the underlying problem. Only then will you solution be effective in the long term.

1.6.3 **IDENTIFY CENTRAL PROBLEMS** and the cluster of related problems that stem from each central problem. These problem clusters may cut across your structure of subtopics.

1.6.4 **LOOK AT BASIC RELATIONSHIPS,** which are often the focus of the root problem; for example:

- Relationships between people or groups of people

- Relationships between basic job functions or responsibilities

- Relationships between objective—organizational, departmental, individual job goals

1.6.5 **TRY TO PINPOINT ACCOUNTABILITY.** Ask, "Who is responsible and who has authority in this situation?"

1.6.6 **GET AT THE ROOT PROBLEM.** Try this process:

Step 1: Jot down an initial definition of the problem as you see it.

Step 2: Ask yourself, "What is the purpose of solving the problem? What results are needed?"

Step 3: Dig deeper. Ask, "Why? Why are these results needed?" See if the answer to "Why?" brings you to a deeper, underlying, more basic problem. Keep asking "Why?" until you feel you can go no deeper, that you have reached the most fundamental level for dealing with the problem.

Step 4: Factoring in these new insights, now redefine the purpose of solving the problem, the results needed, and in turn redefine the problem itself.

1.6.7 **KEEP ASKING WHY UNTIL YOU ARE SATISFIED.** Here are some other questions:

Is the organization likely to experience other, related problems after this problem is solved?

After we carry out this solution plan, will there still be a problem?

1.6.8 **SUMMARIZE THE MAJOR PROBLEM** in a single sentence that includes:

- The question that requires an answer or action

- Who is responsible for providing the answer or action

- The immediate answer that is needed

1.6.9 **DETERMINE OTHER KEY ISSUES,** such as

- Recent changes or conflicts. What has caused them?

- Other interested parties. What are their problems?

- Internal operations that may be affected: sales, production, finance, personnel, other? What roles do various functional areas play in this problem?

- Environmental effects in areas such as public relations, relevant markets, government regulations

- Objectives that should be considered—organizational, departmental, individual

1.6.10 **OTHER ISSUES** you may need to address are:

- Issues that are NOT part of the problem

- Future problems that should be anticipated

1.6.11 RELATE THE CASE TO THE COURSE. Think about problems and possible solutions as they might relate to the ideas and principles that have been discussed in class and in the text. Pay special attention to related text chapters.

1.6.12 LET IDEAS GERMINATE. During the next few days, keep this case situation in the back of your mind and jot down any relevant thoughts as they occur. Discuss the case informally with others whenever you get the chance. In other words, let the case "rummage around in your mind" for a few days.

1.7 SYNTHESIZING POSSIBLE SOLUTIONS

1.7.1 DO NOT EVALUATE POSSIBLE SOLUTIONS at this stage. Evaluations tend to block creativity, and you need to generate as many innovative solutions as possible. Evaluate the situation and the problems, but suspend evaluation of solutions while you are brainstorming them.

1.7.2 REVIEW YOUR REDEFINED PROBLEM STATEMENT and the purpose or results you are aiming for.

1.7.3 REVIEW THE ANALYTIC LEVEL AND APPROACH you have selected.

1.7.4 REVIEW FINANCIAL STATEMENTS, if included. Ask about the financial status of the company. Is it lean and healthy? Fat and healthy? Mildly ailing? Severely ill and on the brink of disaster? Pinpointing the financial health gives you some basis for further analysis.

1.7.5 ASK FURTHER QUESTIONS. Answers to one or more of the following questions may aid your analysis.

- *What ideas, facts, or things might be put together or combined? Changed, modified, or rearranged? Substituted for something else?*

- *What items might be magnified, increased, or made larger (such as advantages or assets)? Minimized, reduced or made smaller (such as faults or disadvantages)? Reversed, handled in exactly the opposite way? Broken down into smaller parts and then each segment dealt with?*

- *Can any ideas or items be applied to similar problems or products? Be simplified, removed, or added?*

1.7.6 CONSIDER ROLE PLAYING, especially if an effective solution depends upon the cooperation of two or more factions. You can role-play alone (either mentally or preferably aloud), or (even better) you can do it with another person. Pretend you are a key member of one faction. Discuss the current situation and possible solutions from that viewpoint. Then take the role of a key member of another faction and do the same thing. Get a debate going. This technique can help you identify needs, concerns, and conflicts that pertain to the problem. As you answer the needs with suggestions to fulfill them, you will stimulate new ideas for solution.

1.8 FORMULATING WORKABLE SOLUTIONS

1.8.1 DETERMINE CRITERIA. Decide more specifically what results a good solution must achieve. In other words, set criteria for evaluating alternate solutions. Criteria are specifications of the quality of a good solution would have.

1.8.2 BE CREATIVE. Coming up with good solutions is easier if you relax, don't criticize your ideas, and let them bubble up freely. Keep an open mind. Be willing to change viewpoints and approaches and to try out new ideas. Encourage your curiosity and spirit of inquiry. Let them led you to new ideas.

1.8.3   **FORMULATE ALTERNATE SOLUTIONS.** Go for as many as possible. Keep asking, "What else might work?" Don't evaluate the solutions at this stage. Just keep generating ideas for improvements or for new opportunities.

1.8.4   **CONSIDER ALL TYPES OF ALTERNATIVES.** Here are some examples:

- Handling part of the problem and postponing the rest

- Delaying tactics that buy time for getting more information, hiring consultants, setting up committees, getting a stockholder vote, etc.

- Doing nothing, ignoring the problem

- Closing the operation, selling out, quitting

- Taking legal action

1.8.5   **TALK ABOUT THE CASE.** Verbalize possible solutions with others. This can spur creative thinking and help you to clarify your ideas.

1.8.6   **TRY TO FIND SOLUTIONS.** Look for solutions that will make the best use of all potential assets and opportunities that you think the company has access to.

1.8.7   **ASK WHAT OTHER FACTORS** are significant to this case. Have you considered important legal, political, social, or psychological factors that may be important in formulating the most effective solution to the problem?

1.8.8   **RELATE TO THE COURSE.** Still stuck in formulating solutions? Try listing basic concepts and principles that are covered in the text and that relate to this case. Compare these to your list of key issues and factors in the case. See where you can match up concepts, principles, or suggestions with the needs of the case.

1.9   EVALUATING ALTERNATES & SELECTING A SOLUTION

1.9.1   **LOOK AT THE CRITERIA** you developed earlier, the standards for evaluating alternate solutions to the case. Did you rank each criterion in the order of its importance to this case?

1.9.2   **EVALUATE ALTERNATE SOLUTIONS** according to how well each meets the criteria. Does one solution stand out? If so, you are fortunate. If not, keep working.

1.9.3   **LIST SIGNIFICANT EVENTS** that are likely to occur in the future that might affect each solution or action plan. Here are some factors you might consider.

- Events that must occur before an alternative can be realized
- Events that are dependent on other events occurring
- Costs, expenses, potential profits
- What is the net cash flow in contribution dollars of a given alternative, adjusted for the probability that it will occur? Which costs are relevant and irrelevant?
- Available resources, such as information, budgets, trained staff, tools, equipment, software, facilities
- Efforts involved
- Impact on company strategies, objectives, policies, and procedures
- Attitudes and reactions of the people involved

- Long-range consequences
- New problems that the action plan may create
- Union contracts and relationships
- Morality and legality
- Reactions of customers, the community, competitors, other important segments of the external environment
  - What opportunities and risks do these probable event present that might affect the action plan?

1.9.4 **COMPARE OPPORTUNITY VALUES** of alternate action plans. Keep in mind that when an organization commits resources to one action plan, it normally is forced to pass up other opportunities that require similar resources. What opportunities is the organization likely to pass up by committing to the action plan you are considering? What payoffs are probable from each? What resources will be necessary for each? What tradeoffs are practical between the time and money invested and the possible payoffs for each plan? What specific conditions require specific actions?

1.9.5 **COMPARE ADVANTAGES.** Still stuck? Try using the advantages and disadvantages of each action plan. Then compare lists.

1.9.6 **SYNTHESIZE SOME ACTION PLANS.** Put together a reasonable number of workable alternative actions or programs, usually at least three, to solve each problem cluster. Look for broad strategies and basic objectives that will provide guidelines for solving the problems. Put together specific plans for implementing your recommended solutions. Set up alternatives for resolving key pressing issues and predict the probable outcomes of each alternative.

1.9.7 **EVALUATE THE ALTERNATE ACTION PLANS,** the sets of strategies, goals, and problem solutions by analyzing the data and listing and weighing the advantages and disadvantages of each.

1.9.8 **RANK THE ALTERNATIVES.** If you have used quantitative tools for analysis, you should have some quantitative ranking of the alternate actions the company could take. Next you should do a qualitative assessment of these alternatives. For example, even though alternative number three has a better net present value than alternative number one, is there a more important, overriding, yet non-quantitative reason that you would still recommend alternative number one? Be prepared to defend your choice in class. What arguments are you likely to encounter from your classmates or instructor? How would you respond?

1.9.9 **SELECT A PLAN.** Prepare a set of specific recommendations for action based on your evaluations. Normally, you should assume action must be taken now, not after further lengthy research. Avoid qualifying your recommendations or hedging your bets. Action must be taken. The company cannot be allowed to drift into further difficulty. Be decisive and assertive.

1.9.10 **CLARIFY HOW TO IMPLEMENT THE ACTION PLAN.** Explain how your recommendations can be carried out. Some areas to cover are:

1) **Communicating.** How will the plan be communicated? Must it be sold to the people who are needed to carry it out?

2) **Implementing.** Who will be responsible for each phase of the plan? How will they carry it out? What will they do? When will they do it? Where will they do it?

3) **Controlling.** What types of followup plans should be made? What controls are needed? How will the action plan be evaluated? At what intervals? By whom? How easy will it be to modify the plan? How difficult or expensive will it be to abandon the plan if the results show signs of disaster?

1.9.11   **REVIEW THE GOAL** and purpose for solving this problem. Does one solution stand out as fulfilling this goal and this purpose?

1.9.12   **PAUSE BEFORE YOU MAKE A FINAL DECISION** on the best action plan. Relax and forget the case for at least 24 hours, if possible. Let all the information you've absorbed, and the thinking you done about the case, simmer at the subconscious level for a while. This important step in the creative process can result in new insights, breakthroughs in your understanding, and a more inspired solution.

1.9.13   **VISUALIZE RESULTS** when you are ready to make the final selection. Use relaxation techniques to put yourself into a relaxed state of mind. Close your eyes and picture your first solution being carried out. Let ideas and pictures come up as they will. Don't strain or try to force them. Allow. Give yourself plenty of time to let the results of each solution run its full course. Then jot down your ideas. This process may help you clarify the possible results of following each of the alternate solutions.

1.10 DISCUSSING YOUR ANALYSIS IN CLASS

1.10.1   **DECIDE ON THE FOCUS** of comments you will make in class about the case. Try relating your comments to something the instructor and students can readily grasp. Here are examples:

    1) Relating to previous cases. Does your analysis have any similarities, or marked differences, with cases that have already been discussed in class? Perhaps you can begin your presentation by comparing or contrasting the two situations.

    2) Relating to exhibits. Do key parts of your analysis tie in with one of the exhibits in the case? If so, you might begin with those aspects of the case—a point everyone can identify with.

    3) Relating to instructor summary. Try to envision how the instructor might summarize or diagram your points on the chalkboard. Can your presentation be given in terms of a list or diagram? For example, a list of advantages and disadvantages, of unique distinctions, of key elements of various alternatives. You could structure your presentation to facilitate such a summary.

1.10.2   **UNDERSTAND THE DISCUSSION PROCESS** the instructor usually follows. The process will normally include

    1) identification and analysis of the problem

    2) analysis of the key alternatives

    3) recommendations for specific action

1.10.3   **UNDERSTAND THE DISCUSSION FORMAT** or approach the instructor may use. Some typical formats include:

    1) Instructor asks, student answers. The discussion is mainly between the instructor and one students at a time. The questions may resemble a cross-examination designed to expose the logic of the student's statements. Take it in the spirit it is meant, a learning device.

    2) Instructor takes a position, students plays devil's advocate. You should determine at some point if your instructor's position is untenable. You must think and reason on the spot, using case information, course concepts, and your own experience and common sense.

    3) Instructor poses an extreme situation, one that carries your position or recommendation to the extreme. You are asked to evaluate the situation in terms of your recommendation. The purpose is to force an examination of the logic underlying your recommendation. Stay alert and open to the need to rethink your position.

    4) Student to student. The instructor allows fellow students to challenge the logic or basis for your position. You or other students may rebut the challenge with different analyses, information, or logic.

Be alert to the need to stay on the topic being discussed, to respect others' contributions, and to be willing to put your own ideas out for discussion.

1.10.4 THINK ABOUT KEY QUESTIONS. For example, ask yourself the following types of questions:

- The initial question asked by the instructor to start the case discussion
- Other questions that might be asked by the instructor or other students
- Questions you might ask of the instructor or of other students

1.10.5 YOUR RESPONSE TO THE INITIAL DISCUSSION QUESTION should provide some kind of answer that will stimulate further discussion; for example, "Here's what I thought . . . But I also wondered if . . .?"

1.10.6 LISTEN CAREFULLY to the student who begins the case discussion. Do you agree or disagree with this person's analysis? If you understand your position in relation to the speaker's, you can move more easily into the discussion yourself.

1.11 WRITING THE CASE REPORT

1.11.1 COMPLEXITY. Case assignments that are considered a project calling for a case report that the instructor will evaluate are usually longer, more difficult, and more complex than those assigned for classroom discussion along. You must devote more time to these cases—in reading and analyzing them, in gathering more information perhaps, in developing solutions, and in organizing and writing a clear case report.

1.11.2 SCHEDULING. Estimate the hours you will need to schedule in order to do a good job. Plan for initial reading, second reading and analysis, group work if that is part of the assignment, data gathering if necessary, development of solution plans, organizing the paper and writing the first draft, and rewriting the paper and proofreading the final version.

1.11.3 EXPECTATIONS. Before you begin your analysis, try to determine whether the case is basically a review case. Briefly go over other case assignments you completed earlier, looking for basic similarities or differences. What principal lesson and techniques were covered in these cases that could be applied to the written case assignment? Do you think the instructor will be looking for evidence that you have a good grasp of these concepts and can apply them?

1.11.4 REVIEW. You may find it helpful to prepare two brief lists: 1) Key findings of previous cases and concepts they represent, and 2) major skills you have learned from the course that the instructor may expect you to apply to this case.

1.11.5 PROJECTIONS. Do you think this assignments calls for you to evaluate the future effects of your recommendation? If so, look for quantitative and qualitative support for your recommendations.

1.11.6 SEQUENCING. After you complete your analysis, think about the sequence in which you should present it on paper. What does the instructor need to know first?

1.11.7 LIST YOUR PRINCIPAL CONCLUSIONS. Include your findings and observations, and then list your main supporting evidence for each finding. You may be able to integrate some of these lists info your paper. For example: "I recommend this action for the following reasons: 1). . . 2). . . 3) . . . ."

1.11.8 RECOMMENDATIONS. It may be most helpful if you first state your bottom-line recommendation. Can you sum up in one sentence the principal output of your analysis? If so, you have:

> A recommendation, key message, or thesis statement that should be put at the beginning of the paper. The rest of the paper should focus on the following items.
>
> 1) Why you chose this action plan or key message
> 2) Other alternatives you could have chosen and why you did not
> 3) The evidence supporting your recommendation

1.11.9 A BRIEF SUMMARY PARAGRAPH that summarizes the key issues in the case may be appropriately placed immediately before or after the recommendations, for clarity.

1.11.10 DO NOT REPEAT CASE CONTENT. Merely refer to key aspects of the case as a natural part of discussing problem and solutions. Assume the reader is familiar with the case content.

1.11.11 SEE FURTHER SUGGESTIONS for writing an effective paper in the chapter on Business Research and Reports and the chapter on Business Writing Style. Pay special attention to the effective use of exhibits.

1.12 CREATING YOUR OWN CASES

1.12.1 CLARIFY THE ASSIGNMENT. You need to have a clear picture of how the instructor wants you to develop and present the case. If you are unsure, meet with the instructor to clarify the framework within which the case must be constructed. Ask some questions.

- What sources will you use? Interviews are most common, but you may be allowed to develop cases from newspaper or journal reports of problem situations, or from television or Internet sources.
- Whom will you interview? If interviews are the source, get to work immediately to line up your interviewee, and make backup plans in case your interviewee cancels out.
- Must you write a case key? Does the instructor want only a case study? Or will you prepare a key to the case, the cases analysis and solutions?
- Will the case be analyzed and discussed by your classmates? If so, will you need to provide enough copies for these students?

1.12.2 GATHER CASE INFORMATION. Look for realistic, valid situations and incidents that indicate 1) a problem that needs creative solutions or 2) untapped opportunities that need ideas and actions to create something new or different. If appropriate, reassure interviewees that real names will not be used in the case. Interview questions that often lead to good case studies are those that ask for war stories, horror stories, etc.—and those that ask about the differences between current reality and an ideal situation. Of course, in your interview you will want to ask for success stories also, for comparison and so that the interviewee can report the positive as well as the negative.

1.12.3 WRITE THE CASE PROBLEM. Gather and write enough details of the situation to give readers a clear and realistic picture of what the people in the case must deal with. Remember, that the readers are not familiar with any of the characters or facts in the situation, so you must provide this information. For human relations aspects, give information about personalities, quirks, traits, skills, etc. of key persons. When finances enter the picture, spell out necessary details. Give enough information for readers to make an intelligent assessment of the situation.

1.12.4 DON'T ANALYZE THE CASE FOR THE READER. While you must give enough information for the reader to understand the surface problems. However, you should not state what you think the problems are—or even hint at the underlying problems. It's the reader's job to dig into the case and ferret out the problems and overlooked opportunities. You must give enough information to do that but not so much that you are doing the case analysis yourself.

For example, it's inappropriate to state that, "Ray is jealous of Susan." Instead, you must tell the reader what Ray says and does in this regard, and let the readers come to their own conclusions. In this way, your case should contain clues to the problems or potential problems that the manager and the organization need to address. Don't spell out the problems. A common student error is to give some analysis, and even solution, within the case, leaving little work for the reader to do.

1.12.5 **GIVE ENOUGH "BYSTANDER" INFORMATION.** In order to make the case realistic, you want to give readers just the information they would have if they were bystanders in this situation—hearing what people way, watching what they do, reading memos, etc. What makes a case realistic is that it's like being on the job and trying to figure out what's really going on and what to do about it.

1.12.6 **ASK CASE QUESTIONS.** At the end of the case, ask one or more specific case questions. These are "bottom-line" questions that will guide you and your readers in analyzing the case and developing creative ideas for resolution. These questions might ask what are the key issues, surface problems, root problems, and overlooked opportunities. You might ask what key figures should do. "What actions do you recommend?" "What should ABC Co. do next?" The questions should help readers to focus their attention on the important issues and desired outcomes.

1.12.7 **WRITE THE CASE KEY.** In a separate section entitled "Case Key" write your analysis of the case—your answers to your own case questions. Tell how you reached your conclusions and recommendations—reveal your thinking process—the how and the why. You may need to state which course and textbook concepts, principles, knowledge, and skills you used to solve the case. Relate the case analysis to the relevant chapters in the textbook.

1.12.8 **MAKE COPIES.** If this case is to be analyzed by a class or a work team, make enough copies for everyone. This version should NOT include the Case Key and should be single spaced to save paper. If the case is a project for course credit, the case report you submit to the instructor for a grade should be in double-space format and include the Case Key.

Chapter 2
Business Research Reports

THIS CHAPTER PRESENTS suggestions for conducting business research and writing business research reports. It includes these topics:

2.1 OVERVIEW OF THE RESEARCH PROCESS

THE RESEARCH PROCESS consists of these steps:

- Define a problem you want to solve or formulate a question you want to answer.
- Make a working outline that itemizes the types of information you would like to find and include in your paper.
- Find the types of information you have outlined, probably modifying your outline as you come up with specific information.
- Sift through the information and select what you might want to include in your paper.
- Organize this information, using your outline and modifying it as necessary.
- Write the report.
- Select highlights of your report for making an executive summary or talk.

2.1.1   DEFINING THE PROBLEM OR TOPIC. In business courses, this step often begins with the instructor assigning a topic for you to research or asking you to either pick from a list of topics or develop your own topic.

2.1.2 **THE ANALYSIS PHASE.** When you analyze, you look at the parts of a whole in order to study those parts. This first phase involves analyzing some area of business in order to select a part of it for further study. It also involves looking at many works (books, periodicals, internet, interviews, other sources) in order to select those parts of a work that can help you to answer the question or to solve the problem. When you are selecting sources and taking notes, you are constantly analyzing.

2.1.3 **THE SYNTHESIS PHASE.** When you synthesize, you select and integrate various parts in order to form or understand a whole. This part of the research process involves pulling together the bits and pieces of information you have selected and organizing them into a coherent whole, a report that adequately defines the question or problem and proceeds to answer it, arriving at some conclusions about the issue or situation and perhaps making some recommendations for action. When you are developing and revising the outline for the report, you are doing the major work of synthesizing. The synthesis phase continues with the writing of your paper, using your outline as the guide for organizing and presenting information.

2.1.4 **OBJECTIVITY.** You want readers to view your research as credible, so you must be reasonably objective. This means that you must look at all types of relevant answers to your question, even if they are not the answers you think are "right" or best. You must at least mention important conflicting viewpoints if those viewpoints reflect "reality." In other words, you must keep an open mind and be fair in your evaluations of information and opinions. If your opinion is biased or prejudiced in some way, you should attempt to be aware of it and to state it in the report to help your readers form a clear picture of the situation.

2.1.5 **THE LEARNING PROCESS.** The research process obviously helps you to learn more about a particular area of business. At a deeper level it can help you to learn more about yourself and about how to discipline your thinking, maintain an open mind, and develop your own opinions on important issues. It can also help you develop the knowledge and skills necessary for locating various types of information, finding answers to questions, solving problems, and communicating the process to others. These are skills you will need throughout your career as a student and as a business professional.

2.2 SELECTING A TOPIC;
PRELIMINARY RESEARCH & OUTLINE

The first step of any research project is identifying the topic you will research—the question you want to answer or the problem you want to resolve. Then you must do some preliminary research to determine whether the topic is feasible and how broad or narrow the scope should be. Then you are ready to make a working outline of subtopics you will try to cover. This process allows you to refine your purpose, the topic, and the methods you will use to cover it.

2.2.1 SELECT A WORKING TOPIC

2.2.1.1 **GUIDELINES FOR SELECTING** a topic are usually given by your instructor. Unless more specific guidelines are given, the range of topics will often encompass any subject directly related to the topics covered in the course. At one extreme, you want to be sure your topic is definitely related to the course objectives. At the other extreme, you want to be sure your paper does not merely repeat or rehash material that is covered in the course materials. Instead it should (1) expand on some course topic or issue, (2) explore a course topic or issue in greater depth, or (3) introduce a clearly related topic or issue.

2.2.1.2 **WHETHER YOU SELECT A TOPIC FROM A LIST** provided by the instructor or come up with a topic on your own, select one that (1) expands on an area you are particularly interested in and that you want to know more about or (2) represents a gap in your area of knowledge and skill, an area in which you feel you need more information in order to do a good job. Consider your career goals when selecting a topic. Explore issues that will bring the greatest payoffs in preparing you for the career you have in mind.

2.2.1.3 **IDEAS FOR SELECTING A TOPIC**

(1) START WITH THE COURSE TEXT. Glance through the table of contents, the chapter titles, the headings within chapters, and the index. What topics are particularly interesting to you? Which ones grab you or turn you on? What topics represent gaps in your knowledge that especially need to be filled? Do you feel at a decided disadvantage when it comes to delegating tasks? Or pricing a new product? Is filling in one of these knowledge gaps especially crucial to achieving your career goals? If you select a topic that is introduced in the course text, read thoroughly all text material on that topic to be sure you don't merely repeat it in your paper. You may want to refer to it in brief, general terms in your final paper, but do not rehash it. Next, check for any footnotes or references that relate to the topic and note these as sources for your initial literature search.

(2) GO OVER YOUR COURSE NOTES and other course materials, such as the *Wall Street Journal* or instructor handouts, and think back over class discussions. What issues or topics were raised that especially interested you? Might any of these be the starting point for further exploration?

(3) DO YOU PLAN TO START A BUSINESS OF YOUR OWN? If your career goal is to start a specific type of business of your own, you might want to explore some aspect of starting or operating that type of business. Of course, the aspect you select should be directly related to the course objectives—some appropriate aspect of management for management courses, of marketing for marketing courses, etc.

(4) REVIEW YOUR SPECIAL INTERESTS. Are you especially interested in learning more about a particular business firm or business leader? If you focus on how that company or that leader applies or personifies specific concepts, techniques, or issues covered in the course, you may have the makings of an interesting paper.

(5) CONSIDER AN INTERNATIONAL FOCUS. Perhaps your career plans include working in or doing business with another country or in the international division of a domestic firm. Or perhaps you would simply like to know more about business operations in a particular foreign country. Again, if you focus on how course-related concepts, techniques, or issues are viewed or applied in another country, you may be able to build a productive paper on such a topic.

2.2.1.4 **DEFINE THE PROBLEM OR QUESTION**

(1) GET AT ROOT PROBLEMS. Properly defining a problem is the key to getting at the root cause of it and coming up with solutions that address the "root problem." For example, you might define a problem as "Poor Public Transportation Services." The key to getting at the root problem is to ask "why" questions. Ask "why are public transportation services so poor?" When you get an answer, ask "why" again, or ask "why does that matter?" Keep asking "why" questions until you believe you have arrived at the root question that will get at the root cause of the problem. It might be "Getting Taxpayers to Support an Excellent Transportation System."

(2) FORMULATE A MEANINGFUL QUESTION. A probing question may be the best beginning for your research paper topic. What do you really want to know about the course topic that does not appear in the course materials? Some examples are: "What do I.T. managers (accountants/human resource professionals, etc.) really do?" "How do leaders get people to follow them?" "How can I predict which career (field, professional, company) will be the best fit for me?" "How should I go about pricing electronic equipment when I get my own store?" "How do I delegate tasks?"

Some instructors prefer that you state a hypothesis (that is, assume an answer to your question) and then proceed to support or refute it, still using fairness and objectivity.

(3) START A TENTATIVE OUTLINE. This practice helps you to get organized from the beginning, focusing on finding those "needles" (of relevant info) in the "haystack" (of masses of data).

If you are solving a problem, ask yourself what types of information are likely to provide some clues to the root problem and some possible solutions. Use these categories as items in your tentative outline. (Examples are "inadequate funding," "taxpayer resistance," "publicizing the advantages.")

If you are using the question approach, what other questions flow naturally from your basic question? Use those questions as your tentative outline. (Examples are "Do I.T. managers deal more with people or things?" "What level of technical expertise is necessary?" "What is a typical I.T. manager's profile?")

2.2.2 *DO SOME PRELIMINARY RESEARCH*

2.2.2.1 PRELIMINARY RESEARCH IS ESSENTIAL before settling on a topic (and submitting it to your instructor, if approval is required). Such research allows you:

(1) to learn what type of research has been done on the topic

(2) to be sure adequate data is readily available

(3) to discover which subject headings, key index words, and related works might be most helpful in finding the information you will need

(4) to see how your topic can be further limited or (in rare cases) broadened

(5) to determine what the major sections of the paper might cover and in turn prepare a working outline

(6) to reserve or request materials that are not immediately available.

2.2.2.2 DO NOT TAKE EXTENSIVE NOTES YET. Take brief notes about the reference sources you find and their locations so you can easily find your sources again. You may want to make photocopies of source pages you are fairly sure you will refer to again. This procedure will save time in the long run because you won't have to relocate these sources. For internet sources, bookmark them in your web browser and paste and copy relevant articles into your computer files, organized according to your tentative outline.

2.2.2.3 RECORD POTENTIAL REFERENCES in any way that works for you. If you use index cards or lined sheets for note taking, use a separate sheet or card for each reference. Then they will be easy to alphabetize by author's last name for your final list of references.

2.2.2.4 EACH REFERENCE NOTATION SHOULD INCLUDE:

(1) reference or bibliographical information as shown in "2.5.7 Documenting Your Sources" in this manual

(2) for books, the library call number, so you can find it later.

(3) page numbers and other notations for easy retrieval of the information

(4) your evaluations of how valuable the source will probably be to you in preparing your paper. You may devise a rating scale of 1 to 5 or A, B, C to indicate importance or value of the material.

2.2.3 *MAKE A WORKING OUTLINE*

2.2.3.1 OUTLINING ORGANIZES THE WORK. As you do your preliminary research, you started a tentative outline. Now it is time to review what you have, determine what else you need, turn your tentative outline into a preliminary outline, and refine your problem statement or basic question.

2.2.3.2 ANALYZE YOUR ASSUMPTIONS. What are you assuming in your approach to the topic? Are your assumptions realistic and logical? Do they reflect a bias or prejudice? If the premises upon which your research is based are faulty, the entire project will lack credibility. For example, the student who selects the question "How should I go about delegating tasks?" makes several assumptions, including:

(1) That the organization she joins will have a hierarchical structure of authority and responsibility.

(2) That the organization structure will contain a chain of command that empowers managers to delegate tasks to persons directly under them in the chain.

(3) That each person in the organization will have areas of responsibility and authority that are fairly well defined along with the specific tasks and duties they are expected to perform.

If one of the assumptions is that the job position will automatically endow her with unquestioned authority that will automatically elicit complete obedience and loyalty from her subordinates, her research will be built on a shaky foundation.

2.2.3.3 LIST MAJOR STATEMENTS OF FACT. Review the information you have so far. List in any order, as they come to mind, major statements about what you already know and have learned from the preliminary research on the topic. Then look for obvious gaps that must be filled in order to answer your questions or resolve the root problem. Note these gaps at the bottom of your list.

2.2.3.4 MAKE A WORKING OUTLINE. Use one of the approaches discussed in Section 2.4.1.

2.2.4 *REFINE YOUR PURPOSE, TOPIC, AND METHOD*

2.2.4.1 REFINE YOUR PROBLEM STATEMENT OR QUESTION AND YOUR TOPIC. Question, Problem, Purpose, Issue, Thesis, Theme, Subject, Topic, Controlling Idea—any of these terms may refer to why you are doing this particular research and what you expect to gain from it. They reflect your Problem Statement or your Meaningful Question. If your instructor wants a statement of purpose, examples are:

> *To determine some effective pricing policies for a small electronics store*

> *To apply principles of delegation in a small one-owner business*

If a problem-solving approach is needed, your refined problem statement might be:

> *How to develop the best pricing policies for a small electronics store*

> *Finding the key do's and don'ts of delegating tasks*

If a question approach is used, the refined question might be

How do I become successful at delegating tasks?

How can I match my professional profile with a specific corporate culture?

The corresponding titles for these papers might be

Assessing the Fit of a Professional Profile with a Corporate Culture

Pricing Policy for the Small Electronics Firm

Delegating in a Small One-Owner Business

2.2.4.2 **NARROW YOUR TOPIC** if it is too broad. Trying to cover too much territory in a term research paper is one of the most common errors students make. Ask yourself, are entire books written (or could be written) about this topic? If so, it is obvious that you could only give it the most superficial, incomplete coverage in a term paper.

2.2.4.3 **AN EASY WAY TO NARROW YOUR TOPIC** is to examine carefully the major sections you developed in your preliminary outline. Ask yourself if one or two of those sections could be developed into a manageable topic. If so, you can salvage most of the preliminary work you have already completed.

2.2.4.4 **AN EXAMPLE OF AN INITIAL OUTLINE** for a 20-page student paper is shown here:

DELEGATION

I. History

II. Various Schools of Thought

III. A Model Approach

IV. Application to a Small One-Owner Business

After determining that all these areas could never be adequately discussed in a 20-page paper, the student focused on the main question he wanted to answer through his research project. He realized that the last section of the outline was the area he should focus on: How should I handle delegation as the owner of a small business? Since basic delegation techniques were covered in the course text, he could focus on the specific application of those techniques to the business he planned to enter upon graduation.

2.2.4.5 **ASK SUBORDINATE QUESTIONS** in order to determine what the major sections of your paper should cover. Now that you have done some preliminary research and refined your topic, what questions naturally come to mind? In our example, the student developed the following subordinate questions:

What are some typical problems?

How can these problems be avoided or overcome?

What is a model (ideal) approach to delegation by the small business owner?

2.2.4.6 **REFINE YOUR WORKING OUTLINE AND TITLE.** Convert the questions into the major sections of an outline. Rewrite the title so that it shows exactly the area your paper will cover. For example, "Delegation" is much too broad a topic. It implies every sort of delegation in every sort of situation, business and otherwise, throughout history. The student considered Delegation in a Small Mail Order Firm, but could find no library materials on such a narrow part of delegation. There appeared to be adequate information, however, on Delegation in a Small One-Owner Business.

2.2.4.7 AN EXAMPLE of a refined outline for this project:

> *DELEGATION IN A SMALL ONE-OWNER BUSINESS*
>
> *I. Some typical problems*
>
> *II. Suggestions for avoiding or overcoming problems*
>
> *III. A model approach to delegation in the small business*

With this outline, each major type of problem will become a heading under "Some typical problems," and each major suggestion will become a heading under "Suggestions for avoiding or overcoming problems." If the writer finds there are only two or three major problem areas, she may decide to make each of those areas a major section of the paper and further divide each section into a discussion of the problem, followed by a discussion of the solution. The model approach might be divided by distinct phases of the delegation process.

2.2.4.8 WORKING OUTLINE is the appropriate term for your tentative outline at this point. Throughout the research project you will be working with your outline, revising various parts of it, as you gather, analyze, and organize the information for your paper. It is important to remember that the outline is never "cast in concrete." It is a tool for logical, efficient, guided effort in the research and writing of your paper and should be changed as your knowledge and understanding progress. It should not become a rigid structure that limits your creativity. See the section xx for guidance in making and working with an outline.

2.2.4.9 DETERMINE THE BEST METHOD for finding the answer to your overriding question. In the example just given the writer decided to first research the literature to see what had been written on his topic. If the library material was inadequate to answer his overriding question, he planned to develop a brief survey to send to some small business owners. If he needed further information, he planned to personally interview some of the owners who had responded to the survey.

2.2.4.10 YOUR METHOD MAY BE LIMITED TO LIBRARY RESEARCH in most of your projects. Even then, you should determine the procedure for developing and carrying out your research, what types of information you should gather, and what the most appropriate sources are likely to be. Many instructors require you to state your method for achieving the purpose of your research when you submit a preliminary topic and outline for approval. Others may expect such a statement in the final paper.

2.3 GATHERING THE INFORMATION

2.3.1 FIND THE RIGHT INFORMATION

2.3.1.1 SEE THE CHAPTER ON FINDING BUSINESS FACTS, for details on the types of business information that is available in published form and on the Internet. Consider also getting first-hand information through interviews, surveys, company records, and similar sources.

2.3.2 ANALYZE SOURCE MATERIALS

2.3.2.1 ANALYSIS. Perhaps the most demanding phase of the research report project is finding, analyzing, evaluating, and selecting the most appropriate information for answering your question and achieving your purpose. Analysis involves looking at various PARTS of books, periodicals, and other words in order to study their relationship and usefulness for your project.

2.3.2.2 ANALYTICAL QUESTIONS that may be helpful to ask when you evaluate information:

What is the significance of this bit of information in relation to my problem or question?

How does this information contribute to the answer to my subordinate questions?

How does this information help to

1) explain some aspect of my topic

2) define some aspect of my topic

3) support or refute some viewpoint, method, or approach directly related to my topic?

How essential is this information to the overall effectiveness of my paper?

Would my paper be just as effective without this information?

2.3.2.3 EVALUATE ALL INFORMATION for reliability and probable usefulness, keeping the information about sources, credentials, and authors in mind.

2.3.2.4 EVALUATE INFORMATION FOUND IN ENCYCLOPEDIAS is usually too general to be of much use in the business paper. Such general information may help you grasp a concept. At the end of the entry, you may find helpful references that lead to more specific sources.

2.3.2.5 EVALUATE AUTHOR CREDENTIALS. These are often given within the book or article you use. You can look up such information on the Internet or in one of the Who's Who publications. Does the author have adequate credentials in the area being discussed? Some news magazines and newspapers don't give the author's name. You must then rely on the credibility of the publisher.

2.3.2.6 EVALUATE THE AUTHOR'S OBJECTIVITY. Ask these kinds of questions:

- Are all sides presented?
- Does the author give a balanced presentation?
- Do you detect evidence of prejudice and/or attempts to manipulate or sway the reader to the author's viewpoint?
- Does the author use emotional language?
- Does the author make accusations?
- Where accusations appear, are they substantiated by documented evidence?
- Are there more statements of opinion than of fact?
- When opinions are given, do they seem logical in light of the facts given?
- Are the facts well documented?

2.3.2.7 WHEN AUTHORS' VIEWPOINTS CONFLICT. Does the opinion of one of your authors conflict with that of another author? This is not an unusual situation, and you must decide which viewpoint you consider more relevant or valid. It may be helpful to note the dates of publication. Does the author of the later publication have the benefit of new information? It may also be possible to find a review of the two authors' works. Or you may use both opinions to show two sides of an issue and leave it to the reader to determine which viewpoint is best.

2.3.2.8 **EVALUATE THE PUBLISHER** of the book or journal. Those which have established reputations in scholarly areas are usually very careful about what they print. For example, articles published by the Academy of Management, a scholarly organization, will carry more weight for your purposes than those published in popular newsstand magazines. If a work is privately printed or does not mention the publisher, its reliability may be questionable.

2.3.2.9 **EVALUATE THE TIMELINESS** of the information. Check the date of publication. Most business research involves current issues. Unless you are including the history of a situation, you will probably want to limit your sources to those published within the past five years. The term "revised" indicates a work has been updated, while the term "reprinted" means an earlier edition has been merely duplicated, so you should use the earlier date in your evaluation.

2.3.3 TAKE NOTES

2.3.3.1 **PHOTOCOPY.** Most students find that photocopying pages from source materials at the library is the most efficient first step to note taking. Make a notation on each page (or stapled/clipped set of pages) giving complete information about the source document, including page numbers (see suggestions for documentation in this chapter). Make another notation that indicates where in your working outline this information will fit (IIIA, for example). Such notations make it immeasurably easier to organize your information when you are ready to write the report.

2.3.3.2 **PARAPHRASE.** From these photocopied pages, or from the original source, you must provide relevant information in your paper in one of these forms:

1) paraphrase in your own words

2) summarize in your own words, or

3) copy verbatim for use in quotes

For this step use the size of note cards or paper that works well for you. Just remember

(a) to leave space at the top for labeling each part according to its place in your outline

(b) to write on one side of the paper only so notes will be easy to organize and keep straight.

2.3.3.3 **EACH NOTE SHOULD HAVE A PURPOSE.** It should either

(1) help answer one of your subordinate questions, or

(2) suggest a significant new subordinate question that should be answered in order to adequately address the problem or question. This second point indicates that you will continuously be evaluating and analyzing your material, your question or problem statement, your outline, and your method during the entire research.

2.3.3.4 **PLAGIARISM.** You must be sure to give credit to your sources for any facts or ideas that are not your own or general knowledge, even though you have paraphrased or summarized that fact or idea in your own words. Failure to give credit is plagiarism, a serious offense that can result in a failing grade on the paper, in the course, and even expulsion from your school. See section 2.5.7 for how to properly document your sources.

2.4 OUTLINING & ORGANIZING THE INFORMATION

First you must select an organization pattern for your report. Then you must go through a synthesis and review process that allows you to arrange the information within your organization pattern. Next you update your working outline, following outlining conventions.

2.4.1 SELECT AN ORGANIZATION PATTERN

Look for an appropriate way to organize the major statements you have listed that reflect the types of information you have gathered. These typical patterns are explained below:

1) Order of Importance

2) Criteria for Comparison of Choices

3) Cause & Effect

4) Chronological Order (time-based)

5) Logical Order

6) General to Particular (overview, then details)

7) Particular to General (details, then overview)

8) Spatial Order (by location)

2.4.1.1 **ORDER OF IMPORTANCE** - putting the most important ideas or material first and continuing in descending order, ending with the least important. In our example, the writer begins with the most significant or crucial rule for delegating and ends with the least significant.

2.4.1.2 **CRITERIA FOR COMPARISON OF CHOICES** - comparing two or more choices or options by discussing one by one the factors upon which a final choice would be based. The advantages and disadvantages of choosing a particular method, approach, process, or machine might be compared. In our example, the writer might compare two or more approaches to delegating by first listing some criteria (standards, or results) that an effective approach should produce, such as (1) motivates delegatee to achieve, (2) results in more productive use of time for delegator. The paper is then organized so that each criterion becomes a major section and the way each approach measures up to a criterion is discussed within that section. The outline for the example just given is shown here.

> A. *Motivational Aspects of Delegation*
>
> > *1. Approach A*
> >
> > *2. Approach B*
>
> B. *Time Managements Aspects of Delegation*
>
> > *1. Approach A*
> >
> > *2. Approach B*

2.4.1.3 **CAUSE AND EFFECT** - showing how actions, events, or attitudes (causes) lead to certain end situations or results (effects). In our example, the writer might first discuss ineffective or nonexistent delegation and its results, then effective delegation and its results, comparing these choices. A pattern often used is: problem, cause, effect, solution.

2.4.1.4 CHRONOLOGICAL ORDER - presenting information in a time sequence, usually a historical sequence from the beginning of a certain era to its end or to the present. In our example, the writer might explore the evolution of delegation practices, showing how more and more freedom and authority have been passed to subordinates since the beginning of the Industrial Revolution.

2.4.1.5 LOGICAL ORDER - presenting material in a step-by-step fashion, starting with what you can assume the reader already knows, presenting new information, and subsequently building on the reader's grasp of that information to discuss additional information. Our writer might begin with an example of delegation in the home or classroom and move on to explain the process of delegation step-by-step. Writers can use logical order also to discuss, step-by-step, various kinds of values, attitudes, characteristics, phenomena, situations, or events.

2.4.1.6 GENERAL TO PARTICULAR - making a broad, general statement and then backing it up with particular examples or arguments (also called *deductive* reasoning). In our example, the writer might state that the adoption of modem management delegation techniques results in greater productivity. Each major section of the paper might then show how a particular aspect of delegation resulted in greater productivity, or the types of productivity that resulted, or ways in which productivity was enhanced.

2.4.1.7 PARTICULAR TO GENERAL - giving examples or arguments that lead one to a broad, general conclusion or statement (also called *inductive* reasoning). Here our writer might use each major section to discuss an aspect of delegation and how that particular aspect boosted productivity, leading to the conclusion that the use of modem management delegation techniques results in greater productivity.

2.4.1.8 SPATIAL ORDER - presenting material according to its geographical location, its location within a particular setting, or through movement from one setting to another such as a journey. In our example, the writer might describe delegation techniques in two or more companies or even in two or more countries, making some comparisons.

2.4.2 SYNTHESIS AND REVIEW

2.4.2.1 SYNTHESIS is the combining of separate parts or elements to form a coherent whole. Now you must determine how best to combine those bits and pieces of information you selected from your analysis of numerous source materials. You want to present a coherent whole, a research report, that defines and offers solutions to your problem or that answers your question. This report must achieve the purpose you set out to accomplish.

2.4.2.2 IDENTIFY THE MAJOR SECTIONS of the report. Ask yourself:

What overall patterns of relationships emerge from the information I have collected? What is the most significant pattern? Look at such relationships as:

- causes and effects
- things that are comparable
- things that are different
- things that conflict
- things that help explain or define essential concepts or issues
- things that serve as an example, model, or application of a concept

Review the organizational patterns discussed in this chapter. When you have determined the most significant pattern, you can identify or verify the outline (organizational pattern) for the major sections of your report. Each major element in the pattern becomes a major section.

2.4.2.3 IDENTIFY SUBSECTIONS. Look for logical subdivisions within major sections. Ask:

What subordinate patterns of relationship emerge from the information I have placed under each major section of the report?

The answers to this question will provide you with the outline for the subordinate sections of the report.

2.4.2.4 ELIMINATE THE LESS RELEVANT INFORMATION. Ask:

What information is not a part of this topic or issue?

What problems lie outside the realm of this problem?

You must weed out information, problems, and issues that are not directly related to your problem or question.

2.4.2.5 REVIEW YOUR QUESTION OR PROBLEM STATEMENT. Is it still the most appropriate one for your paper or should it be revised? In turn, review your subordinate questions and revise if necessary. Check for gaps in logic. You may want to ask someone to read your outline to see how well they understand your thinking.

2.4.2.6 REVIEW YOUR LOGIC. The outline should be a clear reflection of your thinking. Time spent in refining the outline at this point pays big dividends by allowing you to:

(1) correct errors in reasoning, logic, organization

(2) write the paper more fluently and efficiently

(3) produce a more logical, coherent report.

2.4.2.7 UPDATE YOUR TITLE. Your title should indicate as precisely as possible the scope and range of your paper—what the paper covers. The reader should be able to imply what the paper does not cover. The title "Delegation in the Small One-Owner Business" implies that you will cover everything that any small-business owner needs to know about delegating tasks. It also implies that you do not cover other management techniques, nor do you cover delegating in larger size businesses nor in nonprofit or government organizations.

2.4.2.8 EVALUATE AND UPDATE YOUR OUTLINE. After you have gathered the material you need to address your problem or question, and your subordinate questions, review the information to determine if your working outline is still the most effective one. Consider using one of the other organizational patterns discussed in this section.

You may use one organizational pattern (such as cause and effect) for your major sections, and another (such as logical or spatial) for each set of subordinate sections, if such a structure works best for your purpose.

2.4.2.9 USE WORDING SPECIFIC TO YOUR TOPIC. See the outline example below. The introduction and conclusion sections have specific headings instead of the general headings "Introduction" and "Conclusion."

2.4.2.10 OUTLINE EXAMPLE. Here is the final outline of the project mentioned in earlier examples.

DELEGATION IN THE SMALL ONE-OWNER BUSINESS

Purpose: To determine an ideal approach to delegation in the small one-owner business.

I. Understanding why delegation is important

II. Recognizing typical problem areas

    A. Inability to let go of authority

    B. Lack of ability to train subordinates

    C. Limited vision of growth possibilities

III. Finding a better way

    A. Adopting a new perspective

    B. Gaining the necessary skills

    C. Finding the right employees

IV. Creating your own model approach

    A. Developing long- and short-term objectives

    B. Establishing a productive work team

    C. Finding the best system for evaluation and control

V. Letting success motivate you and your employees

2.4.2.10.1 THE OVERALL ORGANIZATIONAL PATTERN here (the major sections) is from the particular to the general, beginning with specific types of problems in delegating, moving to specific ways these problems can be alleviated and how to develop a model system, ending with conclusions about how this process can motivate you and your employees.

2.4.2.10.2 THE INTRODUCTION SECTION of the paper would include the problem statement, or the question, or the statement of purpose, perhaps the method you used, any necessary background information the reader needs to know to understand what follows, and an overview of the key topics covered in the paper.

2.4.2.10.3 THE CONCLUSIONS SECTION might include briefly the broad general conclusions that you have made as a result of the research, personal comments that reflect your thoughts on the topic, what this all means in the scheme of things, and how you recommend implementing these conclusions and ideas in the business world.

2.4.2.10.4 ORGANIZATIONAL PATTERNS FOR SUBSECTIONS may vary. In this example the structural pattern for the subsections under Section II is order of importance. The pattern for the subsections under Sections III and IV is logical order, presenting the material in step-by-step fashion.

2.4.3 FOLLOW OUTLINING CONVENTIONS (COMMON RULES)

2.4.3.1 SYSTEMS FOR USING NUMBER AND LETTERS for outlining the sections of your paper in an outline can vary slightly. Here is a system that is generally accepted:

> *I. . . .*
>> *A. . . .*
>> *B. . . .*
>>> *1. . . .*
>>> *2. . . .*
>>>> *a. . . .*
>>>> *b. . . .*
>>>>> *(1) . . .*
>>>>> *(2) . . .*
>>>>>> *(a) . . .*
>>>>>> *(b) . . .*
>
> *II. . . .*

2.4.3.2 DO NOT USE AN "A" WITHOUT A "B." Using an "A" in an outline, without a "B" is a violation of logic—since you cannot divide a section into one part. If you divide something, you must logically divide it into at least two parts; otherwise it is not divided but is still a whole. Therefore, if you have a 1, you must have a corresponding 2. If you find yourself with a label for only one subsection, fix it by 1) finding a second logical, subsection or 2) restoring the section to a whole and eliminating the single subsection.

2.4.3.3 THREE FORMS OF OUTLINING you should know about are topic, sentence, and paragraph outlines.

2.4.3.3.1 TOPIC OUTLINES are the most commonly used form, and two typical types of this form are 1) nouns and their modifiers and 2) similar types of phrases or clauses. Parallel construction should be used within an outline category, as shown here.

1) NOUNS AND THEIR MODIFIERS

> *a. The difficult boss*
>
> *b. Your supportive employees*
>
> *c. Your problem employees*

2) PHRASES AND CLAUSES. Here is an example of an outline category that uses clauses

> *I. Why delegation is important*
>
> *II. How to recognize typical problem areas*
>
> *III. Where to find the best approaches*
>
> *IV. How to create your own model approach*

Here is an outline category that uses infinitive ("to") phrases:

1. To adopt a new perspective

2. To gain the necessary skills

3. To find the right employees

This outline category that uses gerund ("-ing") phrases:

1. Adopting a new perspective

2. Gaining necessary skills

3. Finding the right employees

This outline category that uses prepositional phrases:

1. From a new perspective

2. With the necessary skills

3. For the right employees

2.4.3.3.2 SENTENCE OUTLINE. Headings are complete sentences with subject and verb. Sometimes the major sections may be nouns and each subsection is a sentence. Some instructors assign this type of outline because the sentences can provide topic sentences for each section of the paper and help guide the student's writing efforts. For business reports, sentences should be short and to the point.

I. Effective managers are good delegators

II. Root problems may be hidden

III. Solutions must address root problems

2.4.3.3.3 PARAGRAPH OUTLINE may be used as a working outline, but is almost never submitted as the final outline. Every heading is a paragraph. The major sections may sometimes be nouns with all subsections consisting of paragraphs. This form provides more guidance for the actual writing of the paper than the other forms. It also gives the reader more detailed information about the paper; for this reason, some instructors require that paragraph outlines be submitted for their approval prior to the submission of the final paper. However, this type of outline is generally considered too detailed for most business purposes.

2.4.3.4 USE PARALLEL CONSTRUCTION for all headings within a category or level of the outline—first level (I, II, III), second level (A, B, C, etc.) First, for each level decide whether to use sentences, a certain type of phrase, clauses, or nouns with or without modifiers. Then use similar grammatical structure for each item at that level. This means that all first-level items (I, II, III, etc.) must have similar structure, such as gerund ("-ing") phrases. However, under item I, the second-level items (A, B, C, etc.) could have a different structure, such as nouns with modifiers. All these second-level items would then be nouns with modifiers.

2.4.3.5 TRANSLATE THE OUTLINE INTO REPORT HEADINGS. Now you have the structure of your report. Remember to translate this structure into headings within your report—to break up solid blocks of text, guide the reader, and make the report more understandable, readable, and interesting. To make headings, do the following:

2.4.3.5.1 DROP THE NUMBERING SYSTEM. Do not retain the I, II, III, or the A, B, C in your heading. Think in terms of newspaper and business magazine articles, which do not use a numbering system for headings.

2.4.3.5.2 USE FORMAT TO INDICATE LEVEL. Indicate whether a heading is level one, two, or three by its format and placement. Styles vary. What is important is to be consistent. If you decide the format for level-one headings will be "centered, all caps, bold, font 16", then use that format for all level-one headings. If level-two headings will be "left, initial caps, bold, 14," then all level-two headings must use that format.

2.4.3.5.3 MAINTAIN PARALLEL CONSTRUCTION. If you prepare your outline properly, using parallel construction, then you simply use that same wording for your headings.

2.5 WRITING THE REPORT

The chapter on Business Writing Style gives detailed information about writing reports as well as other types of business writing. This section gives general tips and suggestions for writing the main text, using headings and visual aids, writing the introduction and conclusion, documenting your sources, and preparing supplementary parts of the report.

2.5.1 GENERAL TIPS

2.5.1.1 REVIEW. Once you have reviewed all your material, your problem statement, question or purpose, and your working outline, you are ready to write the paper according to the outline.

2.5.1.2 AVOID WRITER'S BLOCK. See Chapter 7 for suggestions.

2.5.1.3 AVOID LAST-MINUTE CHAOS. Obviously, starting the project as early as possible in the course term will help avoid chaos. If you find yourself putting off the working on the report, do only one small segment at a time. Promise yourself to work on it for at least five minutes a day for a while. You will probably build momentum after a few short work sessions.

2.5.1.4 LEAVE SPACE FOR REVISIONS. Triple space between lines and provide wide margins for editing.

2.5.1.5 REORGANIZE IF NECESSARY. If, after you have written a large part of the paper, you decide on a drastic reorganization, consider the cut and paste method, using your revised outline as a guide.

2.5.1.6 UPDATE THE OUTLINE. When you have completed the final version of the paper, bring your final outline up to date so that it exactly reflects the structure of the paper.

2.5.1.7 PROOFREAD. Whether you type the paper yourself on an old manual typewriter, use the most sophisticated computer technology, or have someone else do the final draft, what you turn in to your instructor is your responsibility alone. So proofread thoroughly. The instructor can only assume that mistakes are there because you don't know any better and will grade accordingly. If you find minor errors at the last minute, and taking time to correct them would mean a late paper, it is better to correct them neatly in ink and to turn in the paper with errors. Check with your instructor to be sure.

2.5.2 WRITE THE MAIN TEXT

2.5.2.1 BEGIN WITH THE FIRST MAJOR SECTION of your report. Write the introduction later. After you have finished writing all the major sections, you should have a fairly clear picture of what to include in the introduction and the conclusion. Try writing each major section as if it were a separate essay. When you revise and edit, you can introduce transitional passages from one section to another.

2.5.2.2 DO NOT REPEAT TEXT MATERIAL, facts covered in course materials. You may refer briefly to such materials in order to establish the context within which you are discussing some issue, but you should then move quickly into new material.

2.5.2.3 AVOID ACCIDENTAL REPETITION of material by developing a system for identifying notes that have been incorporated into the paper. For example, after you integrate a particular section of your notes into the paper, place a diagonal line through that section so you will know it has been used.

2.5.2.4 GIVE PROPER CREDIT TO YOUR SOURCES. Except when you are expressing your own thoughts and ideas, you must give credit to the author or interviewee that provided you with the information you include in your paper. See the section on "Documenting Your Sources." Usually you will paraphrase what the authors said, giving them credit in an endnote or footnote.

2.5.2.5 USE QUOTATIONS PROPERLY. Sometimes you want to quote an author instead of paraphrasing him or her—perhaps because the words are so appropriate or inspiring, perhaps to give added credibility and weight to your argument. Normally, quotations should be short ones that you weave into your own sentences. Occasionally a longer quotation is needed.

2.5.2.6 IDENTIFY THE QUOTED AUTHOR by name and title or profession.

2.5.2.7 WEAVE DIRECT QUOTES INTO THE TEXT of your paper so that they sound like an integral part of it. See how often you can integrate the quoted author's words into one of your own sentences; for example:

> *The resulting productivity not only "enhances company earnings and the reputation of the manager responsible for this increased level of output," it enhances worker motivation, according to consultant J. B. Preston (Preston 2003, p. 81).*

Typical ways of introducing quotes are:

> ***The famous management guru J.B. Preston says***
>
> ***As finance expert J.B. Preston stated,***
>
> ***According to well-known author J.B. Preston***
>
> ***J.B. Preston, auditing expert, believes that***
>
> ***J.B. Preston is a renowned computer expert whose research indicates that***

When you edit the paper, check to see if there is adequate variety in the way quoted material is handled.

2.5.2.8 DO NOT CONFUSE DIRECT QUOTES WITH YOUR OWN WORDS. Remember that a direct quote is spoken from the author's viewpoint. If you are quoting what an interviewee said, pretend that you have tape recorded her words and are transcribing them.

> *Problem:* Cynthia Gomez said, *"The problems that arise often surprise <u>her</u>. <u>She doesn't</u> want to be caught unprepared."*
>
> *Solution:* Cynthia Gomez said, *"The problems that arise often surprise <u>me</u>. <u>I don't</u> want to be caught unprepared."*

2.5.2.9 DO NOT OVERUSE QUOTES. If you discover sections of the paper that contain strings of quotes with little of your own wording, find some quotes that can be paraphrased.

2.5.2.10 INCLUDE YOUR OWN IDEAS AND OPINIONS where called for. For example, when you report two conflicting opinions of credible authors, it may be appropriate to explain your own evaluation of the issue. Just be sure you make it clear to the reader whether an idea or opinion is your own, or whether it came from one of the source authors. Some sample wording:

> *My evaluation is . . .*   *I concluded that . . .*   *I recommend that . . .*

2.5.2.11 BULLET OR NUMBER ITEMS TO CAPTURE ATTENTION, to highlight some key points, and make your report more readable. See where you can break up solid blocks of text— to make it more appealing and readable, to call attention to key points or information, or to make information more understandable. Use bullets when you block in a list of items. Use numbers for items only if you have a reason for numbers, such as focusing on 7 principles.

2.5.2.12 USE PARALLEL CONSTRUCTION for all items within a numbered or bulleted list.

2.5.3   *USE HEADINGS*

2.5.3.1 YOUR OUTLINE PROVIDES THE HEADINGS. Use headings to clearly identify the major sections and subsections of your report. Just as a good title tells precisely what is in the report (and implies what is not included), good headings give a clear picture of what each section includes. Refine your outline; then use each item as a heading. All newspapers and magazines use headings within articles to make them more readable and informative.

2.5.3.2 HEADING PLACEMENT AND FORM. Normally the number or letter that identifies each part of the outline is not used as part of the heading. Instead placement and form indicate whether a heading represents a major section of the report or a subsection. Here is a generally acceptable system:

> *. . . and most companies had no official policy on this.*
>
> ### *MOTIVATIONAL ASPECTS OF DELEGATION*
>
> *There are three major approaches to using motivation in delegating tasks to subordinates, McClelland's Approach A, Maslow's Approach B, and Fielder's Approach C.*
>
> #### *MCCLELLAND'S APPROACH*
>
> *McClelland's approach incorporates ideas about the socialized aspects of needs that motivate people. There are six steps.*
>
> *THE FIRST STEP. You begin by talking with the worker and . . .*

2.5.3.3 HEADING FORMATS. In this system, all headings are printed in all capital letters. Some systems use different font styles, font sizes, bold, italics, underline, and similar devices to set apart the headings from the text. Regardless of the style you choose, be sure it is generally acceptable, clearly delineates the various heading levels, and that you use it consistently.

2.5.3.4 PLACEMENT OF HEADINGS indicates the section of the report it covers.

(a) Headings that denote level-one sections of the report are usually centered.

(b) Headings denoting level-two sections are usually placed at the left margin.

(c) Headings denoting level-three sections may be indented from the left margin.

(d) Paragraph run-in headings are placed at the beginnings of paragraphs to indicate level-four sections.

2.5.3.4.1 PARAGRAPH RUN-IN HEADINGS may be self-contained, or they may consist of the first few words of the first sentence. Choose one form or the other for a particular section of your report and use it consistently.

> ***THE FIRST STEP. You begin talking with . . .***

> ***THE FIRST STEP is to begin talking with . . .***

2.5.3.4.2 USE PARALLEL CONSTRUCTION for each group of headings. See the discussion of outlines in this chapter, as well as the section Maintain Parallel Construction in the chapter on Business Writing Style.

2.5.3.5 INTRODUCE EACH REPORT SECTION, SEPARATING HEADINGS WITH TEXT. The reader should not see two levels of headings without text between them. After each heading you need text that introduces the section that comes under the heading. This paragraph provides needed transition from the major heading to the grouping of lower-level headings that follow it. It usually provides a very brief overview of what will be covered in the entire section.

> **Problem***:*

> ***MOTIVATIONAL ASPECTS OF DELEGATION***

> > ***APPROACH A***

> **Solution***:*

> ***MOTIVATIONAL ASPECTS OF DELEGATION***

> ***There are three major approaches to using motivation in delegating tasks to subordinates, McClelland's Approach A, Maslow's Approach B, and Fielder's Approach C.***

> > ***APPROACH A***

2.5.3.6 HEADINGS AND TEXT SHOULD STAND ALONE. Do not assume the reader will automatically incorporate the heading information into the text that follows it. Make the first sentence a complete sentence and the first paragraph one that provides all the information you want the reader to know—without relying on the heading. The exception to this rule is the paragraph run-in heading that is a part of the first sentence.

> **Problem***:*

> > ***APPROACH A***

> > ***This is the best approach if the key factor is . . .***

> **Solution***:*

> > ***APPROACH A***

> > ***Use Approach A any time the key factor is . . .***

2.5.4 USE VISUAL AIDS (EXHIBITS)

2.5.4.1 ARRANGE STATISTICS AND FACTS for visual impact and quick, easy comprehension. Some typical devices for doing this are (1) itemized lists (2) tables (3) charts (4) graphs and (5) diagrams. Other devices that aid comprehension are pictograms, drawings, maps, and pictures.

2.5.4.2 ITEMIZED LISTS of information can be helpful in clearly grouping related items and in breaking up long pages of solid type. They can make your report more readable but do not overdo this device.

2.5.4.2.1 USE PARALLEL CONSTRUCTION for all items in a particular list.

2.5.4.3 *EXHIBIT* is a catch-all term that can include all visual aids (except itemized lists) used in a report. You may prefer the term *Table*, *Chart*, and/or *Figure*.

2.5.4.4 GIVE EACH EXHIBIT A NUMBER AND A TITLE that conveys a clear idea of what the exhibit is about and what it includes. Number each exhibit sequentially throughout the report. Put the exhibit number and title at the top. Put any explanatory notes at the bottom. The last item at the bottom should be the source of the exhibit—any documentation or credit that is applicable.

2.5.4.5 EXHIBITS THAT PROVIDE EXTRA INFORMATION but are not necessary to the understanding of the report may labeled as an "Appendix," and placed after the References section of the report. The exhibit should be referred to briefly in the report but not discussed in any detail.

2.5.4.6 PLACE REPORT EXHIBITS NEAR THE DISCUSSION that follows them, if possible, so the reader can easily refer to the exhibit while reading your discussion of it.

2.5.4.7 INTRODUCE AN EXHIBIT by weaving it into your discussion, much as you do with quotes. Identify it by number at least:

> *Much of the increased productivity comes from improved time management, as clearly indicated in "Exhibit 5, Sources of Productivity."*

2.5.4.8 DISCUSS EACH EXHIBIT after it has been introduced in the text and presented physically in the paper. Do not merely repeat data from the exhibit in your discussion; the reader can readily see that information. Instead, determine what sort of analysis needs to be made for the reader or what aspects presented in the exhibit may not be readily grasped and therefore need to be pointed out. Some examples are:

(1) Explanations of what the information means in relation to your overriding or subordinate questions.

(2) The implications of the information for the situations, problems, or decisions being considered in this report.

(3) How this information supports, refutes, ties in with, relates to, compares with, or contrasts to other information in the report.

2.5.4.9 TABLES normally fall into one of two types: (1) One-way tables are simple listings of data with a table. Two-way (cross) tables contain some basic categories in the first column with some values or information for each category in the other column(s).

Example of one-way table:

> *TABLE 16. TYPES OF JOBS AVAILABLE*

> *Officials and managers, GS 10 to 16*
>
> *Professional and technical staff, GS 8 to 14*
>
> *Secretarial and clerical- GS 2 to 8*

Example of two-way (cross) table:

> *TABLE 25. EMPLOYMENT PARTICIPATION RATES, 1974 AND 1980*

Job Category	1974	1980	Change
Officials and managers	10.0%	14.7%	47.0%
Professionals	17.7	26.6	50.2
Technicians	21.5	31.5	47.8

2.5.4.10 LABEL EACH COLUMN IN THE TABLE carefully so the reader can understand the table without having to refer to the text. Choose column headings that are descriptive, mutually exclusive, and show limits or scope of the material presented in the column.

2.5.4.11 CHARTS AND GRAPHS usually fall into one of three basic categories: line graph, bar chart, or pie chart. While you can use numerous variations, if you understand these basic types, you should be able to devise some effective exhibits.

2.5.4.11.1 LINE GRAPHS are best for showing progress or trends over a period of time or fluctuations during a period of time. For example, you might show how sales have gone up or down (fluctuated) during certain months. Or you might shown an overall upward sales trend for a period of years.

Example of a line graph:

EXHIBIT 8. SALES TRENDS, AVCO, 1980–1990

2.5.4.11.2 PIE CHARTS are the best means of showing a whole amount and the proportion within the whole that each of its various parts represents. It is commonly used to show (a) income, and the contribution various sources of income make to the whole, (b) budgets or expenditures, and the portion each type of expenditure takes from the whole budget, (c) constituencies or distinct groups of people, and the proportions represented by the various subgroups.

Example of a pie chart:

EXHIBIT 15. SOURCES OF INCOME, AVCO, 1989

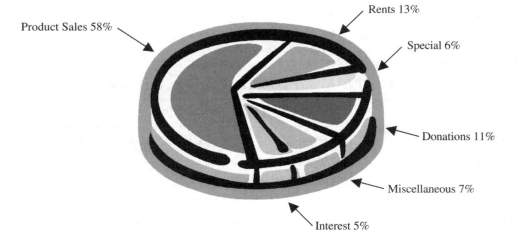

2.5.4.11.3 BAR CHARTS are most effective for making comparisons of events that occurred during the same period of time. You could compare the sales figures for various regions of the country for a particular year, with each bar representing a region. You could likewise compare sales figures of various salespersons, various companies, various branches of a company, various products.

Example of a bar chart:

EXHIBIT 12. COMPARISON OF SALES BY REGION, AVCO, 1989

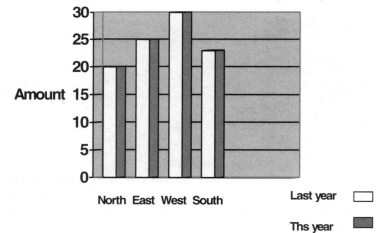

2.5.5 WRITE THE INTRODUCTION

2.5.5.1 REPEAT THE TITLE of the paper at the top of the first page of the report, even though you attach a cover page that includes the title. The first page of the report usually has a two-inch margin above the title.

2.5.5.2 WHAT YOU INCLUDE IN YOUR INTRODUCTION will depend on the nature of your particular project and the expectations and requirements of your instructor. You can include some of the kinds of information listed here, but rarely if ever would you need to include all of them.

(1) VERY BRIEF BACKGROUND information or explanation that is necessary for the reader to understand the project.

(2) THE TOPIC, its scope (what you do include) and its limits (other aspects of the topic, further analyses or issues that you do not attempt to include).

(3) WHY YOU CHOSE THIS TOPIC, its significance, the overriding question you want to answer, your purpose for the project, perhaps the subordinate questions you attempt to answer.

(4) THE MAJOR STRUCTURAL PATTERN of the report, whether from cause to effect, general to particular, or other, that reflects your approach to the topic.

(5) THE METHOD you used to achieve your purpose—the types of research, the types of sources, your reasoning approach.

(6) AN OVERVIEW or brief summary of the major findings; i.e., the key idea contained in each of your major subsections. Perhaps an overview of the conclusions arrived at through these findings.

(7) THE TIMELINESS OF YOUR RESEARCH, its significance for today's students and business persons, its relationship to current problems and issues, the timeliness of your sources.

(8) DEFINITIONS of special terms you use in the report.

(9) A BRIEF BUT SIGNIFICANT ANECDOTE, quote, example, or human interest story that leads directly into your topic.

2.5.5.3 IF YOU HAVE DIFFICULTY in writing the introduction, the reason may be that this section is strictly your own creation. It is not based on the ideas and facts of other authors. However, the introduction does have a structure that can guide you. Review the kinds of information that are often included in introductions as discussed earlier in this chapter, select the ones that apply to your project, decide on a sequence for discussing them, and put them into outline form under the main heading "Introduction."

Now pretend you are holding a conversation with a classmate. You feel confident and relaxed about telling your friend about your research project. Put on paper, freely and rapidly, what you would say, using your outline as a guide. After you have covered every subcategory, evaluate and edit the entire introductory section. Tie each subcategory together in a way that makes sense and moves logically from one idea to the next.

2.5.6 WRITE THE CONCLUSION

2.5.6.1 USE THE SAME APPROACH to writing the conclusion that you used to writing the introduction.

2.5.6.2 WHAT YOU INCLUDE in the conclusion will, again, depend on your project and your instructor's expectations. Some types of information to consider are:

(1) A BRIEF SUMMARY OR WRAP-UP of the most significant findings and how they help answer your overriding question (and perhaps your subordinate questions) and/or achieve your purpose. In this summary you should briefly analyze and evaluate your main points, then point out the significance of each and how they lead to your conclusion(s).

(2) A REVIEW OF THE STRUCTURAL PATTERN, its development and conclusion.

(3) LOGICAL CONCLUSIONS you arrived at as a result of reading, analyzing, and synthesizing the information you found in your source materials. Identify these conclusions as your own so it is clear they are not the ideas of your source authors:

   My conclusions are . . . I therefore conclude that . . .

(4) YOUR PERSONAL OPINIONS about key factors, authors' ideas, and any other aspects of the topic you think are significant. Again, be sure to make it clear where opinions are yours so that the reader cannot mistake them for those of a source author.

(5) RECOMMENDATIONS you would make concerning action that should be taken on the key issue or related issues. How you plan to incorporate the findings and conclusions into your own decisions and actions. Your recommendations to fellow students for using this information.

2.5.6.3 THE PLACEMENT of the conclusions/recommendations section may vary, especially in papers for business courses. The most common placement is immediately after the findings or main text of the report. However, some instructors look for the conclusions/recommendations at the beginning of the report, usually immediately after a brief introduction. This follows the business practice for reports in many organizations. Such placement makes it easy for the reader to find the meat of the report or the bottom-line information without having to leaf through the entire report, especially where there is an appendix at the back of the report, where conclusions are normally placed.

2.5.7 DOCUMENT YOUR SOURCES

2.5.7.1 DOCUMENT PHARAPHRASED SOURCES. You must document all information and ideas that you paraphrase or summarize in your report; that is, any information that is not from your own experience or your own thoughts. Exceptions: The sources of some passages or sayings—such as well-known verses of the Bible ("do unto others," sayings from Shakespeare ("a rose by any other name"), or words from the Declaration of Independence ("all men are created equal")—are so obvious that they do not need documentation.

2.5.7.2 DOCUMENT QUOTED SOURCES. When you do not paraphrase, but instead quote the author word for word, you must put the passage in quotation marks (or their equivalent). These are called "direct quotes." Paraphrased or summarized material must be identified with a source note or footnote. See section "2.5.7 Documenting Your Sources" for further information.

2.5.7.3 THE METHOD YOU CHOOSE for documenting your sources will depend on your instructor's preference and your convenience in writing and keyboarding the final draft of the paper. APA, MLA, and Chicago Manual of Style are typical methods.

The two major types of standard documentation are:

(1) Chapter endnote (scientific) method

(2) Traditional footnote method

A recent survey of business professors indicates that the large majority will accept any standard form of documentation as long as it is used consistently and properly [Carr-Ruffino 1986]. Since the chapter endnote method is much easier to type, we will focus on that method here. If your instructor requires traditional footnotes, consult a manual of style for writing research papers or theses and dissertations [Turabian 1996 or 1977].

2.5.7.4 **THE CHAPTER ENDNOTE METHOD** of documenting a paper includes:

(1) A LIST OF REFERENCE SOURCES at the end of the paper, which includes all your sources in traditional bibliographical form, arranged alphabetically by author's last name, as well as interviewees and other sources of information. If the author's name is not given, use the next element in the entry. Title the section "References."

(2) AUTHOR'S LAST NAMES AND DATE may be used in parenthesis within the paper to show your documented source of material.

(3) A NUMBERING SYSTEM may be used alternatively. Your list of references is numbered sequentially. Instead of using author's last name and date, you may use the number of the documented source, as shown in your References section.

(4) ASIDES OR INCIDENTAL INFORMATION of the type sometimes placed in traditional footnotes are omitted where possible. If needed, they are included in the main text, or put in parentheses in the main text. Footnotes to exhibits are placed directly under the exhibit instead of at the bottom of the page.

(5) MATERIAL WITHIN THE PAPER is documented by placing in brackets or parentheses the author's last name and the date of publication, or number of the source as shown in the list of references.

(6) QUOTED MATERIAL from a book or article requires that you include the applicable page number(s). Here is an example:

> *Researcher Robert J. House has said, "Managers can increase workers' motivation to perform by using the path-goal approach [House 1989, p. 327]:*

> *Researcher Robert J. House has said, "Managers can increase workers' motivation to perform by using the path-goal approach [2, p. 327]:*

The numbering system endnote shows the reader that this information was taken verbatim from page 327 of entry number 2, as shown in the list of references at the end of the report. Entry number 2 reads as follows;

> 2. House, Robert J. "Path-Goal Theory of Leader Effectiveness," *Administrative Science Quarterly* (September 1989), pp. 321–28.

If you make a general reference to an entire source, you do not need a page number(s):

> ***Another approach to motivation has been developed by psychologist David McClelland [5] and others over the past twenty years.***

The source note is usually placed within or at the end of the first sentence in which you refer to a particular source. Sometimes it is appropriate mention the source author's name when you use ideas or information from that particular source. Many times, however, it is awkward or monotonous to do so and a source note alone will suffice.

2.5.7.5 **FORMAT FOR REFERENCES** that are listed in the references page at the end of your report will vary with the type of source. Standard forms for common types of sources follow.

2.5.7.6 **BOOKS.** Most entries simply require (1) the author's name, (2) the title, (3) the city of publication, (4) the publisher's name, and (5) the year of publication. An example:

McClelland, David Q, and David G. Winter. Motivating Economic Achievement. New York: Free Press, 1989.

(1) MULTIPLE AUTHORS. The sources are alphabetized by author's last name, so normally you will put an author's last name first (McClelland, David C.). With more than one author, the other author's names are listed in regular order (David G. Winter).

(2) EDITORS' names are used for books that are a compilation of articles or chapters, each written by a different author. For some books, the name of translator(s) or compiler(s) is given instead of an author's name or along with the author's name. Note the way the publisher has handled the book's authorship and follow that format.

(3) EDITION NUMBER should be included if there is more than one edition of the book, and the volume number of multi-volume sets should be included. A modem reprint of a book originally published many years ago should be noted. Some examples:

Cansedo, Carlos. *A New Decade (Poems: 1970–1980)*. Ed. John Loy.   Translators. John Loy and Jaime Rodriguez. New York: Dover Publications, 1980.

Linde, Shirley, ed., *The Language of Our Times,* Vol. II, 2 vols. 1932; reprint Chicago: The University of Chicago Press, 1985.

The first example gives the author (Carlos Cansedo) of a collection of poems that has been selected and arranged by an editor (John Loy) and translated from Spanish into English by two translators (John Loy and Jaime Rodriguez). The second example is for a source that does not list an author (it includes the works of many authors) so it is listed by the name of the editor (Shirley Linde). The source is the second volume of a two-volume set that was originally published in 1932; it is a modem reprint published by the University of Chicago Press in 1985.

2.5.7.7 **PERIODICALS.** When your source is a journal, magazine, or newspaper, you will normally need to include (1) the author's name(s), (2) the title of the article, (3) the name of the periodical, (4) the publication date, (5) volume and issue number, where available, and (6) the page numbers where the article may be located. Some examples:

Gunther, Max, *"Charisma" Journal of Communication*, 32, Spring 1989, pp. 52–54.

Baack, Jane, "Skills Women Managers Need," *Women in Management Review*, 22, 3, pp. 12–18.

2.5.7.7.1 **VOLUME AND ISSUE NUMBERS.** Volume number can be indicated by the number alone. Most readers will know by its position within the reference that the number refers to the volume. Issue within the volume may be indicated by month or season, or by issue number, placed after the volume number.

2.5.7.7.2 **ARTICLES WITH NO AUTHOR DESIGNATION.** News magazines sometimes include articles that list no author. In such instances, the references entry begins with the next element in the normal sequence of a reference, the title of the article. If you use author's last name endnote method, use the first word of the article to make it easy for the reader to find the source in the References section.

"Trajectories of Genius, The," *Time*, May 16,1990, p. 79

2.5.7.7.3 **BOOK REVIEWS.** The reviewer is considered the author of a book review. The reviewer's name is listed first, followed by the title and author of the book being reviewed, and finally the column or article title, the periodical or book title, and other publication information about where the review was published.

Williams, Jean, review of *Computer Cadence*, by John Forman in "Business Reviews," *California Business,* February 1988, p. 24.

In this example Jean Williams is the author of a book review on the book *Computer Cadence*. The review was published in the Business Reviews column of the journal *California Business*.

2.5.7.7.4 NEWSPAPER ARTICLES usually have a section designation, such as A, B, C, etc. in addition to a page number. Smaller newspapers may have page numbers only.

Wood, Sylvia. "Women Do Count." THE NEW YORK TIMES, December 14, 1986, B-5.

2.5.7.8 INTERNET SOURCES must include enough information for readers to find the material and evaluate it. Include author's name, title of the article, name of the website, date the article appeared, and url (website address).

2.5.7.9 INTERVIEWS, LECTURES, THESES, ETC. Use common sense about what facts to include and the form to use. Normally you should include the name of the interviewee, lecturer, or writer; the person's title and the organization he or she is affiliated with; the title or topic of the information; and the place where the interview or lecture took place. Information given about theses, dissertations, monographs, etc. should guide the readers to finding the source if they wish to read the entire document. Here are some examples:

McGafferty, Virginia. Vice President, Republic National Bank. Personal interview on women in middle management positions. Dallas, Texas, October 10, 1988.

Simpson, Thomas. Attorney at Law, Simpson & Fensterman. Lecture on "Adapting to New Labor Laws." Long Beach, California, April 2, 1989.

Tindale, Martin. "New Approaches to Motivation." Unpublished masters thesis. School of Business, University of Texas, Austin, Texas, 1990.

2.5.8 *PREPARE SUPPLEMENTARY PARTS*

2.5.8.1 SEE EXAMPLES of supplementary parts in the Sample Report at the end of this chapter.

2.5.8.2 SUPPLEMENTARY PARTS normally expected for every report are the Cover Page, Outline, and References section. Your instructor may also require an Executive Summary. For papers longer than 10 pages, a Table of Contents is helpful and normally replaces the outline. If you want to include additional material that needs no discussion within the text of the report, you can add this material as an Appendix.

2.5.8.3 NUMBERING OF SUPPLEMENTAL PAGES. The Cover Page is not numbered. Pages that come before the text or main body of the report, such as the Outline or Table of Contents and Executive Summary are not numbered unless they exceed two or three pages. In that case, use lower case roman numerals centered at the bottom of each page. Pages that come after the report proper, such as the References section and the Appendix continue the numbering sequence and placement used in the report proper.

2.5.8.4 A COVER PAGE is needed as the first page of the report packet. Its purpose is to readily identify the paper and provide space for instructor comments. Include information your instructor will need, such as: title of the paper, your name, course identification, date or semester due, perhaps school name, project identification, and group members. Lines are centered horizontally and vertically on the page. See the Cover Page Examples at the end of this chapter.

The Cover Page is normally divided into two or three major sections, with top and margins of at least two inches (12 lines), side margins of at least one inch, and spacing between sections so that the whole appears well balanced. Typical sections include:

(1) TITLE AND AUTHOR in the top section. The title is highlighted by using large font size, perhaps bold and italic, or all capitals, and placing it on the top line. Your name is given a few spaces down.

(2) COURSE IDENTIFICATION, SUBMISSION DATE, AND OTHER NEEDED INFORMATION are included in the next section, which is spaced several inches further down the page. If this information takes more than three or four lines, divide it into two sections. Include course information, such as course number, section, and title; the professor's name; and the date the paper is submitted. Other items that are sometimes needed are: assignment or project identification, school name, campus location (city or branch), and group members' names for group assignments.

2.5.8.5 **AN OUTLINE** is required by most instructors. Place it immediately after the Cover Page. If a Table of Contents is used, it normally precludes the need for a separate outline.

2.5.8.6 **A TABLE OF CONTENTS** is helpful for papers longer than 10 pages. This page consists of your Outline. Omit the identifying numbers and letters used in the Outline. Add a "Page Number" column to the right of the topics list and show the page number where each section begins. Major sections and subsections are designated by their form and placement. See the Report Example at the end of this chapter.

2.5.8.7 **AN EXECUTIVE SUMMARY** of the report may be required by your instructor. It is normally placed immediately before the report proper. See the discussion in this chapter on how to write an executive summary.

2.5.8.8 **A REFERENCES SECTION** is essential for all research reports, since it provides documentation of the sources of your information. This section may begin immediately after the last paragraph of the report. The title "References" is shown in the same format as a major heading of the report. Entries are arranged in alphabetical order by authors' last names. If a numbering system is used for endnote, each entry in the References section must be numbered sequentially. Each entry may be single spaced; double space between entries. Use hanging indentation, indenting the second and succeeding lines of each entry so that the beginning of each last name is easy to spot. See the Report Example at the end of this chapter.

The references section may include sources referred to in the report as well as sources used only as background information. A separate bibliography is not necessary for most business reports—only for extensive research reports.

2.5.8.9 *APPENDIX* is the term used for all additional materials you want to submit with the report but which you do not discuss within the report. You should briefly refer to these materials within the report, however, informing the reader of their existence and their location (page number) in the report packet. If you include extensive additional materials and if they can be readily categorized, give each category a letter and title:

Appendix A, Statistics   *Appendix B, Case Examples*   *Appendix C, Source Documents*

2.6 SELECTING INFORMATION FOR A TALK

2.6.1 **SEE THE CHAPTER ON TALKS** for extensive suggestions on this topic. The suggestions given here apply specifically to making a talk (oral presentation) that is based on a written report assignment.

2.6.2 **A TALK** that is based on a term research project and written report is a typical course assignment. The amount of detail you provide for this presentation depends on the time limits imposed by your instructor. Normally the class time made available for these oral reports is insufficient to cover your entire report in detail. You must select a few highlights that you think will be most interesting and helpful to fellow students.

2.6.3 **AVOID TEDIUM AND BOREDOM** in your presentation. Try to put yourself in the place of a typical classmate, tuning in to those areas of your project that are probably the most meaningful and interesting to the most people. Remember that droning on and on with dry facts and statistics causes most listeners to tune out, even those with some interest in your topic. Also, if you present too many general concepts or ideas without fleshing them out with examples, brief stories, supporting facts, and illustrations, listeners usually fail to grasp many of the concepts and perceive the presentation as dry.

2.6.4 **GRAB LISTENER INTEREST** by using human interest illustrations, stories, anecdotes and examples. At the same time, try to bring each listener into the picture. Here's an example:

Suppose you had put all your money and energy into starting up a sportswear boutique. Now you have the opportunity to expand, to make your career dream come true, but you are already stretching your time and energy to the breaking point . . .

2.6.5 **HOLD LISTENERS' INTEREST** by keeping them in the picture and by focusing on the most interesting concepts (from the major findings, the major sections of your report). Then back up each of these concepts with brief, hard-hitting, convincing information. Try to present your supporting facts in the form of stories, examples, illustrations, and anecdotes that involve the listeners.

2.6.6 **USE VISUAL AIDS.** Use at lease one aid, even if it's only a list of your three or four major sections or ideas. Simplify statistics and present them as vivid, easy-to-grasp visual aids that you weave into your discussion. Use them to accent your presentation, to explain a concept, to convince your listeners that a concept is valid. Do not dwell on them. Your presentation should move along quickly.

2.6.7 **LEAVE A LASTING IMPRESSION** on your classmates by involving them in your conclusions; for example:

- *What would you plan to do, given this information? What would your next step be?*
- *Would you trust yourself to find the right people and turn over whole areas of your precious business to them?*
- *Do you think you could find the right balance between trusting your employees and using control systems to check what they do?*

2.7 WRITING AN EXECUTIVE SUMMARY

We will discuss two types of executive summaries here.

(1) SUMMARY OF YOUR REPORT. Your instructor may require that you present an executive summary of your own research paper or report.

(2) SUMMARY OF AN ARTICLE OR BOOK. Your assignment may be to write an executive summary of an article(s) or book(s) from the literature.

2.7.1 GENERAL TIPS

2.7.1.1 AN EXECUTIVE SUMMARY IS a compact package of the highlights or key points contained in a more extensive presentation, such as a report, article, book, meeting, interview, or program. The summary may be as brief as one short paragraph, but it normally runs from a half-page to one page in length (when single-spaced, typewritten).

2.7.1.2 BUSINESS EXECUTIVES must cope with information overload, and the executive summary is one way to digest the large quantities of wide-ranging information that today's executives and professionals must be aware of.

2.7.1.3 BUSINESS INSTRUCTORS often assign executive summaries of course-related materials so that:

1) students become accustomed to writing them

2) instructors can quickly peruse new information uncovered through student research efforts; that is, to help instructors stay abreast of news in their fields.

2.7.1.4 THE PROCESS of preparing the summary includes:

(1) evaluating and analyzing potential source materials (where the source is not your own report)

(2) selecting the key points to include

(3) presenting the key points, along with any personal opinions, reactions, or evaluations expected of you.

2.7.2 EVALUATE AND ANALYZE SOURCE MATERIAL

2.7.2.1 THE FIRST STEP in planning a summary of an article or book is to briefly peruse the source material and evaluate it for:

(1) CREDIBILITY, considering the author's credentials, the publisher's reputation, the coherence and logic of the material itself, its apparent accuracy, and the suitability of any analytical tools the author uses.

(2) RELEVANCE and relationship to course objectives and course content. Don't bother with material that is essentially covered in the course text or supplements, nor with material that is only marginally related to key course topics. If in doubt, either skip it and find more suitable material or check with the instructor.

(3) CONTRIBUTION to greater understanding of the course material. Does the material help to explain course concepts, provide examples or applications of principles or strategies presented in the course, expand significantly upon a key concept, or in some way enhance important course material?

2.7.2.2 READ THE MATERIAL THOROUGHLY, continuing to evaluate it. At the same time analyze it, using the guidelines given next.

2.7.2.3 ANALYZE THE MATERIAL AND MAKE NOTES or underline key passages as you answer certain questions:

(1) PURPOSE: What is the main purpose the author(s) or speaker(s) is trying to achieve? In other words, what is the thesis? This information can usually be surmised from the title and key information in the introduction.

(2) ORGANIZATIONAL PLAN: What is the format or organizational pattern for presenting the information?

In rank order with most important information first? By the criteria that will be used in comparing choices and making a decision? By the way that certain causes produce certain effects? In chronological order? In logical order with each step building on information from previous steps? From a general conclusion backed up by supporting arguments or information? From particular arguments or information leading to a general conclusion? By spatial order, such as various locales?

2.7.2.4 FIGURING OUT THE ORGANIZATIONAL PLAN will make it much easier to move through the material and select key points.

2.7.3 SELECT KEY POINTS

2.7.3.1 IDENTIFY THE MAJOR SEGMENTS of the presentation. What constitutes a major segment will vary from key chapters of a book to key paragraphs of a newspaper article.

LECTURES, INTERVIEWS, FILMS, PROGRAMS and other verbal presentations are fairly easy to summarize if you can tape them. Then you can work with the playback to your heart's content as you select key ideas. If you must depend on notes taken on the spot, try to outline them according to main ideas followed by supporting arguments or information under each idea. Most anecdotes or stories can be skipped except for noting the point they make.

2.7.3.2 UNDERLINE KEY POINTS in each segment. Pay special attention to the beginning and the end of each segment, the places where topic sentences or thesis statements are most often found. Look for overviews and summaries of each segment, which often give the key ideas presented in the segment. Try to put the key information into one sentence, a one-liner that gives the bottom-line message of what the segment is all about.

2.7.3.3 WHAT TO INCLUDE? If you are unsure about whether to include certain information, include it in the first pass. You can always edit it out later.

2.7.3.4 DETERMINE YOUR REACTION OR RESPONSE TO IDEAS presented in the material. Jot down your opinions, evaluations, or conclusions. Keep in mind the relationship of the material to course content because you may want to include such links as part of your reaction to the article or book.

2.7.3.5 WRITE A FIRST DRAFT that includes all the material you noted, both your reactions and the key points. You may want to simply string together this material and worry about an organization plan and transitions later. Does the material fit onto one page (or other limits set by the instructor)?

2.7.3.6 EDIT EXCESS MATERIAL. You may use one of the following methods or some combination of methods to further refine the material.

(1) SELECT THE MOST IMPORTANCE SENTENCE, the one you would present if you could present only one sentence. Then select the least important sentence, the one you would omit if you needed to omit only one sentence. Keep repeating this process until an acceptable length is reached.

(2) SELECT THE ORGANIZATION PLAN you will use for the summary, and arrange the material accordingly. Omit material that now seems unnecessary. Then start identifying most important and least important sentences, further trimming the length as necessary. See the section on Paragraph organization in this chapter for ideas.

(3) REWRITE SENTENCES, weeding out unnecessary words, combining sentences that discuss closely related ideas, and using similar methods to achieve conciseness.

2.7.4 *PRESENT THE INFORMATION*

2.7.4.1 **PREPARE THE FINAL DRAFT,** adapting some of the techniques used in writing reports to the writing of the summary, as follows:

2.7.4.2 **USE AN ORGANIZATIONAL PLAN.** Decide on an organizational plan best suited for presenting this particular material and your opinions, a plan that makes it easy for the reader to quickly grasp the significance of the material and the key information it contains.

2.7.4.3 **INTRODUCTION.** The executive summary always has some sort of introduction. Usually the most important information is contained here, such as the purpose of the material, its significance, importance, and relationship to course content.

2.7.4.4 **CONCLUDING SECTION.** Sometimes the executive summary has a brief concluding section. Frequently the summary writer's reactions, opinions, conclusions, and other evaluations are contained here. Sometimes a wrap-up of how the material relates to course content is included.

2.7.4.5 **TRANSITIONS.** Use transitional words, phrases, and occasionally sentences to tie the summary together and show how ideas relate to one another. See the tips on making transitions in Chapter 6 on Business Writing Style.

2.8 WRITING OTHER TYPES OF REPORTS

OTHER REPORTS refers to those reports that are not essentially library research reports. Reporting survey results (from questionnaires and interviews) is covered in Chapter 4. Types of report included here are:

2.8.2 Work experience reports

2.8.3 Reports on past work experience for current course credit

2.8.4 Internship reports

2.8.5 Field observation reports

2.8.6 Reports of other term projects

2.8.1 GENERAL TIPS

COMMON REQUIREMENTS for all types of reports are discussed earlier in this chapter. They include

- An outline, introduction, main text organized around a few key points, and conclusion are essential parts of most reports.

- Sources are documented with endnotes or footnotes and a References section.

- Some data may need to be presented in a table, chart, or graph form.

- Additional information can be placed at the end of the report as an appendix.

2.8.2 THE WORK EXPERIENCE REPORT

2.8.2.1 LOOK FOR CONNECTIONS between your on-the-job experience and course content. Reports on work experience are often one of the requirements for getting school credit for the experience.

2.8.2.2 GET AS MUCH INFORMATION as you can about the course or program for which credit will be given. The more you get, the easier it will be to select those aspects of your work experience that are most relevant. Some sources of information are the bulletin or catalog, department or program brochures, course outlines and similar materials on file in department offices, course textbooks, and handouts.

2.8.2.3 SELECT ONE OR MORE KEY PRINCIPLES, techniques, approaches, or topics that are covered in the course or program, and which you learned about on the job. Which ones were part of company policy or practice? Which ones were violated by company policy or practice? Which ones did employees violate in practice? Which ones were connected in some way to your work situation or experience?

2.8.2.4 CONVEY THE BIG PICTURE of your work situation. Show that you understand the organization's role and standing in its industry, field, and society at large. Give a brief overview of the organization—its purpose, objectives, strategies, structure, perhaps a brief account of its history, and where it is headed.

2.8.2.5 CONNECT THE WORK YOU DID to this big picture, how your work contributed to the team, departmental and organizational objectives, and perhaps how your job and your department related to other jobs and departments.

2.8.3 REPORTS ON PAST WORK EXPERIENCE FOR COURSE CREDIT

2.8.3.1 SOME SCHOOLS offer course credit for past work experience based on the student's written report of knowledge and skills gained through the experience.

2.8.3.2 DETERMINE THE EVALUATION METHOD that will be used for your report. (See tips in the preceding section.)

2.8.3.3 REPORT ON APPROPRIATE KNOWLEDGE AND SKILLS

(1) COURSE KNOWLEDGE AND SKILLS. Are evaluators looking for knowledge/skills comparable to those acquired in certain campus courses? If so, request a copy of the course objectives and content, normally on file in the department that offers each course. Consider

organizing your paper according to each course objective that you have fulfilled through the work experience.

(2) GENERAL KNOWLEDGE and understanding. Are evaluators (at your school) looking for how the general knowledge you gained as a working person has prepared you for a higher level of understanding of course material? Do they relate this to general education requirements? To university objectives for student achievement? If so, get a copy of general education objectives and requirements and/or university objectives. Consider organizing the paper by objectives, discussing how the work experience led to achievement of each objective or a similar aim.

2.8.4 *REPORTS ON INTERNSHIP EXPERIENCE*

2.8.4.1 **TAKE AN EXECUTIVE APPROACH** to reporting your internship in order to discuss your experience from a more advanced level than merely telling what happened. Executives understand the big picture and how each facet of the organization fits in. They make analytical appraisals of key opportunities and threats faced by the organization and of the productivity and effectiveness of the organization.

2.8.4.2 **UNDERSTAND THE BIG PICTURE** as discussed earlier in this chapter and incorporate that overview, as well as the part you played in it, into your paper. You should understand how the project you completed or the work you performed tied in with the department's and organization's purpose and objectives. State what your contribution was to this overall effort.

2.8.4.3 **MAKE AN ANALYTICAL APPRAISAL** of the organization and of your work within or for the organization. What opportunities did you observe -opportunities the organization could seize, opportunities for you or others within the organization? What problems did you observe—barriers to achieving organizational goals, problems to achieving group or individual goals? What threats—to company survival, to success in achieving goals? Think in terms of opportunities on the one hand and problems/threats on the other. What is your opinion of the relative productivity and effectiveness of the organization—its policies, systems, procedures, practices? Of the departments, groups, individuals within the organization? Of the way people and groups worked together, communicated, cooperated?

2.8.4.4 **BASE YOUR ORGANIZATION** pattern on the type of information the instructor requires and on the way the instructor plans to evaluate your paper. Some typical patterns are given in the section Make a Preliminary Outline.

2.8.4.5 **FOCUS ON THE USEFULNESS** of the report to the organization you worked for. If your internship involved a project that you completed for the benefit of the company, perhaps your report should be organized and written in the manner that will make it most practical for the company to use. Check with your instructor about this approach.

2.8.4.6 **SELECT ONE (OR MORE) COURSE PRINCIPLE,** technique, approach, or topic that applies to the job situation you are reporting. Organize your paper around the ways in which that principle(s) was applied in the organization, or what you learned about that topic from your experience with the organization.

2.8.4.7 **SELECT KEY FACTORS** that you experienced or observed on the job, factors that tie in with the specific course principles or techniques you have chosen to focus upon, factors that illustrate application or violation of such principles.

2.8.4.8 **IF YOU TIE JOB EXPERIENCE TO COURSE** work, consider organizing the paper around course principles and techniques as applied to the work experience. Some typical patterns are:

(1) a discussion of applications of each principle or technique

(2) adherence to principles as compared to violations of them

(3) various aspects of a principle and how each aspect was handled

(4) various types of company policy, procedure, practice, or personal job experience in relation to the principle

2.8.4.9 **DO NOT USE A CHRONOLOGICAL APPROACH.** Starting with what happened when you first started the job and discussing key events week-by-week or month-by-month may be the easiest for you to organize your experience, but it is not the best way to convey the significance of that experience to readers. If you use this approach in making notes or writing a first draft, you will need to change it when you rewrite the next draft.

2.8.5. *REPORT OF FIELD OBSERVATION*

2.8.5.1 **RELATE TO THE BIG PICTURE.** Show that you have some understanding of the industry, field, location, and economy where the company operates. If you observe only a segment of the organization, understand how that segment fits into the overall picture.

2.8.5.2 **OBSERVE WITH AN ANALYTICAL EYE.** Keep in mind company mission, goals, strategies, opportunities, threats. Look for areas of effectiveness and ineffectiveness, examples of opportunities and threats being handled well, botched, or ignored. Keep in mind course principles and content that you might see in action in the organization.

2.8.5.3 **A FREQUENT PURPOSE** for conducting a field observation is to make an analysis of some system within an organization(s), such as production system design, planning/operation tools or techniques used in a production facility, wage and salary system, or information and communication systems.

2.8.5.4 **AN INTERVIEW** of one or more of the organization's executives is frequently a part of the field observation. Sometimes an executive makes a prepared talk to the group, followed by a question/answer session. Formulate some key questions ahead of time. (See the chapter on Surveys, Questionnaires & Interviews.)

2.8.5.5 **ORGANIZE YOUR REPORT** of the field observation on 1) the key factors that reflect concepts covered in the course, 2) key aspects of the system or operation you were assigned to observe and analyze, or a similar organization pattern.

2.8.6 *OTHER TERM PROJECTS*

2.8.6.1 **THE APPLICATION** of course knowledge to a real or hypothetical work situation is one type of assignment that has many variations. Examples include devising:

(1) a marketing plan for a product or service

(2) a base salary system for a specific job(s)

(3) a business plan for startup or expansion of a business

(4) developing and analyzing a case study (See Chapter 1)

2.8.6.2 **DETERMINE THE KEY FACTORS** of the project. Think in terms of selling the plan to the people who will determine its fate.

What do they need to know?

What do they want to know?

How can you organize the paper to meet those needs?

What reservations or biases are they likely to have about approving the plan?

How can you break through those blocks to get them to consider the plan?

How can you present the information in the most persuasive way?

Should you begin by pointing out a problem or need that's likely to grab their attention and then showing how the plan solves the problem or meets the need?

2.8.6.3 **ORGANIZE THE PAPER** according to the key factors.

REFERENCES

1. Carr-Ruffino, Norma. *Requirements for Written and Oral Assignments in College Business Courses,* Survey of U. S. Business Professors, 1986.

2. Carr-Ruffino, Norma. *Writing Short Business Reports.* New York: McGraw-Hill Book Company, 1980.

3. Turabian, Kate L. *A Manual for Writers of Term Papers, Theses, and Dissertations,* 6th ed. Chicago: University of Chicago Press, 1996.

4. Turabian, Kate L. *Student's Guide for Writing College Papers,* 3rd ed. Chicago: University of Chicago Press, 1977.

2.9 REPORT EXAMPLE

NOTE: This sample report is given to illustrate how the various parts of a report fit together. The report text is abbreviated to conserve space.

TIME MANAGEMENT FOR MANAGERS

By Jane Reina

Term Research Report

MGMT 462 (12) Introduction to Management

Dr. G. Oscar
December 1, 20xx
Wesleyan College

TABLE OF CONTENTS

i

EXECUTIVE SUMMARY

Effective time management is based on skill in setting objectives and priorities. This means managers must have the ability (1) to formulate clear, specific objectives, (2) to rank objectives in order of their importance for success on the job and for fulfillment as a manager, (3) to select those activities most likely to lead to the achievement of each objective, (4) to rank activities according to importance, and to incorporate these activities into a daily "To Do" list. This daily list helps managers direct their energy and make decisions.

Three important areas for using time-saving techniques are

(1) getting cooperation from others

(2) learning to minimize interruptions

(3) streamlining paperwork.

Managers need the cooperation of the boss, the work team, and peers to effectively manage time. Couching discussions in terms of commonly-held objectives is a key to gaining that cooperation. Managers also need large blocks of uninterrupted time in order to complete time-consuming projects. This can be accomplished by establishing a daily quiet hour, scheduling "open-door" times, and screening telephone calls.

To streamline paperwork managers must develop a system that includes procedures for sorting and handling mail, for writing letters and other documents, for minimizing papers to be filed, and for organizing material kept on file. The goal should be: *After sorting, handle each piece of paper only once.*

Managers who learn how to incorporate these skills into their daily work lives will grow in productivity, professionalism, and promotability.

ii

Time Management for Managers

By Jane Reina

*"Yesterday is a canceled check.
Tomorrow is a promissory note.
Today is ready cash. Use it!"*

This statement by an anonymous philosopher vividly conveys the importance of making the most of the present moment. When we think about it, the present moment is all we really have.

The major purpose of this research project is to determine the basis for good time management. A subordinate purpose is to discover some workable techniques for making the best use of the work time available to managers and their subordinates.

An understanding of good time management is essential for any manager who wants to be successful. All the skills that managers acquire are affected by their attitudes toward time, the way they use their time, and the way they expect their work teams to use time. The time management approach that is used affects management style and supervision techniques—how managers delegate, for example. It has a profound impact on managers' own motivation and the motivational climate they create within their departments. Time management practices can create or alleviate problems for managers and their subordinates.

Setting Objectives and Priorities

Before managers can direct their energies into channels that are most productive for them, they must know what they are trying to achieve. Time management rests on management by objectives, which implies effective action rather than merely efficient action, getting results rather than merely making an effort [Reddin 20xx]. To lay the necessary foundation for using time effectively, managers must become skilled at setting objectives and priorities

The process includes the following [Lakein 20xx]:

(1) Formulating specific objectives that include a single key result, preferably one that is specific and quantifiable, a target date for completion, and if possible the cost or budget allowed for the project.

(2) Using a system for categorizing and/or ranking objectives so managers can always know which goals hold top priority.

(3) Identifying the activities most likely to lead to achievement of each objective.

(4) Using a system for categorizing or ranking activities so managers can always know which activities should receive top priority.

(5) Using a daily "To Do" list that incorporates and ranks the activities previously formulated, and any other necessary activities.

An exercise to help students learn to formulate clear, specific objectives is included in the appendix to this paper. I believe it is essential that all managers learn to use this type of process so that they become aware of when they are directing energy toward top-priority goals and when they are not.

Most people have vague goals, but a goal should be specific enough so that on a future targeted date, people know for sure whether or not they have achieved the goal. It helps to include a deadline date and an amount. Exhibit 1 compares vague and specific goals. Which type do you think is most likely to be achieved?

2

EXHIBIT 1. VAGUE VERSUS SPECIFIC GOALS

Vague Goals	Specific Goals
To make more money	To earn $50,000 nest year
To move up in the company	To be General Manager by 20xx
To get ahead inlife	To have a net worth of $500,000 by 20xx
To go back to school	To have an MBA by 20xx
To have more free time	To take at least a month's vacation
To travel more	To travel to Asia for 3 weeks in 20xx

Source: The Promotable Woman by N. Carr-Ruffino

Setting Deadlines

It is important to set deadlines for completing activities and achieving objectives—for both managers and their subordinates. It is also important to observe them. According to Parkinson's Law: "Work expands to fill the time available for its completion" [Bliss 20xx, p.52].

People who do not have a deadline tend to put off getting started on a task and to dawdle once they do start [Carr-Ruffino 20xx]. Some keep working toward perfection rather than being satisfied with reasonable effectiveness or excellence. Perfectionism is extremely costly. In fact, it is prohibitive over the long term. Successful business people adopt the principle of "sensible approximation." They ask themselves, "If my life depended upon doing this task in half the time I have allocated, what shortcuts would I take? Is there really any reason not to take them?"

It helps to set intermediate deadlines for long-term projects [Lakein 20xx]. This keeps people working at a fairly steady pace rather than procrastinating and being swamped near the final deadline date.

3

Scheduling the Day

Managers who do not plan their days end up doing tasks as they occur. This means that other people's actions may determine their priorities instead of the goals managers have set for themselves. It also means, as Edwin Bliss [20xx p.81] points out, that managers will make "the fatal mistake of dealing primarily with problems rather than opportunities." They are likely to be solving other people's problems instead of working on that new idea, system, or proposal. One of the most productive uses of time is planning ahead. The better a project is planned in advance, the less time it takes to complete it successfully. Therefore, busy-work should not crowd out planning time.

The activities that managers have determined are needed in order to achieve their objectives should be scheduled into a daily "To Do" list [Lakein 20xx]. The key to successful use of such lists lies in actually using them. Refer to your "To Do" list every morning and check it regularly during the day to be sure you are making the best use of your time all through the day. Especially good times for checking the list is just after an interruption, when two activities are beckoning at the same time, and when energy or interest are running out. Any format and materials are acceptable as long as they work for you. However, the use of small pieces of paper should be avoided. Use large lined sheets of paper, tablets, DayTimer notebook, or similar format to organize the day's reminders.

Take a few minutes in the afternoon before going home to work on the "To Do" list for the following day. This gives a feeling of closure and completion to the workday. It also gives a preview of tomorrow so you can think about it and sleep on it tonight.

4

The activities that managers have determined are needed in order to achieve their objectives should be scheduled into a daily "To Do" list [Lakein, 20xx, p. 93]. The key to successful use of such lists is actually using them. Managers should refer to their "To Do" list every morning and check it regularly during the day to be sure they are making the best use of their time all through the day. Especially good times for checking the list is just after an interruption, when two activities are beckoning at the same time, and when energy or interest are running out. Any format and materials are acceptable as long as they work for the manager using them. However, the use of small pieces of paper should be avoided. Put everything on one sheet of paper or in one notebook.

Using Time-Saving Techniques

Effective managers learn to weed out time-wasters that creep into their well-planned days and to replace them with time-savers—whether the source of the waste is the boss, the work team, peers, or the system. It is important to get the cooperation of others, to minimize interruptions, and to handle paperwork efficiently.

Getting Cooperation from Others

Managers' best time management efforts can be sabotaged by bosses, workers, and peers [Lakein 20xx]. Therefore, managers must try to foresee and circumvent as many obstacles as possible.

Your Managers

If the boss pushes the manager to complete an item that is low on the priority list, the manager should tactfully discuss the conflict rather than meekly complying. The discussion should be couched in terms of achieving objectives and doing what is best for the boss.

5

Your Work Team

Encourage your work team to think about time management and to speak up when they are asked to do things they think are ineffective or time-wasters. Managers often waste their workers' time by communicating instructions poorly or in other ways delegating ineffectively—for example, when they do not select the right job for the right person or do not train the person properly. Managers also waste workers' time by interrupting them unnecessarily.

Your Colleagues

The heads of other units or departments in the company can create all sorts of bottlenecks and delays in your plans. When discussing the need for action with peers, stress how the completion of the task in question helps achieve a specific objective. If the objective is tied in with an organizational objective, the common goal may motivate them to cooperate.

Streamlining Paperwork

Many articles and books have been written about handling the "paper explosion" and avoiding paper-pushing all day. Time management expert W. J. Reddin [20xx] states that the less paperwork an organization produces, the more effective its planning system is likely to be. When people are preoccupied with documenting actions, they spend less thought and energy on actually doing the things that contribute most to achieving specific objectives.

The first step in streamlining paperwork is to work out a plan for minimizing and organizing the flow of paper. Managers must establish procedures for sorting and handling their mail effectively, minimize the time they spend writing letters and. other documents, minimize the number of papers to be filed, and see that their files are organized so they can easily access them.

6

The second step is to establish this goal: Once the daily incoming mail is sorted, handle each piece of paper only once. This is a goal, not a rigid rule, but it is surprising how consistently the goal can be reached (Lakein 20xx).

Handling Mail Effectively

A workable system for sorting and handling mail is a prerequisite to handling each piece of paper only once. Mail should be divided into categories that work best for each manager. Some typical categories are [Carr-Ruffino, 20xx]: (1) Immediate action-high priority, (2) Pending action-high priority (needs research, consultation, or approval), (3) Can be done later—low priority, (4) To read later, file, or distribute, (5) Throw away.

Organizing Correspondence

Writing letters and reports in minimal time is also an integral part of handling each piece of paper only once (Grossman 20xx). Train your assistant to handle routine correspondence.

Streamline reports by developing standard procedures for authorizing and auditing new forms and periodic reports. The procedures should provide a double check for duplication of effort, real need, and distributions lists. Can some reports be combined? Can routine reports be computerized?

Keeping Lean Files

The third aspect of handling each piece of paper once is minimizing and organizing the papers that must be filed [Grossman 20xx]. Ask, "What are the probabilities of our ever needing this piece of paper again? If we eventually need some information it contains, could we get it elsewhere? What would happen if we did not have a written record of it?" Many people ask, "Could we possibly need this ever again?"

7

Work with your assistant to find an overall paperwork system that works best. The system might include such categories as "followup," "current projects," "to read," "creativity," and "travel," as well as a general file [EXECU*TIME 20xx]. The key to a workable system is to experiment until the best combination is found and then to actually use the system consistently.

Conclusion

The basis for all good time management is skill at setting objectives, identifying appropriate activities for each objective, ranking these items according to their importance, and incorporating them into a daily "To Do" list that directs energy into the most productive channels. Once managers have become skilled in this area, they are ready to adopt and devise various time-saving techniques.

Managers must have cooperation from their manager, workers, and colleagues if they are to manage time most effectively. Communicating in terms of common objectives is a key to getting this cooperation. Managers who must work on large projects must also have blocks of uninterrupted time in order to work most effectively.

Another area where time-saving techniques pay off is in streamlining paperwork. Managers who know how to handle important paperwork without becoming swamped with trivia are more likely to achieve their objectives. Good managers learn how to organize their paperwork, handle most pieces of paper only once, and prioritize their correspondence according to importance. Managers who learn to incorporate these skills into their daily work lives will find themselves becoming more productive—and promotable.

8

References

Bliss, Edwin C. *Getting Things Done*. New York: Scribner, 20xx.

Carr-Ruffino, Norma. *The Promotable Woman*. Franklin Lakes, NJ: Career Press, 20xx.

EXECU*TIME. "The Time Traps That Can Be Set forYou by Others," www.excu*time.com August 20xx.

Grossman, Lee. *Fat Paper*. New York: McGraw-Hill, 20xx.

Lakein, Allan. "How to Get Control of Your Life," *Administrative Quarterly*, 2, 10, November 20xx, pp 45–49.

Reddin, W. J. *Effective Management by Objectives*. New York: McGraw-Hill, 20xx.

9

Appendix

A Time Management Skill Builder: How Do You Spend Your Time and Energy?

Purpose: To track how you spend your time for two weeks—and assess how well you're managing your activities. To track your energy-level patterns—and assess whether you're scheduling demanding, important activities during high-energy times of the day.

Step 1. Review your goals. Get in touch with your current goals. What are your current job goals? Project goals? How do they fit in with your overall career goals? With the three or four top-priority goals in your life?

Step 2. Set up a weekly time log. Use a calendar that has enough space to write in your activities, or set up your own weekly time log sheets using Snapshot #1 as a guide.

Step 3. Track your activities, energy levels, and work pace. Pick two weeks that are fairly typical and log all your activities. Include all waking hours and weekends. Note times when your energy level is especially high or low. Also note any variations in the work pace you prefer at various times.

Step 4. Summarize your activities. Calculate some totals for time spent on various types of activities, such as writing reports, reading background material, making routine phone calls, commuting, shopping, socializing. Calculate the approximate percentage of the total time you spend on each major type of activity.

Step 5. Analyze your patterns—energy level and work pace. Are your highs, midranges, and lows fairly persistent? If not, what factors seem to make a difference? Chart a typical day's energy-level pattern and a typical day's work pace pattern. How do weekends differ from work days? Why the variation?

Step 6. Identify time-wasters and energy drains. Does the amount of time you're spending on each type of task adequately support your top-priority goals? If not, how can you re-prioritize your activities? Are you making best use of your high-energy times? If not, how can you change the timing of your activities? Do some activities or situations regularly waste your time or drain your energy? List them.

10

2.10 OUTLINE EXAMPLE

An Outline is needed for most papers, unless a Table of Contents is provided.

Outline

I. **Introduction**

II. **Setting Objectives and Priorities**
- A. **Setting Deadlines**
- B. **Scheduling the Day**

III. **Using Time-Saving Techniques**
- A. **Getting the Cooperation of Others**
  1. The Boss
  2. Workers
  3. Peers
- B. **Streamlining Paperwork**
  1. Handling Mail Effectively
  2. Streamlining Correspondence
  3. Keeping Lean Files

i

2.11 COVER PAGE EXAMPLES

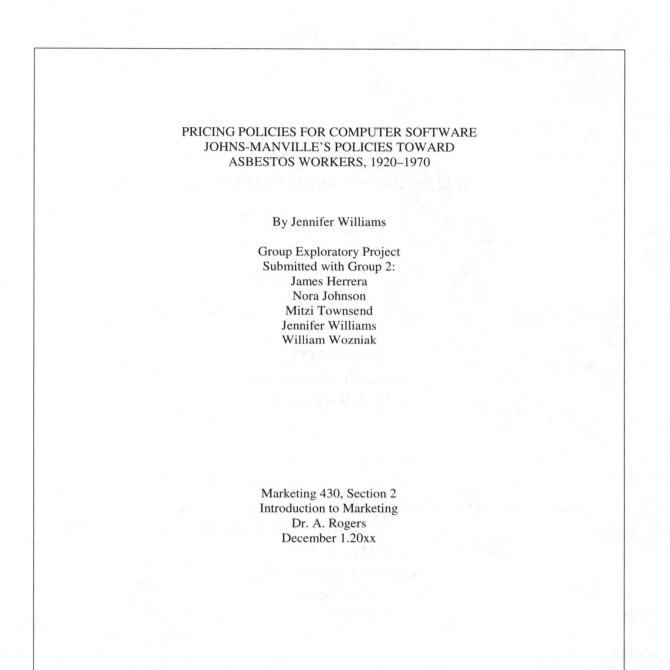

PRICING POLICIES FOR COMPUTER SOFTWARE
JOHNS-MANVILLE'S POLICIES TOWARD
ASBESTOS WORKERS, 1920–1970

By Jennifer Williams

Group Exploratory Project
Submitted with Group 2:
James Herrera
Nora Johnson
Mitzi Townsend
Jennifer Williams
William Wozniak

Marketing 430, Section 2
Introduction to Marketing
Dr. A. Rogers
December 1.20xx

STRESS AND THE WOMAN MANAGER

By Robin Agnost

MGMT 342-02
Women in Management
Dr. J. Worthington

May 15, 20xx
California State University
at Sacramento

Chapter Three
Finding Business Facts:
Getting the Information You Need

Published resources are essential for most business research and term papers. Research projects virtually always require a search of the literature in the topic being investigated in order to access the thinking of leaders and experts on the subject. Library research is also desirable for some case analyses for expanding or updating the information given in the case. In addition, knowing where to find the information you need may be valuable for making career decisions and other purposes. This chapter discusses ways of accessing information from the following types of sources:

3.1   Government Publications

3.2   Business References—General Sources

3.3   Specialized Sources of Specific Data

3.4   Statistical Sources

3.5   The Internet

3.1 GOVERNMENT PUBLICATIONS

Huge quantities of primary data, most collected for governmental use, become sources of secondary data for the business community. Data include reports, statistical publications, bibliographies, and periodicals. Citations are divided into four categories: Indexes; Census Data; Selected Sources of Data Generated by the Federal Government; and Selected Sources of Data Generated by the States.

3.1.1 INDEXES

Business Service Checklist (Washington, DC: Dept. of Commerce). Published weekly as a guide to U.S. Dept. of Commerce publications and to key business indicators.

Business Services and Information: The Guide to the Federal Government (New York: Management Information Exchange, Wiley, 1978). Guide used for identifying U.S. government publications. Appendix with phone numbers and agency addresses.

The Federal Register (Washington, DC: Division of the Federal Register, National Archives). Published daily. Contains all official regulatory matter issued by all national agencies and governmental bodies.

Code of Federal Regulations, DC: Division of the Federal Register, National Archives), Published quarterly, revised yearly. A code of regulations first published in the Federal Register.

C/S Index to Publications of U.S. Congress, Adier, James B. (U.S. Government, Washington, DC). Published quarterly with annual cumulations, 1970 top present. Basic source for working papers of Congress. Abstracts of congressional documents. Two sections indexes and abstracts. The subject title indexes use entry number referrals.

Monthly Checklist of State Publications (Washington, DC: Superintendent of Documents, GPO). Published monthly. A record of state documents and publications received by the Library of Congress.

Guide to U.S. Government Publications, Andriot, John L., ed., (U.S. Government, McLean, VA: Documents Index.) Published annually since 1973. Annotated guide to publications of the various U.S. government agencies.

Selected United State Government Publications (Washington, DC: Superintendent of Documents, GPO). Biweekly. Covers documents received by that office which are of some general interest and will be listed for sale.

3.1.2 CENSUS DATA

The Bureau of the Census is by far the largest publisher of comprehensive statistical data. Its catalog, which is published monthly with annual cumulations, contains good, descriptive lists of all census publications. The Census Bureau publishes only its most widely used censuses and surveys. Much more information is available, usually on computer tapes. This information provides limitless possibilities for subject cross-classifications or area tabulations.

The following sampling of information available through the census surveys is divided into three parts: Census Data Index; Census of Population Data; and Specific Census Data Sources.

3.1.2.1 CENSUS DATA INDEX

Bureau of the Census Catalog of Publications: (Washington, DC: Department of Commerce, Bureau of the Census). Published quarterly with monthly supplements and annual cumulations. Complete index of Census Bureau data, including publications and unpublished materials.

3.1.2.2 CENSUS OF POPULATION DATA

Census of Population (Series PC) (Washington, DC: Department of Commerce, Bureau of the Census). Issued every 10 years. Detailed characteristics of the population for states, counties, cities, and towns in a series of reports (PC [1] AD) that give data on number of inhabitants, general population characteristics, and general social and economic characteristics. Separate "Subject Reports," Series PC2), cover statistics on ethnic groups, migration, fertility, marriage and living arrangements, education, employment, occupation and industry, and income.

3.1.2.3 SPECIFIC CENSUS DATA SOURCES. Produced and published to be used as major economic indicators.

Census of Agriculture (Washington, DC: Department of Commerce, Bureau of the Census). Issued every 3 years. Reports data for all farms by county and state.

Census of Business (Washington, DC: Bureau of the Census). Issued every 3 years. Contains statistical data on retail and wholesale trade and on selected service industries. Arranged geographically and by Standard Industrial Classification (SIC) codes with subject reports. Issued for years ending in "2" and "7," the census is supplemented by "Monthly Retail Trade," "Selected Services Receipts," and the "Monthly Wholesale Trade" series.

Current Business Reports: Monthly Retail Trade and Accounts Receivable (Washington, DC: Bureau of the Census). Published monthly. Includes information on monthly sales for retail stores by kind of business, region, selected states, and Standard Metropolitan Statistical Areas (SMSAs). Also contains data on department stores and end-of-month accounts receivable. These reports are issued several weeks after the end of the month reported, a companion series, *Current Business Reports: Advance Monthly Retail Sales,* providing preliminary data, is issued one week after the month reported. These cumulate into an *Annual Retail Trade* series and finally into the *Census of Business* every five years.

Current Business Reports: Monthly Wholesale Trade (Washington, DC: Bureau of the Census). Published monthly. Contains monthly figures for wholesale inventories and sales arranged by kinds of business and geographic divisions. The reports are issued several weeks after the end of the month reported and cumulate into the *Census of Business* every five years.

Census of Construction Industries (Washington, DC: Bureau of the Census). Issued every 3 years. Compiled using data from government and private organizations and reports from construction firms. Contains detailed data on construction establishments; number employed; payroll; payments and expenditures; assets; depreciation; and income. A comprehensive source of statistical data on the construction industry.

Census of Governments (Washington, DC: Bureau of the Census). Issued every 3 years, for years ending in 2 and 7. Important source for detailed statistics on federal, state, and local governmental finance, including: governmental organization; taxable property values; public employment; governmental finance; local governments; tax revenues; holdings of selected public-employment retirement systems; construction expenditures; and typical studies.

Census of Housing (Washington, DC: Bureau of the Census). Issued every 10 years.

> *Volume I: States and Small Areas.* A presentation of detailed occupancy characteristics, structural characteristics, equipment and facilities, and financial characteristics for each state, and a U.S. summary.

> *Volume II: Metropolitan Housing.* A collection of data on SMSAs having 100,000 or more inhabitants, with cross-classifications of housing and household characteristics for analytical use.

> *Volume III: City Blocks.* A collection of data descriptions of conditions and plumbing facilities, average number of rooms, average contract monthly rents, average valuations, total population, number of housing units occupied by nonwhites, and number of persons per room.

> *Volume IV: Components of Inventory Change.* A description of the physical changes that have taken place since the last census for the SMSAs with more than one million inhabitants.

> *Volume V: Residential Financing.* Gives ownership and financial information.

Census of Manufacturers (Washington, DC: Bureau of the Census). Issued every 3 years. Supplies data on U.S. manufacturing firms categorized under the headings of Final Area Reports and Final Industry Reports:

Final Area Reports presents statistics on value added by manufacturing, employment, payrolls, new capital expenditures, and number of establishments.

Final Industry Reports includes a series of separate reports on value of shipments, capital expenditures, value added by manufacturing, cost materials and employment for approximately 450 manufacturing industries. The data are classified by geographic region and state, employment size, class of establishment, and degree of primary products specialization.

Census of Mineral Industries (Washington, DC: Bureau of the Census). Issued every 3 years. Provides detailed data on the number of mineral industry establishments with data on employment, payrolls, assets, expenditures, consumption, costs, shipments, and receipts. This information is presented by industry, geographic area, and subject. Vol. 3 of the 1972 *Census of Manufacturers* includes indexes of production for individual mineral industry groups. This data is not issued in any other form.

Census of Retail Trade (Washington, DC: Bureau of the Census). Issued every 3 years. Compiles data for states, SMSAs and counties, and cities with populations of 2,300 or more by type of business. Data include number of establishments, sales, payroll, and personnel.

Census of Selected Services (Washington, DC: Bureau of the Census). Published every 5 years. Includes data on hotels, motels, beauty parlors, barber shops, and other retail service organizations. Survey also includes information on number of establishments, receipts, payrolls for states, SMSAs, counties, and cities.

Census of Transportation (Washington, DC: Bureau of the Census). Issued every 3 years for years ending in "2" and "7." Provides travel data on the civilian populations, truck inventory and use, and shipment of commodities by manufacturers. Most of this data is not publicly available elsewhere. This work is the most important cumulative general source for U.S. transportation data.

Census of Wholesale Trade (Washington, DC: Bureau of the Census). Issued every 3 years. Presents statistics for states, SMSAs, and counties on number of establishments, sales, payroll, and personnel for kind of business.

Census Tract Reports (Washington, DC: Bureau of the Census). Issued every 10 years. Detailed report on population and housing.

Construction Reports (Washington, DC: Bureau of the Census). Each of the 10 sub-series in this series provides current statistical data on some specific aspect of the housing industry. Six of the most important periodicals: Vacant Housing Units (quarterly), Housing Starts (monthly), Housing Authorized by Building Permits and Public Contracts (monthly), Building Permits, Sales of New One Family Homes (monthly), and Construction Expenditure of State and Local Tax Revenue (quarterly).

Highlights of U.S. Export and Import Trade (Washington, DC: Bureau of the Census). Published monthly. Compiled using data from the Bureau of Customs. Reports unadjusted and seasonally adjusted data on trade by commodity group, country and world area, U.S. customs regions and districts, method of shipment, and end use category. Issued two months after month of coverage. The most comprehensive of several regular trade statistical series.

3.1.3 SELECTED SOURCES OF DATA GENERATED BY THE FEDERAL GOVERNMENT

Categories include statistical and national economic indicators, congressional developments, international commerce, localized databases, consumer interests, and the environment. Pertinent publications for specific industries and activities are listed under "domestic commerce."

3.1.3.1 STATISTICAL AND ECONOMIC INDICATORS

American Statistical Index (Washington DC: Congressional Information Service). Published monthly with annual cumulations, 1970 to present. Important source for identifying statistical publications published by the U.S. government. Indexes and abstracts statistics on numerous topics from the publications of many government agencies. Index volume contains four separate indexes that list publications by subject and name; by geographic, economic, demographic categories; by title; and by agency report numbers. Abstract volume gives brief descriptions of the publications and their content.

Business Conditions Digest (Washington, DC: Department of Commerce, Bureau of Economic Analysis). Published monthly. Supplemented weekly by Advance Business Conditions Digest. Provides a look at many of the economic time series found most useful by business analysts and forecasters. Presents approximately 600 economic tune series in charts and tables. Appendixes provide historical data, series descriptions, seasonal adjustment factors, and measures of variability. Economic measures listed include: selected components of the national income and national product; measures of prices, wages, and productivity; measures of the labor force, employment, and unemployment; data on federal, state, and local government activities; measures of U.S. international transactions; and selected economic comparisons with major foreign countries. An essential economics reference tool.

Economic Indicators (Washington, DC: Superintendent of Documents, GPO). Published monthly. A digest of current information on economic conditions of prices, wages, production, business activity, purchasing power, credit, money, and federal finance. Gives monthly figures for the past two years; frequently goes back as far as 1939.

Measuring Markets: A Guide to the Use of Federal & State Statistical Data (Washington, DC: Department of Commerce, GPO, 1974). Materials published by state and federal governments, which are useful in marketing research. Sources for population, income, employment, sales statistics, and some state taxes are included. Examples demonstrate the use of federal statistics in market analysis.

Statistical Abstract of the United States (Washington, DC: Department of Commerce, Bureau of the Census, GPO). Published annually, 1879 to present. Arranged in 34 categories, it is a reliable source for statistical summaries of the economy, business, population, and politics. Emphasis is on information of national scope, plus tables for regions, states, and some local areas. Table of contents, introductory text to each section, source notes for each table, and bibliography of sources are extremely useful guides to additional material. Subject index. *Historical Statistics of the U.S.: Colonial Times to* Washington, D.Q: Department of Commerce). 2 volumes. A supplement to the Statistical Abstract of the United States, it correlates data.

Survey of Current Business (Washington, DC: Department of Commerce, Bureau of Economic Analysis, GPO). Published monthly, 1921 to present. Official source of Gross National Product,

National Income, and International Balance of Payments. Important reference for business statistics, including general economic and industrial statistics for specific products plus articles analyzing current business situations. Subject index. Statistics are indexed in American Statistical Index (see above). Companion publication: Business Statistics, weekly and biennial volumes that provide historical data for statistical series in surveys of current business.

3.1.3.2 CONGRESSIONAL DEVELOPMENTS. These entries focus on activities of Congress and the federal government.

Commerce Business Daily (Washington, DC: Department of Commerce, Office of Field Operations). Published daily. Lists US government procurement invitations, contract awards, subcontracting leads, sales of surplus property, and foreign business opportunities. Addresses are included. A code indicates which notices are intended wholly or in part for small businesses. The organization, by general subject categories, is not immediately apparent but can be grasped quickly by those searching regularly for particular kinds of contracts.

Congressional Quarterly (Washington, DC: Congressional Quarterly, Inc.). Published weekly, with quarterly cumulated index and an annual *CQ Almanac,* a compendium of legislation for one session of Congress. An excellent weekly service for up-to-date news on all activities of Congress and the federal government. Each issue includes the status of legislation and congressional voting charts. A record of the government for one presidential term is published every four years as *Congress and the Nation.*

U.S. Government Manual (Washington, DC: GPO). Published annually. An indispensable official handbook of the federal government. Describes personnel, purposes, and programs of most government agencies.

3.1.3.3 INTERNATIONAL COMMERCE

Commerce Today (Washington, DC: Department of Commerce). Published biweekly. Gives current information on commodities and foreign countries, especially those of interest to the foreign trader. Other phases covered include industrial developments, laws, and regulations of foreign countries.

Foreign Commerce Handbook: Basic Information and Guide to Sources (Washington, DC: U.S. Chamber of Commerce). Published every five years. Useful guide to foreign commerce sources.

Foreign Economic Trends and Their Implications for the United States (Washington, DC: Bureau of International Commerce). Pamphlets issued semiannually or annually for each country. Perhaps by the US Foreign Service/Embassies. Contains one summary table, a narrative of economic trends, and an analysis of possible implications of these trends for U.S. foreign trade.

International Economic Indicators and Competitive Trends (Washington, DC: Bureau of International Economic Policy and Research). Published quarterly. Compiled using data from the International Trade Analysis staff. Presents a variety of comparative economic statistics for the U.S. and seven major competitor nations, with an analysis of the economic outlook.

Overseas Business Reports (Washington, DC: Bureau of International Commerce). Published annually. Compiled using data from the Office of International Marketing. Each report deals with a group of countries' basic economic structure, trade regulations, practices and policies, market potential and investment laws. Designed to aid business in gaining access to, and increasing its share of, foreign markets.

3.1.3.4 DOMESTIC COMMERCE

3.1.3.4.1 CLASSIFICATION MANUAL

Standard Industrial Classification Manual (Washington, DC: U.S. Government Printing Office, 1973). Classifies establishments by type of activity in which engaged, to facilitate the collection, tabulation, presentation, and analysis of data, and to promote uniformity and comparability in presenting statistical data collected by various agencies of the U.S. government, state agencies, trade associations, and private research organizations. Covers entire range of economic activities.

3.1.3.4.2 SPECIFIC INDUSTRIAL INFORMATION. This section is a sampling of reports on industrial information by many governmental departments, bureaus, agencies, and committees.

AIRLINES

Handbook of Airline Statistics (Washington DC: Civil Aeronautics Board). Published annually. Data updated monthly by Air Carrier Financial Statistics. Maps, tables. Compiled using data from the Bureau of Accounts and Statistics and the U.S. Civil Aeronautics board. Includes airline statistics for trends in passenger, freight, express, and craft expenses and depreciation; promotion, sales, and administrative expenses; and data on capital gains, interest expenses, income taxes, subsidies, dividends, investment, long-term debts, and rates of return on stockholders' equity. An essential source for background information and statistical data on the status of commercial air transportation in the U.S.

FAA Statistical Handbook of Aviation (Washington, DC: Federal Aviation Administration). Published annually. Maps, tables. Compiled using data from federal government agencies and industry organizations. Statistical data on civil aviation activity such as airports, scheduled air carrier operations, and accidents. A convenient reference for current and retrospective statistics on the aviation industry.

BANKING AND FINANCE

Corporation Income Tax Returns (Washington, DC: Internal Revenue Service). Published annually. Charts, graphs, tables. Compiled using data from estimates based on a sample of all tax returns filed during a specified period. Serves as a detailed report on corporate sources of income, assets, dividends, deductions, credits, income tax, and tax payments. Statistics are conveniently classed by industry, size of total assets, and size of business.

Federal Reserve Bulletin (Washington, DC: Board of Governors of the Federal Reserve System). Published monthly. A source of statistics on banking, deposits, loans and investments, money market rates, securities prices, industrial productions, flow of funds, and various other areas of finance in relation to government, business, real estate, and consumer affairs.

Statistical Bulletin (Washington, DC: Securities and Exchange Commission). Published monthly. Charts, tables. Compiled using data from the NY and American Stock Exchanges, other registered U.S. exchanges, and periodic surveys by the SEC. Summarizes new securities offerings, trading, stock price indexes, and round lot and odd lot trading. Valuable to those interested in the operation and regulation of security exchange activities.

BROADCASTING

Statistics of Communications Common Carriers (Washington, DC: Federal Communications Commission). Published annually. Graphs, tables. Compiled using data from monthly and annual reports filed with the FCC. Contains detailed financial and operating data, by company, for all telephone and telegraph companies and communications holding companies engaged in interstate and foreign communication service, and for the U.S. Communications Satellite Corporation. Invaluable for information about specific utilities and the communications industry in general.

CONSTRUCTION

Construction Review (Washington, DC: Bureau of Domestic Commerce). Published monthly. Tables. Compiled using data from federal, state, and local government agencies and trade associations. Provides current and retrospective statistical data on all aspects of the construction industry, by geographic area. Brings together virtually all current government statistics pertaining to the industry. Issues also include brief articles.

HIGHWAYS

Highway Statistics (Washington DC: Federal Highway Administration). Published annually. Data pertinent to motor fuel, motor vehicles, driver licensing, highway user taxation, state highway financing, highway mileage, and federal aid for highways. An important source for highway transportation data.

Highway Transportation Research and Development Studies (Washington, DC: Federal Highway Administration). Published annually. A compendium describing current highway research and development activities at the federal, state, industry, and university level.

Highway Safety Literature (Washington, DC: National Highway Traffic Safety Administration). Published semimonthly; no charge. Abstracts recent literature on highway safety. International coverage. Arranged topically.

MARKETING

Marketing Information Guide (Washington, DC: Department of Commerce). Published monthly. Annotations of selected current publications and reports, with basic information and statistics on marketing and distribution.

MINING AND PETROLEUM

Minerals Yearbook (Washington, DC: Bureau of the Mines). Published annually. Three volumes. Statistics on metals, minerals, and mineral products, along with economic and technical developments and trends in the U.S. and foreign countries. Volume 1: Metals, Minerals, and Fuels; Volume 2: Domestic Reports; Volume 3: International Reports. Data usually apply to information gathered two to three years before date of publication.

Sales by Producers of Natural Gas to Interstate Pipeline Companies (Washington, DC: Department of Energy). Published annually. Gives sales by size groups, states, and pricing areas; sales to individual purchasers; and pipeline companies' purchases from producers, as well as their own production.

Statistics of Interstate Natural Gas Pipeline Companies (Washington, DC: Department of Energy). Published annually. Statistical compendium of financial and operating information. Includes income and earned surplus, gas operating revenues, customers and sales, capital stock and long-term debt, gas utility plant, gas accounts, physical property, and number of employees for specific companies, with industry compilations.

Mineral Industry Surveys (Washington, DC: Bureau of the Mines). Published irregularly. Charts, graphs, maps, tables. Statistical data on metals, nonmetals, and fuels, regarding production, consumption, shipments. Information also provided on fatal and nonfatal injuries, hours worked, and reports and developments in industrial safety and health programs.

PRINTING AND PUBLISHING

Printing and Publishing (Washington, DC: Bureau of Domestic Commerce). Published quarterly. Tables. Compiled using data from the Departments of Commerce and Labor. Statistical report on printing, publishing, and allied industries, issued four months after the month for which data is reported. Covers foreign trade by country and product, sales and profits, employment, and earning by industry.

RAILROADS

Rail Carload Cost-Sales by Territories (Washington, DC: Interstate Commerce Commission, Bureau of Accounts). Published annually. Includes data for rail carload mileage cost scales by district, region, type of car, and unit costs for various weight loads by type of equipment. Data grouped into seven regions of the U.S. by carriers with revenues of $5 million or more. An invaluable source of cost breakdowns for rail operations.

TRANSPORTATION

Transport Economics (Washington, DC: Interstate Commerce Commission). Published quarterly. Tables. Provides analysis and summary of operating statistics, finances, equipment, and employment for carriers in interstate commerce (such as rail, motor, water, air, and pipeline). Supplements and cumulates into Transport Statistics in the United States.

Transport Statistics in the United States (Washington, DC: Interstate Commerce Commission). Published annually. Six parts issued separately. Transport statistics on traffic operations, equipment, finances, and employment as they relate to railroads, water carriers, pipelines, motor carriers, freight forwarders, and private car lines.

UTILITIES

Electric Power Monthly (Washington, DC: Department of Energy). Statistics on production, fuel consumption, capacity, sales, and operating revenues and income. December issue includes data on peak loads, energy requirements, and system capacities for the previous ten years and estimates for the following ten years. Supplemented by and cumulated from National Electric Power Generation and Energy Use Trends, which is published quarterly.

3.1.3.4.3 AGRICULTURE

Agriculture Statistics (Washington, DC: Department of Agriculture). Published annually. Compiled using data from USDA counts and estimates, census statistics, the Department of Labor, the Foreign Service, and other federal agencies. The annual agriculture reference book. Includes statistical data on acreage, yield and production of crops, commercial crops, prices paid and received by farmer, livestock production, market supplies and prices, imports and exports, farm resources, income and expenses, consumption and family living, and agricultural programs. Historical series limited to the last ten years. An indispensable tool for agribusiness. Well indexed for quick access to specific information.

Statistical Summary (Washington, DC: Department of Agriculture, Statistical Reporting Service). Published monthly. Designed for ready reference, this report summarizes statistical data estimated for or collected on prices, sales, stocks, and production of agricultural products, such as fibers, grains, vegetables, nuts, fruits, seeds, livestock, milk, and dairy products.

3.1.3.4.4 LABOR

Area Trends in Employment and Unemployment (Washington, DC; Manpower Administration). Published monthly. Described area labor market developments land outlooks for 150 major employment centers, with separate brief summaries for selected areas, including those with concentrated persistent unemployment and underemployment.

Area Wage Surveys (Washington, DC: Bureau of Labor Statistics).

Handbook of Labor Statistics (Washington, DC: Bureau of Labor Statistics). Published annually. The basic statistical reference book on U.S. labor characteristics and conditions. Includes retrospective data and assembles in one volume the major BLS labor statistical series. Ceased publication with 1981 annual.

Monthly Labor Review (Washington, DC: Bureau of Labor Statistics). Published monthly. Reviews labor issues, including employment, wages, collective bargaining, industrial relations, labor law, and foreign developments. Contains statistics and book reviews.

3.1.3.4.5 SMALL BUSINESS

Small Business Bibliographies (Washington, DC: Small Business Administration). Published irregularly. Briefly describes particular business activities. Substantial bibliography includes federal, state, and nongovernmental publications. Preface to each issue may be helpful to those seeking career information.

3.1.3.4.6 PATENTS AND TRADEMARKS

Index of Patents Issued from the U.S. Patent Office (Washington, DC: Patent Office). Published annually. Two volumes. *Volume 1* indexes patents listed in the year's issues of the *Official Gazette* by name of patentee. Entries include a general designation of the invention, patent number, date of issue, and classification code. *Volume 2* indexes patents by subject of invention as indicated by the classification code number identified in the Manual of Classification. A convenient appendix is a list of libraries receiving current issues of U.S. patents and of depository libraries receiving the *Official Gazette*.

3.1.3.5 LOCALIZED DATA BASES

County and City Data (Washington, DC: Department of Commerce, Bureau of the Census). Published irregularly. Various statistical information for counties, cities, SMSAs, unincorporated towns, and urbanized areas. For each county, 196 statistical items are given. Provides information supplemental to the *Statistical Abstract* (See 3.1.3.1).

County Business Patterns (Washington, DC: Department of Commerce, Bureau of the Census). Published annually. Contains county, state, and U.S. summary statistics on employment, number and employment size of reporting business units, and taxable payrolls for approximately 15 industry categories. Statistics are particularly suited to analyzing market potential, establishing sales quotas, and locating facilities.

3.1.3.6 CONSUMER INTERESTS

Consumer Legislative Monthly Report (Washington, DC: Department of Health and Human Services, Office of Consumer Affairs). Published monthly when Congress is in session. Lists and briefly describes consumer related bills introduced into the current Congress. Though summaries of bills are very brief, inclusion of bill sponsors and committees referred to gives access to further information. Topical arrangement and index are convenient to use.

3.1.4 SELECTED SOURCES OF DATA GENERATED BY STATE GOVERNMENTS

This list categorizes sources of economic data. Much of the information generated at the state level is prepared by agricultural and/or business colleges of state universities.

Department of Geology or Conservation. Monographs are available from this department in most states, describing the geology of various geographic areas. Water supply, fish and game conservation, and mineral resources are described.

Department of Health. Public health statistics on state births and deaths are usually published monthly. Some states publish data on diseases.

3.2 BUSINESS INFORMATION—GENERAL SOURCES

In addition to specialized business references, some general business sources include the business reference librarian in your local library as well as business-related dictionaries, encyclopedias, almanacs, yearbooks, handbooks, and manuals.

3.2.1 BUSINESS REFERENCE LIBRARIAN

The business reference librarian should be consulted as a timesaving first step in gathering business facts. This specialist has the best sources at his or her fingertips and can give expert guidance. Ask about any booklists concerning specific areas. The librarian may also provide information about special library collections, books scheduled for publication, and about books held in other business reference libraries in the general area and in university, public, and corporate libraries.

3.2.2 DICTIONARIES

Dictionaries are useful for checking the meaning, spelling, or pronunciation of words, terms, and phrases.

Dictionary of Economics and Business. E.E. Nemmers, (Totowa, N.J.: Rowman & Littlefield). Paperback giving brief definitions.

Dictionary of Management. Derek French and Heath Seward, (New York: International Publications Service). Defines about 4,000 management and economic terms and techniques used by managers. Includes abbreviations and brief descriptions of major associations and organizations.

International Dictionary of Management: A Practical Guide. Hano Johannsen and G. Terry Pag, (Boston: Houghton Mifflin). Covers the entire area of business and management.

Lexicon of American Business Terms. James F. Filkins and Donald L. Caruth, (New York: Simon & Schuster). Brief dictionary containing 3,000 of the most common business terms.

Trade Names Dictionary. Donna Wood, ed., (Detroit: Gale Research Co.). Two volumes. A guide to trade names, brand names, product names, with addresses of their manufacturers, importers, marketers, or distributors. Supplemented periodically by *New Trade Names*.

3.2.3 ENCYCLOPEDIAS

Encyclopedia. of Business Information Sources. Wasserman, Paul, C. Georgi, and J. Woy (Detroit: Gale Research). Quick survey of basic information sources. Provides specific citations, dealing with a single point, with the business manager in mind. Includes reference words, periodicals, trade associations, statistical sources, and data bases.

3.2.4 ALMANACS AND YEARBOOKS

3.2.4.1 Almanacs are collections of current factual information covering a broad range of topics.

Almanac of Science & Technology (New York: Harcourt Brace Jovanovich. Facts on what's new, what's known.

World Almanac and Book of Facts (New York: Newspaper Enterprise Association). Published annually. Facts on diverse subjects.

3.2.4.2 Yearbooks are fact books providing current information. They usually give more information than almanacs.

Commodity Year Book (New York: Commodity Research Bureau). Published annually. Statistical yearbook with data on production, prices, stocks, exports, and imports for more than 100 commodities.

Statesman's YearBook (NY: St. Martin's Press). Published annually. First three sections are factual data about international organizations, U.S. and Commonwealth countries. Final section provides descriptive data and statistics on other countries, including history, government, population, and commerce.

3.2.5 HANDBOOKS AND MANUALS

Business handbooks and manuals are excellent reference tools that present concise introductions to the concepts, procedures, and techniques for specific managerial functions. These compendiums are well organized and indexed, providing easy access to the precise information needed.

Advertising Manager's Handbook. Stansfield, Richard H., (Chicago; Dartnell Corp.). Reference book on advertising strategies. Case studies included. Covers such topics as the campaign concept, copy, art, budgeting, and media selection.

Foreign Exchange Handbook: A User's Guide (The). Walmsley, Julian (NY; Wiley Interscience). Provides an in depth coverage of major currency markets. Discusses some of the economic and technical influences on currency and money markets. Other topics covered include financial futures and gold markets, payment systems, and exposure management and control. Provides standard foreign exchange calculations and money market formulas.

Handbook of Forecasting: A Manager's Guide (The). Makridakis, Spyros and Steven C. Wheelwright, eds., (NY: Wiley-Interscience). Explains which forecasting methods work and which do not.

Handbook of Modern Accounting. Davidson, Sidney and Roman Well, eds., (NY; McGraw), Defines important terms and procedures. Covers recent developments, their implications and applications.

Handbook of Selling: Psychological, Managerial, and Marketing Bases. Grikscheit, Mary M., Harold C. Cash, and W.J.E. Crissy (New York: Wiley). Discusses selling strategy and tactics. Deals with how to organize information about a customer and answer customer objections.

Office Administration Handbook. Fettridge, Clark and Robert S. Minor, eds., (Chicago; Dartnell Corp.). Discusses methods of handling office, personnel, and administrative problems.

Personnel Administration Handbook. Scheer, Wilbert E. (Chicago; Dartnell Corp.). Reference book for personnel managers or administrators. Covers wage and salary, labor relations, interviewing, recruiting, hiring, measuring work performance, merit increases, and terminations.

Strategic Management Handbook (The). Albert, Kenneth J., ed. (NY: McGraw). Discusses concepts, principles, and practices of strategic management. Contains how to material, highlighted with real life cases and examples. Written by experts from management consulting firms, Fortune 300 companies, and top business schools.

3.3 SPECIALIZED SOURCES OF SPECIFIC DATA

Some specialized sources of specific data include online data bases, periodicals, financial guides, directories, biographies and doctoral dissertations.

3.3.1 ONLINE DATA BASES

The information explosion can be attributed to computer technology, which has revolutionized the search for business facts. By using a database, which is an organized collection of information in a particular subject area, decision makers benefit from the accessibility and adaptability of massive resources now available. This tool is an expensive one, but is certainly cost-effective when measured by time savings. Total cost depends on the data bases selected for the search, the amount of time used, and the number of references retrieved.

The actual process of a computer search is a simple one. A questionnaire is completed, specifically describing the problem and indicating important authors, journals, or key facts useful in retrieving references. While the search is being completed, computer, librarian, and researcher interact in redirecting and redefining. Citations can be printed immediately or mailed.

Interactive search services and directories can be helpful The business databases are divided into three areas: bibliographies, statistics, and directors.

3.3.1.1 INTERACTIVE SEARCH ACCESS. Three major vendors that offer online interactive search access to hundreds of databases are:

Bibliographic Retrieval Services **(BRS),** Scotia, NY

DIALOG/Lockheed Information Services, Palo Alto, CA

SDC Search Service, System Development Corp., Santa Monica, CA

BRS and DIALOG offer general bibliographic data, and some of their databases overlap. SDC emphasizes technical and statistical information.

3.3.1.2 BIBLIOGRAPHIES. Online interactive search access to various bibliographic databases.

ABI/INFORM.   1971 to present, 134,636 records. All phases of business management and administration. Stresses general decision sciences information that is widely applicable. Includes specific product and industry information. Scans 400 primary publications in business and related fields.

Management Contents (Skokie, IL: Management Contents, Inc.). 1974 to present, with monthly updates. Current information on a variety of business and management related topics for use in decision making and forecasting. Articles from 200 U.S. and foreign journals, proceedings, and transactions are fully indexed and abstracted. Areas include accounting, design sciences, marketing, operations research, organizational behavior, and public administration.

Monthly Catalog of U.S. Government Publications (Washington, DC: U.S. Government Printing Office). Published monthly with annual cumulations (see entry under 1.1 Government Publications Indexes). 101,401 records of reports, studies, fact sheets, maps, handbooks, and conferences.

New York Time Information Bank (see entry under 3.3 Periodicals).

PAIS International Bulletin (NY: Public Affairs Information Service). Published monthly, 1976 to present. Worldwide coverage of more than 800 journals and 6,000 nonsocial publications; 137,653 citations.

Predicasts Terminal System (Cleveland: Predicasts, Inc.). Bibliographic and statistical database providing instant access to many business journals and other special reports for searches of current articles, statistics, geographic location of companies. Abstracts a wide range of periodical abstracts and indexes.

3.3.1.3 STATISTICS. In-depth statistics easily adapted for a wide variety of manipulations.

Economic Time Series:

Business International/Data Time Series (Business International Corp.). PTS/U.S. Time Series (Predicasts, Inc.)

Marketing Statistics:

BLS Consumer Price Index (Department of Labor, Bureau of Labor Statistics).

BLS Producer Price Index (Department of Labor, Bureau of Labor Statistics).

Financial Statistics:

Disclosure II (Washington, DC: Disclosure, Inc.). 1977 to present. Updated weekly. Extracts of reports filed with the U.S. Securities and Exchange Commission by publicly owned companies. 11,000 company reports provide a reliable and detailed source of public financial and administrative data. Source of information for marketing intelligence, corporate planning and development, portfolio analysis, legal and accounting research.

3.3.1.4 DIRECTORIES OF COMPUTER-BASED SERVICES Listings can be found in the following directories:

Directory of Computer Based Services (Washington, DC: Telenet Communications Corp.). Issued annually. Lists data banks, commercial service bureaus, educational institutions, and companies that offer interactive computer based services to the public through the nationwide Telenet network. Lists databases that may be accessed, a brief description of the contents, and who offers the database.

Directory of Online Information Resources (Rockville, Md.: CSG Press). Easy-to-use guide to 225 selected publicly accessible databases, file descriptions, coverage, and size. Subject and source; index; phone and address list of data base suppliers.

3.3.1.5 DIRECTORIES. Arranged by subject, title, geographic location, and code number.

Directory of Mail Order Catalogs, CA TFAX

EIS Industrial Plants (Economic Information Systems, Inc.).

Foreign Traders Index (Department of Commerce).

Trade Opportunities (Department of Commerce).

3.3.2 BIBLIOGRAPHIES

Bibliographies, lists of printed sources of information on a topic, are the most important starting point for business facts. They can quickly lead the business executive or student to original available sources of information on a specific topic.

Bibliographic Index. A Cumulative Bibliography of Bibliographies (Bronx, NY: H.W. Wilson Co.). Published three times annually. Lists by subject, sources of bibliographies containing 30 or more citations of books, pamphlets, and periodicals.

Bibliography of Publications of University Bureaus of Business and Economic Research: The AUBER Bibliography (Boulder, CO: Association for University Business and Economic Research). Published annually. Bibliography of publications that do not appear in other indexes. Written by bureaus of business and economic research and members of the American Association of Collegiate Schools of Business. Includes books, series, working papers, and articles published by each business school. Divided into two parts: subject and institution. Author index.

Business Books in Print (NY: R.R. Bowker). Published irregularly. Data for more than 31,500 books and periodicals indexed by author, title, and business subjects. Directory of publishers.

Business Information Guidebook (A). Figueroa, Oscar and Charles Winkler, (NY: AMACAM). Useful first point of reference for locating sources of business information.

Business Literature (Newark, NJ: Public Library of Newark, Business Library). Published 10 times each year; annotated lists of current topics.

Business and Technology Sources (Cleveland: Cleveland Public Library). Published quarterly. Bulletin developed to cover one subject per issue; lists numerous other publications concerning the topic.

Business Reference Sources: Annotated Guide for Harvard Business School Students. Daniella, Loma M., comp., (Boston: Harvard University Baker Library). Comprehensive annotated bibliography of entire field of business covering selected books and reference sources.

Core Collection: An Author and Subject Guide (Boston: Harvard University Baker Library). 1971 to present, revised annually. Selective listing of more than 4,000 business books listed by author and subject.

Encyclopedia of Business Reference Sources. Wasserman, Paul, C. Georgi, and J. Woy, (Detroit: Gale Research Co.). Survey of basic information tools covering 1,215 subject sources (see 2.3 Encyclopedias). Includes reference works, periodicals, trade associations, statistical sources and online data bases.

Management and Economics Journals: A Guide to Information Sources. Tega, Vasie G. (Detroit: Gale Research Co). Bibliography of periodicals.

Management Information Guides (Detroit: Gale Research Co.). A group of bibliographic references to business information sources in many fields. Each volume includes general reference works, film strips, government and institutional reports. Two examples of this source are:

(1) ***Public Relations Information Sources*** Norton, Alice, [Management Information Service Guide #22] (Detroit: Gale Research Co.). Annotated bibliography of general sources, public relation tools, and international public relations.

(2) ***Service to Business and Industry*** (NY: Brooklyn Public Library, Business Library). Published 10 times a year; annotated bibliographies covering current business topics.

Subject Catalogue: A Cumulative List of Works Represented by Library of Congress Printed Cards (Washington, DC: U.S. Library of Congress). Published quarterly, with yearly and five year cumulated editions, 1950 to present. Annotated bibliography on every subject from all parts of the world. Cross-referenced subject headings. A good starting point.

Use of Management and Business Literature. Vernon, K.D.C., ed., (Woburn, MA; Butterworth). Bibliography includes a description of British publications and library practices, forms of business information, and surveys of literature in corporate finance, management, accounting, organizational behavior, manpower management and industrial relations, marketing, computers, and quantitative methods and production.

Where to Find Business Information: A Worldwide Guide for Everyone Who Needs the Answers to Business Questions. Brownstone, David M. and Gorton Carruth, (NY: John Wiley & Sons). List of 3,000 current foreign and domestic, private and public business information sources

3.3.3 PERIODICAL DIRECTORIES, PERIODICALS INDEXES, PERIODICALS, NEWSLETTER DIRECTORIES, & NEWSPAPER INDEXES

3.3.3.1 PERIODICAL DIRECTORIES are helpful reference tools for finding major industry publications relevant to a specific area.

Business Publication Rates and Data (Skokie, IL: Standard Rate and Data Service, Inc.). Published monthly. Index to business, trade, and technical publications arranged by "market served" categories.

Ulrich 's International Periodicals Directory (NY: R.R. Bowker Co.). Published annually. Subject index of more than 55,000 entries for in-print periodicals published worldwide. Contains "Abstracting and Indexing Services" chapter.

3.3.3.2 PERIODICAL INDEXES are valuable sources of current information for a broad scope of subjects. Abstracts provide the added feature of descriptive notation.

Accountants Index (NY: American Institute of CPAs). Published quarterly with annual cumulations. Comprehensive index of books, pamphlets, government documents, and articles on accounting and related fields. Author, title, and subject index.

Business Periodicals Index (NY: Wilson Company). Published monthly with quarterly and annual cumulations, 1938 to present. Cumulative subject index covering 270 business periodicals. Subject categories are very specific. Separate book review index in annual volume.

Cumulative Index (NY: Conference Board). Published annually. Useful subject index for wide range of studies, pamphlets, and articles that the Conference Board research firm has published in the areas of business economics, corporate administration, finance, marketing, personnel, international operations, and public affairs. Covers material published during the past 20 years, with emphasis on the most recent 10 years.

Current Contents: Social and Behavioral Sciences (Philadelphia: Institute for Scientific Information). Published weekly, 1961 to present. Reproduces the tables of contents of journals in business, management, economics, computer applications, and other disciplines in social and behavioral sciences. Worldwide coverage of 1,330 journals. Subject, author, and publishers' address indexes.

Predicasts' F&S Index United States (Cleveland: Predicasts, Inc.). Published weekly, with monthly, quarterly, and annual cumulations, 1960 to present. Index covering company, industry, and product information from business-oriented periodicals and brokerage house, reports in the US Information arranged by company name, SIC number, and company according to SIC groups.

Predicasts' F&S Index International. Same as above, except that it gives information about the rest of the world, excluding Europe.

Predicasts' F&S Index Europe. Same as F&S International, but with coverage of European continent only.

Index of Economic Articles (Homewood, IL: Richard D. Irwin, Inc.). Published annually. Bibliographies from 200 English language journals on articles, communications, papers, and proceedings discussions. Classified index and author index.

Management Contents (Skokie, IL: G.D. Searle & Co.). Published biweekly. Reproduction of the tables of contents of a selection of 150 of the best business/management journals. Each issue can be scanned for significant articles. Now available as online data base.

Public Affairs Information Service Bulletin (PAIS) (NY: Public Affairs Information Service). Published weekly, 1915 to present. Cumulations five times each year and annually. Selective subject index of current books, yearbooks, directories, government documents, pamphlets plus 1,000 periodicals relating to national and international economic and public affairs. Factual and statistical information. Brief annotations of entries. Now available as online data base.

Work Related Abstracts (Detroit: Information Coordinators). Published monthly with annual indexes, 1972 to present. Abstract of articles, dissertations, and books concerning labor, personnel, and organizational behavior. Loose-leaf format. Arranged by subject in 20 categories. Subject index. Subject headings list published annually.

3.3.3.3 BUSINESS PERIODICALS feature articles of use and interest to business managers and students. Specialized journals report new research findings and developments. Two examples of general business periodicals are:

Business Week (NY: McGraw). Published weekly. Business news magazine with concise articles on new business trends and developments. Special issues; Survey of Corporate Performance and Investment Outlook. Indexed in BPI, F&S, PAIS (see indexes).

Fortune (NY: Time Inc.) Published monthly. Topics of general interest cover new products and industries, politics and world affairs, biographical information. May issue: Fortune 300, largest U.S. industrial corporations. Indexed in BPI, F&S, and PAIS (see indexes).

Other general business periodicals include: Across the Board; Barren's National Business and Financial Weekly; Business Briefs; Boardroom Reports; Columbia Journal of World Business; Commerce Business Daily; Commercial and Financial Chronicle; Dun's; Forbes; Nation's Business; and Supervisory Management.

3.3.3.4 ACADEMIC JOURNALS are also important; three examples are:

Business Horizons (Bloomington, Indiana University Graduate School of Business). Published bimonthly. Readable articles, balanced between practice and theory, of interest to management and academicians. Indexed in BPI, F&S, and PAIS.

Harvard Business Review (Boston: Harvard University Graduate School of Business Administration). Published bimonthly. Professional management journal featuring practical articles on all aspects of general management and policy. Indexed in BPI, F&S, and PAIS.

Journal of Business (Chicago: University of Chicago Business School). Published quarterly. Scholarly journal geared to professional and academic business and economic theory and methodology. Includes short subject list of books. Indexed in BPI, F&S, and PAIS.

Each major industry issues publications containing specific information concerning their field. Some examples are:

Advertising Age (Chicago: Crain Communications, Inc.). Published weekly. February issue, "Agency Billings" provides data on advertising agencies ranked by billings for the year. August issue, "Marketing Profiles of the 100 Largest National Advertisers," provides data on leading product lines, profits, advertising expenditures, and names of marketing personnel.

Safes Management (NY; Bill Communications, Inc.). Published semimonthly. "Survey of Buying Power," published in July and October issues, is a prime authority on U.S. and Canadian buying income, buying power index, cash income, households, merchandise, line sales, population, and retail sales information. National and regional summaries, market ratings, and metro-market and county-city market data by states.

Some important management journals are: The Journal of Creative Behavior; California Management Review; Human Relations; Administrative Science Quarterly; Academy of Management Review; Sloan Management Review; Academy of Management Journal; Organizational Behavior and Human Performance; Industrial and Labor Relations Review, Personnel Psychology.

3.3.3.5 NEWSLETTERS of trade associations and professional societies can provide valuable business facts and services. The following directories are useful in finding the appropriate newsletter:

National Directory of Newsletters and Reporting Services (Detroit: Gale Research Co.). Lists and provides information on newsletters and publications closely akin to newsletters issued regularly by business, associations, societies, clubs, and government agencies. Features reference guide to national and international services, financial services, association bulletins, and training and educational services. Cumulative subject, publisher, and title indexes.

Oxbridge Directory of Newsletters (NY: Oxbridge Communications, Inc.). Published annually. Lists 3,000 U.S. and Canadian newsletters in 145 subject areas.

3.3.3.6 NEWSPAPER INDEXES are helpful sources of information about current events and newsworthy materials not appearing in other types of periodicals.

New York Times Index (NY: The New York Times Co.), Published every two weeks with annual cumulations, 1831 to present. Detailed index, summarizing and classifying news alphabetically by subject, persons, and organizations. Cross references. Also online data base from 1969.

Wall Street Journal Index (NY: Dow Jones Company, Inc.). Published monthly with annual cumulations, 1938 to present. Complete report on current business. Subject index of all articles that have appeared in the Journal, grouped in two sections: Corporate News and General News.

3.3.4 BUSINESS, ECONOMIC, AND FINANCIAL GUIDES AND SERVICES

3.3.4.1 BUSINESS SERVICES are information agencies that compile, interpret, and distribute data on specific subjects. These guides are kept up to date by revised and supplemental data issued on various schedules.

Babson's Business Service (Babson Park, MA: Business Statistics Organization, Inc.). Issued in three bulletins:

Business Inventory Commodity Price Forecasts. Published monthly. Pertinent discussions on business topics as well as short sketches of supply, demand, price, and buying advice of major commodities.

Business Management Sales and Wage Forecasts. Published monthly. Covers current problems on labor and wages; keeps abreast of current developments in sales and buying power, Babson's Washington Service is published by the same organization.

Babson Weekly Staff Letter covers current trends and business problems.

Business and Investment Service (NY: International Statistical Bureau, Inc.). Published weekly. Analyses of production in basic industries. Includes political analyses of interest. Section entitled "Selected Securities Guide" presents stock market trends and indexes, as well as earnings and prices of stocks in selected industries. Additional services available are a quarterly security list; a monthly trend of distribution; a foreign newsletter; and postwar reports.

Chase Manhattan Foreign Trade Service (NY; Chase Manhattan Bank). Published annually with additional supplements. Service for Chase Manhattan Bank customers gives foreign exchange and export trade information for many countries.

Directory of Business and Financial Services. Grant, Mary M. and Norma Cote, eds. (NY: Special Libraries Assn.). Guide to existing national and international business, economic, and financial services describing 1,051 publications issued by 421 publishers. Each listing includes coverage, frequency, price, and addresses. Arranged alphabetically by title; publisher and subject index use referral numbers.

Dun and Bradstreet Credit Service (NY: Dun and Bradstreet). Published every two months. Collects, analyzes, and distributes credit information on manufacturers, wholesalers, and retailers. Includes general information on the character, experience, and ability of the enterprise, plus a highly detailed statement covering the antecedents, methods of operation, financial statement analysis, management programs, and payment record for each entry. Also operates a foreign division.

John Herling's Labor Letter (Washington, DC: John Herling's Labor Letter). Published weekly. Gives current information on labor topics, legislation, and opinions in Washington.

The Kiplinger Washington Letter (Washington, DC: Kiplinger Washington Agency). This is a condensed and confidential letter to subscribers. It analyzes economic and political events and attempts some forecasting. The news service features continuous events and reports from the "grass roots" membership. Additional publications include: *Kiplinger Tax Letter*, published biweekly, which reviews federal tax legislation, and *Kiplinger* Agricultural Letter, published biweekly, which gives pertinent developments affecting agriculture, products, and financial data. Special features pertinent to subject area. All titles indexed m Moody's Complete Corporate Index (pamphlet).

Moody's Stock Survey (NY: Moody's Investors Service). Published weekly. Presents data on stocks including recommendations for purchase, sale, or exchange of individual stocks. Discussions on industry trends and developments.

Standard and Poor's Corporation Services (New York). Offer comprehensive investment data weekly, with annual cumulations. Their publications include: *American Exchange Stock Reports; Bond Outlook; Called Bond Record; Convertible Bond Reports; Daily Dividend Record; Facts and Forecast Service (daily); Industry Issues; The Outlook; Stock Reports; Over the Counter and Regional Exchanges; Standard NYSE Stock Reports.*

Standard Rate and Data Service (Wilmette, IL). Issues 12 volumes of publishing rates and data on the following areas: Business Publications (monthly); Canadian Advertising (monthly); Consumer Magazine and Farm Publications (monthly); Direct Mail Lists (semiannually); Networks (bimonthly); Newspapers (monthly); Print Media Production Data (semiannually); Spot Radio (monthly); Spot Television (monthly); Transit Advertising (quarterly); Weekly Newspaper (semiannually); plus a Newspaper Circulation Analysis.

Trading Areas and Population Data in Eastern United States (NY: Hagstrom). Issues a number of maps of the metropolitan New York, Philadelphia and adjacent areas. These are city, county, and special area maps giving detailed information useful to marketing and forecasting.

United Business and Investment Report (Boston). Published weekly. This investment service offers a commentary on the current situation with a forecast of business, financial, and economic conditions.

3.3.4.2 LOOSE-LEAF SERVICES offer efficient, up-to-date information, especially for business law topics and taxes. Laws, regulations, rules, orders, and decisions, along with explanations and interpretations are set up in loose-leaf volumes. Weekly or biweekly packets include new revisions. The following are the major loose-leaf services.

Bureau of National Affairs, Inc., Washington, DC. Issues reports on government actions that affect labor, management, and legal professions. Some of its reports are:

Daily Report for Executives. Overnight service. Discusses such topics as legislation in Congress, tax and transportation rulings, and price and cost trends.

Daily Labor Report. Overnight service. Discusses important labor management agreements, major NLRB and court decisions.

Business International Corporation, New York. Publishes information about worldwide business problems and opportunities, emphasizes international management, laws, regulations and business forecasts. Its loose-leaf services are:

Financing Foreign Operations (NY: Business International). Published weekly. Eight-page weekly report for managers of worldwide operations.

Investing, Licensing and Trading Operations Abroad (NY: Business International). Published monthly. Current information for each country on foreign investment, competition, and price.

Commerce Clearing House Services, Chicago. Publishes more than 100 loose-leaf reports, covering topics in tax and business regulatory law. Publications include *Federal Banking Law Reports, Government Contracts Reports, Contract Appeals Decisions, Insurance Law Reports.*

Prentice-Hall Services, Englewood Cliffs, NJ. Publishes loose-leaf reports covering the latest laws and regulations. Gives comments and interpretations of the laws. Publications include: *American Federal Tax Reports, Tax Court Service, Tax Ideas, Prentice-Hall Management Letter.*

3.3.5 DIRECTORIES

Directories provide brief data on companies, organizations, or individuals. They are used for a variety of purposes: to determine the manufacturer of a specific product; to check companies located in a particular area; to verify company names, addresses, and telephone numbers; and to identify company officers.

Business Organizations & Agencies Directory. Kruzas, Anthony T., and Robert C. Thomas, eds. (Detroit: Gale Research Co.). Supplies exact names to write, phone, or visit for current facts, figures, rulings, verifications, and opinions on business matters. Names agencies, associations, groups, federations, organizations, and contact people.

Consultants and Consulting Organizations Directory (Detroit: Gale Research Co.). Indexes over 8,000 firms, people, and organizations involved in consulting. Main arrangement is geographic, with subject, personal name, and organization name indexes.

Corporate 500: The Directory of Corporate Philanthropy (Detroit: Public Management Institute). Data about corporate philanthropy of the nation's 500 largest corporations. Lists eligible activities, corporate headquarters, board and committee members, contact people, and grant recipients.

Directory of Industry Data Sources: U.S. and Canada. Benjamin, William A., ed. (Cambridge, MA: HARFAX). Three volumes. Includes more than 13,000 annotated entries describing a wide range of information sources on 60 industries. Arranged in 5 parts: general reference sources; industry data sources; directory of all publishers mentioned in part 2; extensive subject and title indexes.

Directory of Special Libraries and Information Centers. Darnay, Brigitte, T., ed.. (Detroit: Gale Research Co.). Three volumes: Special Libraries and Information Centers in the United States and Canada; Geographic and Personnel Indexes; New Special Libraries. Provides information about holdings, services, and personnel of more than 16,000 special libraries, information centers, documentation centers.

Directory of Corporate Affiliations (Skokie, IL: National Register Publishing Co. Inc.). Published annually with quarterly updates titled *Corporate Action*. Lists 5,000 American parent companies with their 16,000 divisions, subsidiaries, and affiliates.

Government Research Centers Directory. Kruzas, Anthony T. and Kay Gill, eds. *(Detroit:* Gale Research Co.). Identifies research and development facilities funded by the government. Describes research centers, bureaus and institutes, testing and experiment stations, statistical laboratories.

International Research Centers Directory. Kruzas, Anthony T., and Kay Gill. Eds. (Detroit: Gale Research Co). Identifies and describes research and development facilities throughout the world (excluding the U.S.). Includes government, university, and private installations.

Law and Legal Information Directory (Detroit: Gale Research Co.). Guide to national and international organizations, bar associations, the federal court system, federal regulatory agencies, law schools, continuing legal education, paralegal education, scholarships and grants, awards, prizes, special libraries, information systems and services, research centers, legal periodical publications, book and media publishers. Wasserman, Paul and Marck Kaszubski, eds. Paul and Janice McLean, eds. (Detroit: Gale Research Company). Contains profiles on 1,967 individuals and organizations that conduct training and development programs for business, industry, and governments.

Million Dollar Directory (NY: Dun and Bradstreet). Published annually in three volumes. Lists 39,000 U.S. companies worth $1 million or more. Gives officers and directors, products or services, SIC number, sales, and number of employees. Division, geographic, location indexes. Also available as online data base. *National Directory of Corporate Public Affairs: An Annual Guide* (Washington, D.C: Columbia Books, Inc.). Alphabetical listing of over 1500 companies involved in public affairs programs, their PACs, key personnel, type of business, and areas of geographic influence.

National Trade and Professional Associations of the U.S. and Canada and Labor Unions (Washington, DC: Columbia Books, Inc.). Published annually. Listing of trade and professional organizations and labor unions with national memberships. Key word, geographic, and budget size indexes.

Rand McNally International Banker's Directory. Published semiannually. Multi-volume. Referred to as the "Blue Book." Contains names of officers and directors of all banks in the world. Details include basic principles and practices of banking, with the latest information on all domestic and foreign banks, statements, personnel, U S banking, and commercial laws. Also includes the most accessible banking points for 75,000 no banking towns and Federal Reserve Districts and banks.

Reference Book (NY: Dun and Bradstreet Marketing Services Division). Published every two months. Available only to customers of D&B Business Information Reports. Detailed lists of names and addresses of U.S. firms by state, city, SIC code, line of business, estimated financial strength, and credit appraisal. Information can be retrieved in any desired sequence.

Research Centers Directory (Detroit: Gales Research Co.). Lists research institutes, centers, foundations, tones, bureaus, experiment stations, and similar nonprofit research facilities, activities, and organizations in the U.S. and Canada. Identifies special research facilities and their availability for use by outsiders. Contains sections on business, economic, and multidisciplinary programs. Subject research center and institutional indexes.

Research Services Directory *(Detroit:* Gale Research Co.). Lists to profit organizations providing research services on a contract or fee for service basis to clients. Covered research activities include business, education, energy and the environment, agriculture, government, public affairs, social sciences, art and the humanities, physical and earth sciences, life sciences, and engineering and technology.

Standard and Poor's Corporation Records (NY: Standard and Poor's Corp.). Published semimonthly in loose-leaf format, 1923 to present. Corporate news and financial information on American,

Canadian, and foreign companies. Provides company history, officers, and product data. Daily News covers current corporate developments. Indexes to main entry and subsidiaries.

Standard and Poor's Register of Corporations, Directors and Executives *(W:* Standard and Poor's Corp.). Published annually, 1928 to present Vol. 1: Alphabetical list of U.S. and Canadian corporations. Includes product or line of business, SIC code, and number of employees. Vol. 2; Alphabetical list and brief biography of executives in U.S. and Canada. Vol. 3: Indexes corporations by SIC code, geographic area, new individuals, obituaries, and new companies.

Telecommunications Systems and Services Directory. Schmittroth, John, Jr., ed.. (Detroit: Gale Research Co.). 3 parts. Four indexes, cumulative in each part. Provides descriptions of communications systems serving the need for rapid and accurate transmission of data, voice, text, and images. Covers voice and data communications networks, teleconferencing, videotext, teletext, electronic funds transfer, telex, facsimile, and two-way cable television.

The Directory of Directories. Ethridge, James M., ed., (Detroit: Gale Research Co.). Nearly 7,000 informative, up-to-date listings of directories, 2,100 subject headings and cross-references.

Thomas Register of American Manufacturers (NY: Thomas Publishing Co.). Published annually. Comprehensive U.S. directory restricted to manufacturing firms. Vols. 1–7 are indexes to manufacturers by product; Vol. 7 includes a list of trade names. Vol. 8 lists manufacturers by company name, including information similar to Standard & Poor's Register. Vols. 9–12 are compilations of manufacturers' catalogs.

3.3.6 BIOGRAPHIES

Biographical reference books are useful sources of information regarding people, living or deceased. They provide dates of birth and death, nationality, and information about occupations.

Dun and Bradstreet's Reference Book of Corporate Management (NY: Dun and Bradstreet). Published annually. Directory of top executives arranged by company, birth date, college, and employment history.

Marquis Who's Who Publications/Index to All Books (Chicago: Marquis Who's Who, Inc.). Published annually. An index to 230,000 biographical sketches currently contained in Marquis' Who's Who volumes.

Who's Who in America (Chicago: Marquis Who's Who, Inc.). Published every two years. Biographies of prominent living Americans.

Who's Who in Consulting (Detroit: Gale Research Co.). Reference guide to professional personnel engaged in consultation for business, industry, and government.

Who's Who in Finance and Industry (Chicago: Marquis Who's Who, Inc.). Published every two years. Contains brief biographies of financial and industrial, national and international leaders.

3.3.7 DOCTORAL DISSERTATIONS

Somewhat obscure sources of research are the unpublished doctoral dissertations required in university Ph.D. programs. These are clearly indexed and available on photocopies or microfilm:

American Doctoral Dissertations (Ann Arbor, MI: University Microfilms International). Published annually. A complete listing of all doctoral dissertations accepted at American and Canadian universities. Arranged by board subject classification and, under each heading, alphabetically by name of university. Author index. Publication is slow.

Dissertation Abstracts International (Ann Arbor, MI: University Microfilms International). Published monthly. Section A: The Humanities and Social Sciences; Section B: The Sciences; Section C: European Dissertations. Informative abstracts of dissertations submitted by more than 345 cooperating institutions. Arranged in same categories as American Doctoral Dissertations; each issue is a detailed "Keyword Title Index," DATRIXII offers a personalized search service for all past and current dissertations.

3.4 STATISTICAL SOURCES

Statistics are an absolute necessity to decision makers. They are becoming increasingly valuable and available through computer online data bases. The most comprehensive compilations are provided by governmental agencies, universities, and trade associations. These statistics determine U.S. and regional business trends. Data are also gathered for specific industries. Examples are banking and monetary statistics; labor and marketing statistics; and plant and equipment expenditures studies. Other sources concentrate on important international statistics and foreign economic trends.

Statistical sources are divided into two major sections: 1) indexes and selected statistics sources for general information, and 2) international and industrial marketing statistics.

3.4.1 INDEXES

Predicasts Forecasts Predicasts, Inc., (Cleveland: University Circle Research Center). Published quarterly, cumulated annually. Abstracts business and financial forecasts for specific U S industrial products and the general economy. Presents composite data for economic, construction, energy, and other indicators.

Standard and Poor's Trade and Securities Statistics (NY; Standard and Poor's Corp.). Loose-leaf, with monthly supplements. Current and basic statistics in the following areas: banking and finance; production and labor; price; indexes (commodities); income and trade; building and building materials; transportation and communications; electric power and fuels; metals; auto, rubber and tires; textiles, chemicals, paper; agricultural products; security price index record.

Statistics Sources: A Subject Guide to Data on Industrial, Business, Social, Educational, Financial and Other Topics for the U.S. and International. Wasserman, P.J. O'Brien, and K. Clansky. (Detroit: Gale Research Co.). Guide to statistical data. Indexes information from domestic and international sources. Arranged dictionary style; includes selected bibliography of key statistical sources.

3.4.2 SELECTED STATISTICAL SOURCES

3.4.2.1 GENERAL STATISTICAL SOURCES

The Dow Jones Irwin Business and Investment Almanac Levine, Sumner N., ed. (Homewood, IL: Dow Jones. Irwin), Published annually. Tables and graphs. Most basic, comprehensive statistical information on various aspects of business, finance, investments, and economics for recent trends. Includes articles on tax, accounting, and labor developments. Subject index.

3.4.2.2 INDUSTRY STATISTICAL SOURCES

Many business projects involve gathering statistics and/or investment data on a particular industry. The following sources provide useful statistics on leading industries and analyze current trends and future projections.

Guide to Trade and Securities Statistics (*A*)Balachandran, M. (Ann Arbor, MI: Pierian Printing). Specialized guide of composite statistical data available in 30 of the most widely used loose-leaf services and statistical yearbooks. Analyzed on an item-by-item basis, using a subject/keyword approach. Sources are listed and described at the front of the volume.

Real Estate Analyst Reports (St. Louis: Wenzlick Research Co.). Published monthly. Loose-leaf real estate analyses include: The Agricultural Bulletin; As I See It (commentary); Construction Bulletin; Mortgage Bulletin; Real Estate Analyst.

Yearbook of Industrial Statistics (NY: United Nations). Published annually. Supplemented monthly in Monthly Bulletin of Statistics. Vol. 1: General Industrial Statistics. A body of international statistics on population, agriculture, mining, manufacturing, finance, trade, and education. Vol. 2: Supplies internationally comparable data on the production of industrial commodities internationally.

3.4.2.3 MARKETING—STATISTICAL SOURCES

Access to current statistical data is essential to those engaged in market research. Marketing departments attempting to determine sales potential, set sales quotas, or establish effective sales territories are interested in details such as population, number of households, age, sex, marital status, occupation, education level, income, and purchasing power. Much of this information is available from U S government sources. Individual states also publish statistical series, often on a more timely basis than the federal government. Private companies also generate data applicable to marketing functions.

Commercial Atlas and Marketing Guide (Chicago: Rand McNally Services). Published annually, 1884 to present. Includes maps for each state in the U S and a section of maps of foreign countries. Marketing statistics for states and some worldwide data, such as airline and steamship distances, are provided. Also included are population statistics and figures for retail sales, bank deposits, auto registrations, etc., for principal cities.

Editor and Publisher Market Guide (NY: Editor and Publisher). Published annually, 1884 to present. Market data are provided for more than 1,500 U.S. and Canadian cities in which newspapers are published. Included are figures for population, households, principal industries, and retail outlets. Estimates are given by county and newspaper city, and strategic market segment analysis is performed for such items as population and personal income. Total retail sales are arranged by state.

Survey of Business Power Data Service (NY: Sales and Marketing Management). Published annually, 1977 to present. A spinoff of the July and October statistical issues of Sales and Marketing Management magazine. Arranged in 3 volumes: Vol. 1 county and city population characteristics, such as household distribution, effective buying income, total retail store sales, and various buying power indexes; Vol. 2 retail sales by individual store groups and merchandise line categories for the current year; Vol. 3 TV market data, metro area and county projections for population, effective buying income, and retail sales.

3.4.2.4 INTERNATIONAL STATISTICAL SOURCES

International Marketing Handbook (Detroit: Gale Research Co.). Provides a marketing profile of 138 nations. Data regarding transportation and utilities, credit, foreign trade outlook, investment, industry trends, distribution sales, advertising and research, trade regulations, and market profile.

Consumer Europe (Detroit: Gale Research Co.). Provides data on the production, sales and distribution of more than 150 consumer product categories. Focuses on Western Europe.

European Marketing Data and Statistics (London: Euromonitor Publications Ltd.). Published annually. The volume's 70,000 statistics provide current marketing data on the population, employment, production, trade, economy, consumer expenditures, market sizes, retailing, housing, health and education, culture and mass media, and communications of Europe's 26 major countries.

Handbook of the Nations (Detroit: Gale Research Co.). Provides political and economic data for 190 countries. Economic data includes statistics on the GNP, agriculture, major industries, electric power, exports, imports, major trade partners, and the budget.

Index to International Statistics (Washington, DC: Congressional Information Service). Published monthly, with quarterly and annual cumulations. Indexes publications of international intergovernmental organizations, such as the UN, the Common Market, and the World Bank. Geographic index is included.

International Marketing Data and Statistics (London: Euromonitor Publications Ltd.). Published annually. Handbook that supplies statistical tables and latest data for 45 countries in the Americas, Africa, Asia, and Australia. Information is geared toward marketing use.

Japan Trade Directory (Tokyo: Japan External Trade Organization). Provides information about 1,700 Japanese companies and their 8,500 products and services. Three sections: products and services, prefectures and companies, advertising.

World Bank Annual Report (Washington, DC: World Bank). Published annually. Summarizes the activities of the World Bank and International Development Association. Reviews economic trends in developing countries, capital flow, and external public department.

World Business Cycles (London: The Economist Newspapers Ltd.). Provides business and economic data for five decades (1930 to 1980) for many countries. Also provides longer-term data for Great Britain and the U.S.

World Directory of Multinational Enterprises Stopford, John M,, ed. (Detroit: Gale Research Co.). Two volumes. Provides information on 550 multinational corporations, with five year financial summaries. Ranks corporations according to sales, diversification, and other criteria. Wasserman, Paul and Jacqueline O'Brien, *Statistics Sources* (Detroit: Gale Research Co.). Facts and figures on 12,000 subjects for nearly every country in the world. Arranged in dictionary style with cross-references, it cites annuals, yearbooks, directories, and other publications.

Worlds Trade Annual (NY: Walker & Co.). Published annually. Five volumes offering statistics and detailed information on various aspects of the world trade situation.

3.5 THE INTERNET

THE INTERNET CAN BE A GOOD SOURCE OF FACTS if you evaluate the source and give adequate information in your write-up. See the Chapter on Business Research & Reports, the section on Document Your Sources for proper documentation of Internet sources.

3.5.1 Evaluate Credibility

3.5.1.1 ANYONE CAN POST ANYTHING ON THE INTERNET. Articles found here may not go through the "sifting and evaluating" process that editors of newspapers, magazines, and scholarly journals perform. You must at least try top determine the name of the organization that sponsors the website and something of their history and reputation.

3.5.1.2 ASK KEY QUESTIONS. Evaluate the credibility of your Internet sources by asking such self-questions as:

- Is this website monitored or administered? By what organization or person(s)?
- What is the history and reputation of this organization or person(s)?
- What are their biases likely to be?
- What's the purpose of the site?
- Who is the author of the article or message?
- What are his or her qualifications? Reputation? Probable biases?
- Is the information (and the links) relevant, reliable, and current?

3.5.1.3 PREFER EDUCATIONAL (.EDU) AND GOVERNMENT (.GOV) SITES first for credibility. Next, mainstream associations (.org). Last in credibility are commercial (.com) sites, which are all about making money and therefore probably have more bias built in.

3.5.1.4 FIND THE ROOT DIRECTORY OR HOME PAGE. You must determine the organization that is sponsoring the website. You may need to go to the root directory for that.

> For example your search might take you to:
>
> *http://www.aaiusa.org/famous_arab_americans.htm.*
>
> If that webpage doesn't show the organization sponsoring it, you may need to go to
>
> *http://www.aaiusa.org.*
>
> That page is the root directory and will tell you that the website is sponsored by Arab American Institute of USA.

3.5.2 Conduct an Internet Search

3.5.2.1 DEFINE THE TYPE OF INFORMATION you need for this aspect of your project or assignment.

3.5.2.2 ASK YOURSELF WHAT ORGANIZATIONS MIGHT PUBLISH SUCH INFORMATION. You might do an Internet search looking for organizations that deal with this subject matter.

3.5.2.3 DETERMINE KEY WORDS to use for your Internet search. Have alternates for each key word, so you can try different combinations if your first attempt does not bring up the information you need.

3.5.2.4 FORMAT KEY WORDS properly in order to get the results you want. While search engine protocols may vary, here are some typical rules for entering your search words:

3.5.2.4.1 NARROW THE SEARCH by putting quotation marks around the phrase you want to the search to focus on.

<travel, sightseeing and "hotels in Italy" >

3.5.2.4.2 INDICATE TOPICS TO OMIT by using the word "NOT."

<health foods NOT canned>

3.5.2.4.3 FIND SITES THAT COVER TWO OR MORE TOPICS by using the word "AND."

< health foods AND vitamins>

3.5.2.4.4 INDICATE INFORMATION TO INCLUDE AND EXCLUDE by using the plus and minus signs. This is similar to AND and NOT formats. A plus sign before a word or term tells the search engine to retrieve only documents that contain that word. A minus sign before a word or term tells the engine to exclude it from the search.

<health foods + vitamins - canned foods>

3.5.2.4.5 FIND SITES THAT CONTAIN EITHER OF SEVERAL TOPICS by use of the word "OR" between search words.

<chakras OR acupuncture meridians>

3.5.2.4.6 DESIGNATE THE PROXIMITY THAT YOU PREFER by using the words "NEAR."

<major cities NEAR New York>

3.5.2.4.7 INCLUDE PLURALS, SUFFIXES, ALTERNATE SPELLINGS in your commands to the search engine by inserting an asterisk after or in middle of the word. (These are called "wildcards.")

<health*foods>   *<hea*lth foods>*

3.5.2.4.8 ASK FOR MORE INFORMATION by formatting a "nested search" that puts another topic(s) in parentheses within the main topic(s). Some search engines allow this protocol.

<health foods AND (cancer OR American Cancer Association) AND vitamins.

3.5.2.5 TRY VARIOUS SEARCH ENGINES. If one search engine doesn't produce the result you need, try another. Each one tends to produce somewhat different search results, even when you enter the same key words.

3.5.2.6 TRY META-SEARCH ENGINES, such as Copernic. They send your key words to several search engines at the same time.

3.5.2.7 USE ADVANCED SEARCH FEATURES. Refine your search beyond basic key words by clicking on the "advanced search" option of the search engine. By doing this, you can search only certain domains, such as .edu or .gov. The advanced search option can also help you to locate an exact phrase or person, specific dates, or a particular element, such as an audio clip.

3.5.2.8 PROPERLY DOCUMENT YOUR INTERNET ARTICLES in the References section of your report and in the endnotes or footnotes within the papers. Include article title, author, date, newspaper name and page number (or website name and url)—enough information to enable readers to find the original material and to evaluate it.

Source Note: Some Information in this chapter reprinted with permission of Y.S. Multinovich, "Business Facts for Decision Makers," *Business Horizons,* March 1985, pp. 63–80.

Chapter Four
Research Surveys:
Questionnaires & Interviews

THIS CHAPTER INCLUDES suggestions for using surveys to gather business information. The most common survey methods include: 1) questionnaires—both oral and written 2) interviews—both in-person and telephone.

4.1 GENERAL TIPS—DOING SURVEYS

A SURVEY is a data collection tool. Questions are formulated and answers to them are gathered through personal interviews, written questionnaires, or telephone interviews.

4.1.1   **SURVEYS ARE OFTEN USED** to explore, describe, or explain the 1) knowledge, 2) behavior, 3) experience, 4) attitudes, or 5) beliefs of a population of people with regard to a particular subject.

4.1.2   **THE TERM** *POPULATION* refers to a particular group of people and includes every person in that group. The population of business enterprises in Kansas City includes every business in the city.

4.1.3   **THE TERM** *SAMPLE* refers to a subgroup of a population. It is often impossible to survey an entire population, and usually more feasible to survey a sample. Findings and conclusions about the sample are assumed to be more-or-less true for the entire population. For example, you might select 50 businesses that are representative of the type and range of businesses found in Kansas City and survey people in those businesses.

4.1.4   **SURVEYS TEND TO BE RELIABLE** in that the measurements used tend to produce the same results time after time in sample after sample.

4.1.5   **SURVEYS TEND TO BE WEAK ON VALIDITY** because the answers may be poor approximations of direct observations. The questions may not accurately measure what they are supposed to measure. Valid surveys depend on complete and accurate survey answers, which in turn are dependent upon the memory, motivation, knowledge, experience, and ability of the respondents.

4.1.6   **BIASED SAMPLES** are not truly representative of the entire population. For example, if all or most of the sample respondents reside in the Deep South, or if they are all over 50, or under 30, their opinions may be slanted by their environmental experiences, and the sample might not reflect the characteristics of all U.S. residents. To avoid such biases, which can distort results, be sure your sample is either a random sample or a representative sample.

4.1.7 **IF ALL MEMBERS OF YOUR POPULATION** had the same characteristics and were the same in every way, you would not need a sample. One person would represent the entire population.

4.1.8 **A REPRESENTATIVE SAMPLE** reflects key variables of the population. What are the key variables in your population that could affect how people respond to your questions? Age? Sex? Management level? Size of company? Think of people in these categories as subgroups within your population. You need to know, or estimate, what percentage of the whole that each subgroup represents.

For example, if company size is a key factor, you may find that 60 percent of people in your population work for large firms with over 5,000 employees, 30 percent work for mid-sized firms with between 1,000 and 5,000 employees, and 10 percent work for small firms with fewer than 1,000 employees. Therefore, 60 percent of the responses you use in your tabulation and analysis should come from managers at large firms, and so forth. Your sample would then be representative of the population so far as company size is concerned.

4.1.9 **RANDOM SAMPLES** can be selected by a number of methods. Refer to a good research methods text for detailed information about sampling plans, including determining sample size.

4.1.10 **TO COMPENSATE FOR GREATER VARIABILITY** within one subgroup, a disproportionate number of respondents can be used for that particular subgroup, with a smaller proportion of respondents from the subgroup that has less variability.

4.1.11 **SAMPLE SIZE IS IMPORTANT.** When you increase the number of population members that comprise your sample, you decrease the probability of drawing a sample that is extremely different from your population. In other words, as you increase sample size you can expect less variation from sample mean (average response) of one sample and the means of other samples of that population. Also, when the questionnaire or interview includes many items, the sample must be fairly large for purposes of statistical analysis.

4.1.12 **USE AS LARGE A SAMPLE AS IS PRACTICAL.** This is a good rule of thumb for beginning researchers. For most studies, samples of less than 30 are too small, and samples of more than 500 are rarely necessary.

4.2 QUESTIONNAIRES

A QUESTIONNAIRE is a written set of questions asked of a sample of persons in order to get information and/or opinions on a particular topic. The results are tabulated, analyzed, and put into written form.

A QUESTIONNAIRE IS PARTICULARLY USEFUL for describing the characteristics of a large population. A carefully developed questionnaire administered to an appropriate sample can provide you with information about the characteristics of the population from which the sample is taken.

WRITTEN QUESTIONNAIRES ALLOW YOU to standardize your measurements because all respondents answer identically-worded questions. Questionnaires that are self-explanatory can be mailed, allowing you to study larger samples than would be possible with questionnaires that must be administered by an interviewer.

4.2.1 PLANNING THE QUESTIONNAIRE

4.2.1.1 DETERMINE THE INFORMATION YOU WANT and who you want it from. What burning questions do you have that relate to the course objectives and topics? Can you get the answers, or at least some further insight, by studying a particular population? What size and type of sample do you need? Do you need to mail the questionnaire? If so, how will you get your mailing list?

4.2.1.2 THE MAILING LIST you are able to secure may limit your population. If the only mailing list that is feasible, for example, is that of your local Chamber of Commerce, then the local Chamber of Commerce is your population. The limitation of such a population is that your results will reflect only the opinions of this group, not of all local business persons.

4.2.1.3 SOURCES OF MAILING LISTS include biographical books, such as the *Who's-Who*-type books, directories of organizations or individuals, criss-cross directories, and membership lists. The older the source, the more addresses will be out-of-date resulting in a higher percentage of undeliverable questionnaires.

4.2.1.4 YOU CAN PURCHASE MAILING LISTS from firms that specialize in lists, but they are usually expensive. A major advantage is that such lists come in the form of peel-off mailing labels.

4.2.1.5 IF YOU COMPILE YOUR OWN LIST, the easiest approach may be to write the addresses in longhand directly onto mailing label sheets. Copy the sheets before removing and applying the labels to envelopes. Alternatively, you can computerize the list, merge each name into the cover letter as an inside address, and use window envelopes that let the address show through.

4.2.1.6 RETURN RATE IS IMPORTANT to the validity of your survey. Aim for a return rate of about 50 percent. The lower the return rate, the more likely you are to get a biased sample. For example, a recent study of how women feel about their relationships with men indicated that male-female relationships have deteriorated and that there are many problems. Since only 5 percent of the women who received the questionnaire returned it, critics argued that respondents tended to be women who had negative experiences, were bitter, and welcomed the chance to vent their anger. Therefore, the sample may have been biased toward negativity and not necessarily representative of opinions of the population of all U.S. women.

4.2.1.7 THE RETURN RATE WILL DEPEND LARGELY on the interest that recipients have in the topic, the benefits they perceive will result from the survey, the amount of time they have available to devote to such matters, and the length, clarity, and complexity of the questionnaire. A well-chosen sample and a well-written questionnaire will enhance your return rate.

4.2.1.8 PROMISING ANONYMITY to respondents will encourage them to respond initially and will enhance the candor with which they respond. On the other hand, this anonymity makes it difficult to follow up. If you don't know who has failed to respond, you don't know where to direct follow-up efforts.

4.2.1.9 THE AVERAGE RETURN RATE for mail surveys is between 10 and 20 percent, even when surveys are well-written and sent to an interested audience. You may get a higher return rate by getting the leadership of an organization to back your effort. Also, effective follow-up measures may boost your return rate to about 50 percent.

4.2.1.10 FOLLOWUP MEASURES must be planned at the beginning of the project so that you may prepare enough copies of the survey, labels, envelopes, etc. If you have not promised confidentiality, number each name on your mailing list and write that number on the questionnaire so you can later determine who should receive follow-ups. Some types of follow-up are discussed next.

(1) TO INCREASE RETURN RATE mail an identical follow-up questionnaire a few days or weeks after the first mailing. If respondents are anonymous, send the second mailing to everyone, instructing them to disregard it if they have already returned the first questionnaire.

(2) TO ESTABLISH THAT YOUR SAMPLE IS REPRESENTATIVE of your population, mail a short-form questionnaire containing two to five simple questions. The responses can indicate how well the sample represents the entire population you are covering. For example, in a survey on managerial stress, you believe that age, sex, and management level are key factors that affect stress level. Send non-respondents a short follow-up questionnaire asking only for their age, sex, management level, and perceived stress level. Some recipients who did not respond to the full questionnaire will return the short form. If you determine that these recipients who did *not* answer the full questionnaire have similar characteristics in these key areas as those who *did* respond, you can make a case that your sample is representative of your population.

4.2.1.11 PLAN YOUR METHODS FOR TABULATING AND ANALYZING THE DATA. For any large mailing, you will certainly want to do a trial run first. Even prior to your trial run (discussed later), fill out a few questionnaires yourself, tabulate them, and do some analysis. This can alert you to problems and opportunities. Most likely you will use a computer in your tabulation and analysis. Consider the following:

(1) How will responses be transferred from the questionnaire to the computer program?

(2) What statistical treatment will you use? How will data be grouped for statistical analysis? How will the grouping affect the number of respondents you need?

4.2.1.12 ANALYSIS FREQUENTLY CONSISTS of merely determining the percentage of respondents who gave various answer to each question. For a more sophisticated analysis, determine what computer programs are available and appropriate for analyzing the data; for example:

(1) Some type of spread sheet? Often spread sheets can be used to perform simple calculations of the data, then totals can be plugged into a formula to determine correlations, regressions, and so forth.

(2) Some type of data base, perhaps with file management capabilities, so that you can quickly pull out the responses of any subgroup and study them separately?

(3) A comprehensive package, such a The Statistical Package for the Social Sciences (SPSS), that will perform almost any type of statistical treatment?

4.2.1.13 MAKE A TRIAL RUN. Ask a few appropriate respondents to complete the questionnaire before you have it reproduced en masse. Include a couple of questions about problems they had in understanding or completing the questionnaire and suggestions for improving it. Again, tabulate and analyze these responses to work out problems and to recognize overlooked opportunities for getting important information.

4.2.1.14 PLAN YOUR REQUESTS FOR FURTHER INFORMATION. If you are willing and able to send respondents a copy of the results of the survey after you've finished your work, ask them if they want a copy. Offering to give them this information may help motivate them to complete the questionnaire.

Consider meeting with some of the respondents in order to get some face-to-face, in-depth information and case examples. If you have promised anonymity to respondents, you must get their responses to these two questions from a separate form that they can return to you in a separate envelope. Exhibit 4.1 shows a sample *further information form* for this purpose

EXHIBIT 4.1 FURTHER INFORMATION FORM

FURTHER FORMATION

TO: [your name and address]

_____ Yes, I would like to receive a copy of the results of this survey on xxxxx.

_____ Yes, I am willing to talk with you, at my convenience, to further discuss xxxxx, xxxxx, xxxxx, and similar topics.

From:_____

Title:_____

Phone number(s):_____

Firm name & address:_____

_____

NOTE: This form is provided to protect the confidentiality of your responses to the questionnaire.

Of course, your wishes concerning confidentiality of interview responses will also be respected.

4.2.2 *WRITING THE QUESTIONNAIRE*

4.2.2.1 **CONSULT PEOPLE** who have knowledge of your topic before and after writing the questionnaire. Bounce your ideas and your preliminary questions off others to help insure that your questions elicit the information you want in the form you want.

4.2.2.2 **KEEP IT SHORT!** Most people balk at responding to a long, complex questionnaire. They tend to put it aside if they think it will take more than 10 or 15 minutes to answer, seems difficult to understand, doesn't have a clearly stated purpose, or doesn't seem worthwhile or of interest to them.

4.2.2.3 **MAXIMIZE YOUR RETURN RATE.** You must entice, tempt, and woo respondents. Here are some courting techniques:

4.2.2.3.1 **GET A GROUP'S LEADERSHIP SUPPORT.** Get the backing of the leaders of the organization to which respondents belong and use that support persuasively.

4.2.2.3.2 **GET A GROUP'S AGREEMENT.** Get the agreement of the group ahead of time, if possible. Ask them to answer your questionnaire as soon as they receive it.

4.2.2.3.3 MAKE THE SURVEY INVITING AND EASY. If possible, use desktop publishing software to produce a questionnaire that looks professional, compact, and tempting.

4.2.2.3.4 BEGIN WITH AN INTEREST SEDUCER. Make the questionnaire seem fascinating and easy-to-answer. For example, instead of a cover letter, put a brief, persuasive introduction on the top part of page one of the questionnaire. This format allows you to showcase the following items:

(a) Persuasive reasons for the reader to respond

(b) The first few interesting, easy questions.

Readers see this the minute they open the envelope. Aim to draw them into picking up a pen and responding to those first questions at that moment.

4.2.2.3.5 STATE THE SURVEY'S PURPOSE AND USE. Clearly state the purpose of the questionnaire and how it will be used. Point out, or imply, the benefits to the recipient for taking the time to complete it. Focus on benefits that are likely to have value for this particular sample of people. You might promise to send them a copy of the results or even some gift. The benefit may be as simple as a feeling of helping someone with a worthwhile project, but it must be there.

4.2.2.4 PHRASE QUESTIONS CAREFULLY so that recipients clearly understand them and so that responses are valid.

4.2.2.5 PROVIDE FOR THE DEGREE, EXTENT, OR INTENSITY OF RESPONSE. You need to know the degree or extent of each respondent's opinion, feeling, or belief about the various issues. This will increase the meaning and accuracy of your results. See Exhibit 4.2, Question (2), which offers respondents five degrees of importance ranging from extremely important to not important. A simple yes-or-no response to each reason would not allow the respondents to convey an accurate picture of their thinking.

4.2.2.6 MAKE ITEMS EASY TO RESPOND TO—AND TO LATER TABULATE. Structure items so that responses are easy for recipients to make and for you to tabulate.

4.2.2.7 AVOID OPEN ENDED QUESTIONS if you need specific data that results in clear statistical treatment. Open-ended questions are difficult to answer and to tabulate. In Exhibit 4-1, Question (2) would be an open-ended one if respondents were required to think up all the reasons themselves.

Example: *What do you think are the reasons for this under-representation?*

4.3.3.8 OFFER CLEAR CHOICES AS RESPONSES TO QUESTIONS. Make it easy for people to respond and for you to later tabulate their responses. In Exhibit 4.2, Question (1) has three clear choices, and the yes/no/undecided format is adequate to reflect respondent's thinking. Question (2) has three choices plus a write-in option.

List the most-likely responses you can think of.

Label the last choice *Other* and provide space for respondents to write in other responses.

4.2.2.9 OFFER WRITE-IN OPTIONS. They are open-ended and therefore difficult to tabulate; however, they are often necessary in order to get clear, complete responses. To tabulate them, look over all responses and determine some common themes which can become categories. Set up each category as if it were a choice and tabulate.

4.2.2.10 AVOID BIASED OR LEADING QUESTIONS because they lower the validity and credibility of your results. For example, Question 1 in Exhibit 4-2 would be a leading question if it were phrased as follows:

EXHIBIT 4.2 SAMPLE QUESTIONS

1) Do you think women are equitably represented in top management in your company?

_____ (a) Yes _____ (b) No _____ (c) Undecided

2) If you answered "no" to item 1, please rate the following reasons for women's under-representation

	HOW IMPORTANT IS THIS REASON?				
	Extremely				Not at All
a. Not enough qualified women	5	4	3	2	1
b. Reluctance of male top decision makers to include women at the top	5	4	3	2	1
c. Not enough women can visualize themselves at the top	5	4	3	2	1

d. Other (specify): _____

4.2.2.11 DETERMINE DEMOGRAPHIC DATA that is necessary, as well as data that would enhance the study but could be omitted if the questionnaire becomes too long. Data frequently asked of business persons include (1) questions about company size: number of employees, gross annual sales, market share and/or net annual profit, (2) questions about the type of company: products or services offered, types of customer, type of structure types of systems used, (3) questions about the respondent: job title, areas and types of responsibility, number of subordinates, salary range. For some studies such personal data as age, marital status, and number of children are important,

4.2.2.12 DEMOGRAPHIC QUESTIONS should be followed by clear categories that respondents select as most appropriate to their situation. Precise choices are easier to tabulate than open-ended choices. They also provide more accurate responses in sensitive areas such as salary and age. For example, the following would be a poor question:

What is your current annual salary?

Exhibit 4-3 shows a better format for this question.

EXHIBIT 4.3 DEMOGRAPHIC QUESTION

---

(10) What is your current annual salary?

___ (a) Under $25,000

___ (b) $25,000 to $49,999

___ (c) $50,000 to $45,000

___ (d) $0ver $45,000

4.2.2.13 PLACE DEMOGRAPHIC QUESTIONS LAST in most questionnaires. The other questions are normally most important to your study and they are more interesting to the recipient.

4.2.2.14 NUMBER OR CODE each question and response to aid in later tabulation and analysis of the data. The examples given here use numbers to code the questions and letters to code the responses.

4.2.3 REPORTING THE RESULTS

4.2.3.1 BE OBJECTIVE in reporting the results of your survey. Include information that disagrees with your own ideas or predictions as well as information that confirms them. Give the whole story. Report any errors or possible problems with the way you set up the study and gathered the data, as well as conditions or events that might have affected the results.

4.2.3.2 THE WRITTEN REPORT SHOULD INCLUDE the following:

4.2.3.2.1 AN INTRODUCTION that gives a statement of the problem or situation you examined, a review of some relevant literature on the subject, and the purpose of your questionnaire.

4.2.3.2.2 THE METHODS YOU USED to conduct your survey, including the key information about the population, sample, questionnaire, procedures you used in administering the questionnaire, return rate, and other procedures.

4.2.3.2.3 THE RESULTS you got when you tabulated your data and did the statistical analyses.

4.2.3.2.4 A DISCUSSION OF THE RESULTS, including your interpretation of what they mean. Show that you are capable of looking at the results and tying them in with other relevant factors.

4.2.3.2.5 CONCLUSIONS AND RECOMMENDATIONS for action or change. These should flow naturally from your discussion of the results. What does your analysis mean as far as changes that should be made or action that should be taken?

4.2.3.2.6 REFERENCES. A list of all your reference sources.

4.2.3.2.7 APPENDIX, which should include a copy of the questionnaire and may include some of the tables, charts, graphs, figures, and mathematical formulas that are not discussed in detail in the main text of the paper.

4.2.3.2.8 AN ABSTRACT OR EXECUTIVE SUMMARY of the introduction, methods, results, and discussion sections is usually expected. Writing one helps you to focus on the key points made in your survey and to communicate it succinctly to others,

4.2.3.3 SUPPLEMENTARY PARTS OF THE REPORT usually include a cover page and should include a table of contents for papers longer than 20 pages.

4.2.3.4 TABLES, CHARTS, AND GRAPHS are ideal for reporting survey results and are normally used liberally in the main body to illustrate the discussion of the findings. See the suggestions given in Chapter Four.

4.3 INTERVIEWS

4.3.1 DETERMINE THE KIND OF INFORMATION you want. If the interview augments library research, then it should yield information not available through printed matter. Frequently interviews are used to enhance known information, to see concepts in action, to hear about their use firsthand, to make them come alive. You can use information from interviews as real-life examples of concepts and ideas you present in your writing and also as material for case studies.

4.3.2 DETERMINE THE BEST SOURCES of this information. Be sure that a potential interviewee is actually involved in the kinds of activities, responsibilities, or functions that you want information about. An initial conference with your instructor may prevent false starts. Tell the instructor your plans and get feedback about their practicality.

If your research centers around information you will need when you start pursuing your individual career goals, a good source might be someone holding the type of position you would like to have some day. Such an interview can even lead to a valuable job contact when you conduct your job search campaign later on.

4.3.3 MAKE APPOINTMENTS WELL IN ADVANCE of any deadlines for turning in the results of the interview, such as a report or case study. Here are typical problems:

You have difficulty getting an appointment with your first-choice interviewee(s), so you must find and contact other target persons.

- The interviewee postpones or cancels the appointment at the last minute. Busy people often are called to emergency meetings or must take sudden business trips.

- You do not get enough relevant information from the interviewee and must line up other interviewees.

- It takes longer than you expected to develop a written report of the interview.

   Be professional. Anticipate these problems, so you can produce on-time results, not excuses. Most business professors do not accept excuses because most managers in the business world cannot afford to accept excuses instead of results.

4.3.4 DETERMINE THE LENGTH OF THE INTERVIEW. Ask for a reasonable time frame, one that will give you what you need without being an undue imposition on the interviewee. Be sure both of you are clear about the time frame.

4.3.5 **PREPARE A LIST OF QUESTIONS.** Design questions to elicit the information you need from this interview. Be sure to cover all key areas. This list should not be considered a rigid structure that the interview must follow. Often the most important information is offered spontaneously, especially when your attitude promotes a relaxed, informal atmosphere. On the other hand, you want to make the most of the interview session, and the prepared list helps assure that you cover all your bases.

4.3.5.1 CLOSED QUESTIONS are those that make it easy to answer "yes" or "no" without further comment. You may want to use them to get very specific information. Some questions are very closed, while others are moderately closed.

> *Do you prefer the traditional or participative approach?*

> *Would you change jobs, if you had the chance?*

4.3.5.2 OPEN QUESTIONS encourage further discussion of a topic. Questions that start with *"what, why, how, where, when"* are used by reporters to guide interviewees into discussions of particular aspects of a topic. Some questions are more open than others. The most open-ended questions tend to start with "what," "why," or "how."

> *What do you think of this new management idea?*

> *Why are you interested in virtual reality?*

> *How should the company go about achieving this goal?*

> *Who might be interested in this type of job?*

> *Where will the company look for new markets?*

> *When will the company be able to expand to Europe?*

4.3.6 **DETERMINE THE METHOD OF RECORDING** the information. Will you take notes? Or will you use an audio cassette recorder, videotape camera, or some combination of these? Consider using an audio cassette recorder as a backup to other methods. Get the interviewee's permission ahead of time so you both know what to expect. Taking notes helps you record your impressions, what you read between the lines, and nonverbal communication. Audio recordings get the verbal information, and video gets both verbal and visual communication. You may want to take a few brief notes during the interview and follow up with more complete notes immediately afterward.

4.3.7 **DECIDE ON THE INITIAL QUESTION.** This should be a warm-up question to put you both at ease, one that helps you get to know each other better on a fairly personal level. You may change this question once you actually get into the meeting, but preparing an initial question will help prepare you for the interview.

4.3.8 **DECIDE ON THE LEADOFF QUESTION.** The leadoff is the first question that gets down to the purpose of the interview. It normally should be a general, open-ended question intended to get the interviewee started on the topic. From there, the interviewee will often take the lead and one topic naturally leads to another, all relevant and related. Sometimes all or most of your questions will be answered spontaneously in this manner.

4.3.9 **REFER TO OTHER QUESTIONS** you have prepared at these times:

1) any time the interview wanders too far off the main topics for too long

2) whenever the interviewee stops talking and looks to you for another question, and one does not readily come to mind from the context of the interview

3) shortly before the interview is scheduled to end, to be sure all important questions have been answered.

4.3.10   **FOLLOW UP** the interview with a cordial thank-you letter.

4.3.11   **DECIDE ON THE FORMAT FOR THE INTERVIEW WRITE-UP.** The style that you use will depend on the assignment and what the instructor expects.

4.3.12   **INTERVIEWS THAT PRODUCE CASE STUDIES.** When the purpose of the interview is to get information for writing one or more case studies, follow the format suggested in the chapter on Cases, the section on Writing Your Own Cases.

4.3.13   **INTERVIEWS INCORPORATED INTO A REPORT.** These reports are normally research reports. Avoid two common problems:

- Do not put the interview(s) into a separate section of the report.

- Do not use a question-answer format for reporting the interview.

The purpose of assigning students to do interviews as part of a research project is normally to give them a chance to see how the concepts they gathered from written materials is applied in a business setting. Two main contributions of interview material are examples, reinforcement, and recommendations.

(1)   EXAMPLES OF CONCEPTS. Whether it's an idea, concept, policy, practice, or other aspect of a topic, talking with people who put these aspects into actual practice can provide you with excellent examples and brief stories for your report.

(2) REINFORCEMENT OF CONCEPTS. Credible interviewees can lend weight to the concepts you set forth in your paper and to your conclusions and recommendation.

(3) RECOMMENDATIONS. After you gather all the information you can find about a topic, you may still be unsure about what it all means and what should be done about it— your conclusions and recommendations. Interviewees can give you invaluable ideas about this aspect of your project.

4.3.13.1 INTEGRATE INTERVIEW INFORMATION into the topics you cover in your report. Weave information in as examples of ideas or practices, as additional information on a particular topic, or as part of your conclusions and recommendations.

4.3.13.2 USE QUOTES, which can be very effective, especially if they convey the general flavor of the discussion or highlight the thinking of the interviewee.

4.3.13.3   GIVE CREDIT TO YOUR INTERVIEWEES for the information they contributed by using endnotes and footnotes. See the chapter on Business Research Reports, the section on Writing the Report for documentation format.

4.3.14   **INTERVIEW REPORT.** The instructor may ask you to simply report on the interview(s) you conducted. If so, here are some suggestions.

4.3.14.1 THE INTRODUCTION to the paper should clearly establish the topic, purpose, and key issues that were covered in the interview(s). It should clearly identify the interviewees and their organizations with such information as each organization's purpose, its role and status within the field or industry, and the interviewee's job title, responsibilities, role and status within the organization.

4.3.14.2 THE BODY of the report will contain the content of the interview(s). A question-answer format may be appropriate and acceptable to the instructor. If in doubt, ask. The instructor may want the format to be organized around certain topics that you were expected to cover in the interview(s). If so, then you must use a topic format instead of a question-answer format. This means you must first make an outline, then organize the information to fit into the outline topics.

4.3.14.3 THE CONCLUSION should summarize or wrap up the opinions and conclusions that were expressed, including your own. It may do any or all of the following:

(1) Summarize the significance of your findings

(2) Make conclusions about what all this information means

(3) Tell how this information fits into the larger picture of the course project, the course content, the business program, your career concerns, or other framework.

4.3.14.4 ADDITIONAL INFORMATION. You may briefly mention additional materials that you acquired through the interview, such as annual reports, sample business documents, brochures, or product information. You can label these materials as "Appendix," and attach them to the report. If you discuss these materials more thoroughly, they should be included in the body of the report as exhibits, properly labeled and numbered.

Chapter Five
Talks: Speeches, Oral Presentations

ARE YOU WILLING AND ABLE TO GIVE A GOOD TALK? If you are, you already have a competitive edge on most business persons. If you are not, this is a skill that you can learn, and with practice become very good at. Nearly all competent speakers are made, not born. So get busy learning and practicing this profitable business skill.

A CHECKLIST FOR TALK EVALUATION is shown at the end of this chapter. Use it to evaluate yourself when you practice your presentations. Get a friend to listen to you and to use the form to evaluate your presentation. Here are the steps and processes that you will explore:

5.1 SELECTING THE RIGHT MATERIAL

MOST BUSINESS CLASS PRESENTATIONS are based on (1) research reports, (2) field observation reports, (3) work experience reports, or (4) case analyses.

5.1.1 RESEARCH REPORTS

5.1.1.1 LIMITED PRESENTATION TIME is usually a key factor in planning a talk based on a research report. Since you will probably have insufficient time for discussing the entire report, you must choose the most interesting, important facets of your report and organize them into a talk. Put yourself in the place of your classmates as you try to determine what will be most interesting, helpful, and significant to them. If in doubt, discuss the project with some of them or with other friends or relatives who have similar interests.

5.1.1.2 THE MOST COMMON MISTAKE is trying to cover too many major points in the talk, which results in bombarding listeners with more concepts than they can absorb in a short time period. Focus on no more than two or three major points. Then back up those points with stories or interesting details that explain, describe, or support each point.

5.1.2 WORK EXPERIENCE REPORTS

5.1.2.1 THE SOURCE OF THIS TALK may be work done in connection with an internship, consulting, or other work experience for credit. Your instructor may be looking for a talk that shows students how information presented in business courses is applied in actual work experience.

5.1.2.2 THE MOST FREQUENT MISTAKE made in preparing this type of presentation is trying to include too many ideas and details or in giving a day-to-day or week-to week log of the experience.

5.1.2.3 SELECT ONE OR TWO KEY CONCEPTS that everyone in the class has learned in the business program and show how these concepts were demonstrated, used effectively, neglected, or violated in the work situation.

5.1.2.4 ALTERNATIVELY, find another way to relate your work experience to knowledge you have gained in the business classroom and present it in a well-organized way that your classmates can understand.

5.1.3 FIELD OBSERVATION REPORTS

5.1.3.1 FIELD TRIPS, both by groups and by individuals, may be the source of interesting, informative oral presentations. Avoid a chronological sequence of presentation

When we arrived....   Then we were taken to the plant floor....

5.1.3.2 FOCUS ON ASPECTS OF THE BUSINESS operation that most directly relate to your business course. Then base the outline for your talk on either:

(1) key points about how the business operates, tying each point into course concepts, or

(2) key course concepts that are being observed or violated by the business, tying them in with the business operations.

5.1.4 CASE ANALYSES

5.1.4.1 AN EFFECTIVE STRUCTURE for the oral presentation of a case includes:

1) SUMMARY—a brief summary of the case as it was presented in the assignment, to refresh everyone's memory about the key points of the case

2) PROBLEM—a discussion of the major problems that management must address

3) SOLUTION—an explanation of the conclusions you reached and the actions you recommend, your action plan for management

5.1.4.2 THE MOST FREQUENT MISTAKE made in oral presentations of cases is poor organization: jumping into the middle of the case without adequate review, giving solutions before identifying problems, and bogging down in details.

5.2 PLANNING THE CONTENT: GENERAL TIPS

5.2.1   DETERMINE THE PURPOSE

What is the purpose of your presentation? Ask yourself these kinds of questions:

- *What is your instructor looking for?*
- *What do your classmates need to know?*

Decide exactly what end results you want from the talk.

- *When the talk is over, what do you want the outcome to be?*
- *What are you trying to accomplish?*

The answer to such questions as these will help you write the title of your talk. Your purpose should be made clear or, where appropriate, intriguing, in both your opening and closing remarks. Do not try to achieve too many purposes in one short talk; keep it simple.

5.2.2   RELATE THE CONTENT TO THE COURSE. Include clear connections and references to course concepts in your talk.

5.2.3   AROUSE LISTENER INTEREST by the material you select for your talk and by the way you present it. You must be able to put yourself in their place in order to do this. Trying out your ideas informally beforehand can help guide you.

5.2.4   USE LOGIC by giving supporting facts, citing reference sources, etc. See Exhibit 5-1.

5.2.5   USE PSYCHOLOGY to make an impact on listeners by considering human needs, feelings, preferences, and desires. Feelings trigger action; logic is used to rationalize action. So express your feelings, convey others' feelings, and appeal to listeners' feelings, where appropriate. If your talk is a persuasive one, show how your proposal will satisfy a need. Help listeners visualize themselves enjoying specific benefits and payoffs from doing what you ask. See Exhibit 5.1.

5.3 PLANNING THE INTRODUCTION

5.3.1   GOOD OPENINGS attract everyone's attention, present a clear picture of what you will talk about, and set the stage for the rest of your presentation.

5.3.2   AVOID STARTING WITH YOUR NAME AND TALK TOPIC. This opening is so typical and expected that people tune it out—and begin tuning you out. Eyes tend to glaze over as listeners think about what's next in their life. If you need to give your name and talk topic, do it *after* you get listener's attention with your snappy opening lines.

5.3.3   PLAN AN ATTENTION-GETTING OPENING. Your opening is the most important part of your talk. If you do not arouse the interest of your classmates in the beginning, you may never have another chance to get them with you. Your opening should immediately catch their attention and arouse their interest. Make it as startling or surprising as you can. Then let it lead into the theme of your talk.

5.3.4   GOOD OPENINGS that can be very successful include:

- **A question**—personal, startling, and/or unusual
- **A startling statement**—challenging, unusual, personal, surprising
- **An unusual fact or statistic**—startling, not generally known

EXHIBIT 5.1. A Talk That Meets Both Logical & Psychological Needs

Logical	*Psychological*
1. INTRODUCTION	**1. ATTENTION**
	Capture attention, set the stage
Explain the topic	**2. NEED**
	Show listeners how information you have can help them, how it relates to their needs, interests, wants
Give overview	Explain needs or problems of a business situation and relate them to needs or problems listeners may face in the business world.
2. BODY	**3. SATISFACTION**
Key points	Make a few clear major points, tying in to satisfaction of needs, interests, wants
Details	Explain key aspects of the solution to a problem
	4. VISUALIZATION
Examples	Illustrate points, tell stories, give cases. Show how ideas or solution can be applied in business or personal situations
3. CONCLUSION	**5. ACTION**
Summary	Summarize and wrap up points
Conclusions	Explain what this means, the significance for listeners
	Appeal to personal interests and feelings
Recommendations	Call for action that will fulfill needs

- **A great quote**—one that is short, snappy, to-the-point; one that is revealing, made by an appropriate or well-known person, and tells the story in a nutshell

- **Humor**—an amusing slant or a ludicrous aspect (see note that follows)

- **A short anecdote**—a brief story that is humorous, personal, surprising, or otherwise interesting and relevant.

5.3.5 **THE BEST ATTENTION-GETTERS** tend to involve the audience physically (a show of hands, a voice vote) or touch their feelings—through humor, surprise, challenge, a personal revelation, or similar methods.

5.3.6 **UNUSUAL PROPS**—such as dollar bills, toy guns, costumes, bizarre or amusing company products—get attention by dramatizing the opening.

5.3.7 **A NOTE ON THE USE OF HUMOR**: Don't tell jokes if you don't normally feel comfortable doing so. They tend to fall flat or backfire when you're not confident about them. Instead, let your sense of humor bubble up naturally whenever you can. If you do use a joke, be sure it is relevant to your presentation.

5.3.8 **BE SURE THE OPENING IS DIRECTLY RELATED** to your topic and helps introduce it. A dramatic or participative opener is an asset, but only if it is relevant.

5.3.9 **GIVE AN OVERVIEW** of what you are going to cover in the talk, once you have your listeners' attention. If the talk involves mystery and surprise, set the stage. Either way, your introduction should prepare listeners to understand and accept the main points that come next.

5.4 PLANNING THE MAIN POINTS

5.4.1 **DECIDE ON A FEW CLEAR POINTS** and how to illustrate them. Your comfort and enthusiasm always shine through and brighten the talk (just as discomfort and boredom always sabotage it). Therefore, if you select points (a) that you understand and have verbalized to others and (b) that are interesting to you, the talk should go well.

5.4.2 **LIMIT MAIN POINTS**, generally to three or four, so you will have adequate time to explain, clarify, and show how they apply to business situations. The only way to make a lasting impact on listeners is to adequately develop a few major ideas so that they get the picture. When you merely touch on major idea after major idea, none of them is likely to take hold in listeners' minds.

5.4.3 **SELECT SUPPORTING DETAILS** carefully. The goal is to retain listeners' interest and to paint a clear picture of each major idea. Supporting material should include both verbal and nonverbal items; for example:

- supporting facts, statistics
- brief, relevant anecdotes or stories
- explanations
- pictures, charts, graphs, maps, models
- examples, samples
- demonstrations
- applications to business or personal situations

5.4.4 **AVOID LONG STRINGS OF DRY FACTS.** Make the necessary information interesting and understandable by breaking it up, using simplified charts or graphs, interesting examples, humor, brief stories, as appropriate. It is possible to be businesslike and professional and still make the presentation entertaining enough to achieve the goals of listener interest and understanding.

5.4.5 **DEVELOP A GOOD ORGANIZATIONAL PLAN** for the body of the talk. Communicate your plan by stating a point clearly, then developing it fully, and finally summarizing it. Be especially aware of letting listeners know when you are leaving one point and moving on to the next.

> *That gives you an idea of how the ABC approach works. Now let's take a look at the XYZ approach.*

5.4.6 **INVOLVE YOUR AUDIENCE** in every way you can throughout the talk, even if you do not have time to get individual responses from them. Ask them questions that they can answer silently; ask for a show of hands; put them in the picture by such expressions as, "Suppose you had this problem dumped in your lap. What would you do?" If the time assigned for your talk is longer than 20 minutes, plan to get more active audience involvement, such as individual responses, or a brief exercise or self-check that is directly related to your topic.

5.4.7 **SELECT VISUAL AIDS** that will help you illustrate your points. Sometimes a good chart that simply outlines your major points can be sufficient. More suggestions are given later in this chapter.

5.5 PLANNING THE CONCLUSION

5.5.1 **PLAN A CLEAR CONCLUSION** of your talk, one that will reinforce the results you want. Use your concluding remarks to leave a good last impression and to insure a strong listener response by touching their emotions, where appropriate. Make your conclusion agree with your opening. Summarize your main points, tying them in to what your talk means for the listener—the bottom line.

5.5.2 **FAILING TO CLEARLY CONCLUDE** their talks is one of the most common mistakes of beginning speakers. Sometimes they merely stop talking and sit down, as if they can hardly wait to end the ordeal. At other times they give rather vague, "inconclusive" conclusions, and listeners are not sure that the speaker is trying to wrap up the talk. Without a clear conclusion, most listeners have difficulty pulling all the parts of the talk together in their own minds. So don't drop the ball at the end.

5.5.3 **GOOD CONCLUSIONS** may include the following:

- **A summary of points** made and how they lead to a general conclusion
- **What this in formation means** to listeners; how they can use it for their benefit
- **A recommendation** or an appeal for action or change
- **A personal touch** that relates to listeners' feelings, desires, or needs through the use of humor, expression of personal feeling, an anecdote that includes human interest and feeling, etc.

5.6 USING VISUAL AIDS

5.6.1 **DEVISING AND USING VISUAL AIDS** is a skill worth developing because effective visuals contribute so much to the success of a talk. They help you illustrate and reinforce your points, allow your audience to grasp your message both orally and visually, and can help relieve your own tension by giving you something to do besides just standing there.

5.6.2 **TYPICAL VISUAL AIDS** include the following (see also Chapter 2, Reports)

- Charts, graphs, maps, diagrams, sketches, pictures

- Models, samples, examples

- Transparencies, slides, films, tapes

5.6.3 **TRANSPARENCIES USUALLY WORK BEST** for student presentations—if an overhead projector is available in the classroom. Transparencies will accommodate everything from a simple list of your key points to colorful pictures, charts, graphs, etc.

5.6.4 **COMPUTER SLIDES.** Computer software can produce slides that are very effective and professional. However, computer equipment may not be available in the classroom. Even if it is, time constraints often mean that students will not have adequate time for setup of computer-based slides. You can still use the slide software, and print them out as transparencies.

5.6.5 **MAKE EACH VISUAL SIMPLE—FEW WORDS, MUCH WHITE SPACE.** Each one should present only a few words, figures, or items. "White space" is the blank space in and around any text or images that you use. A common problem with visuals is too crowded with words or images, with too little white space. Experiment by adding more white space to your visual.

5.6.6 **USE WORDS, NOT TEXT.** A visual should highlight the information you are giving orally—not give the information itself. You drain the impact of your visual aids when you try to include too much information in one visual.

5.6.7 **DIVIDE UP WORDY OR CROWDED VISUALS.** If the visual you are planning contains more than a few words or images, find a way to divide it up into several visuals that you will present in sequence. Exhibit 5.2 is an example of a visual that is overly complex. If you use adequate font size and white space, this visual will be too long and awkward. The solution is to simply break it apart at logical points and make several visuals from it. In this example there are three logical parts, and the three resulting visuals are shown in Exhibits 5.3, 5.4, and 5.5. Use this same principle for overly complex drawings, images, or maps.

5.6.8 **CLARIFY, DON'T PUZZLE PEOPLE.** Do not use complex maps or diagrams that people cannot easily decipher—these become a puzzle and a problem, not an aid. Remember, the goal is "instant impact" that makes it easy for listeners to share the picture you have in your mind.

5.6.9 **MAKE VISUALS AND LETTERING LARGE.** Everyone in the room should be able to easily read it. Font size for transparencies should be 18, with 16 the absolute minimal size. Letter size for charts that are posted should be at least three inches high for the average 30-foot classroom. The rule is one inch high for each ten feet of viewing distance.

EXHIBIT 5.2. VISUAL AID—TOO COMPLEX

LEADERS	*ENTREPRENEURS*
Focus:	*Focus*:
What's new on horizon	Boosting revenues
Vision of the future	Market opportunities
Strategies for achieving mission, objectives	Competitive challenges
Culture—global, local, corporate	
Inspiration that motivates action	
Major functions:	*Major functions:*
Look for new boundaries	Look for new opportunities
Ask what and why	Ask what and how
Communicate vision, strategies	Innovate to meet challenges
Influence people to adopt, implement them	Take calculated risks
Motivate people to achieve	Capitalize on opportunities
Inspire—produce change	Establish direction
Create the organization needed	
Values:	*Values*:
Awareness of environment	Acting on new opportunities
Adaptability to changing environment	Taking risks and succeeding
Useful change—initiating it	Being a market player
Change orientation:	*Change orientation:*
Challenges status quo	Status quo is irrelevant
Bold approach	As needed to take advantage of new profit potential
Large and difficult changes	Short-term and long-term as needed
Long-term orientation	

EXHIBIT 5.3. VISUAL AID—SIMPLIFIED #1

LEADERS	*ENTREPRENEURS*
Focus:	*Focus*:
What's new on horizon	Boosting revenues
Vision of the future	Market opportunities
Mission and objectives	Finding niches
Strategies for achieving mission, objectives	Competitive challenges
Culture—global, local, corporate	
Inspiration that motivates action	

EXHIBIT 5.4. VISUAL AID—SIMPLIFIED #2

LEADERS	*ENTREPRENEURS*
Major functions: Look for new boundaries Ask what and why Communicate vision, strategies Influence people to adopt, implement them Motivate people to achieve Inspire—produce change Create the organization needed	*Major functions:* Look for new opportunities Ask what and how Innovate to meet challenges Take calculated risks Capitalize on opportunities Establish direction

EXHIBIT 5.5. VISUAL AID—SIMPLIFIED #3

LEADERS	*ENTREPRENEURS*
Values: Awareness of environment Adaptability to changing environment Useful change—initiating it	*Values*: Acting on new opportunities Taking risks and succeeding Being a market player
Change orientation: Challenges status quo Bold approach Large and difficult changes Long-term orientation	*Change orientation:* Status quo is irrelevant As needed to take advantage of new profit potential Short-term and long-term as needed

5.6.10 USE PLENTY OF CONTRAST—DARK ON LIGHT. You must have adequate contrast between the lettering or image and its background, in order to make the contents stand out. Black on white or clear has the greatest impact. Choose large bold fonts.

You can use color to advantage—to add interest or to clarify, but be sure to have adequate contrast. Use strong, dark colors on a very light background or vice versa. Lettering must be very dark against very light in order to be legible. On a light or clear background, choose navy letters, not sky blue; burgundy, not red; dark brown, not yellow or gold.

5.6.11 TEST THE IMPACT OF YOUR VISUAL by walking 30 feet away (or more if your classroom is larger) and viewing it from that distance. If you must squint in order to read any part of the visual, or if you can't really make out a picture, start over. If you don't have access to the equipment beforehand, at least try to imagine how this visual will look from afar.

5.6.12 PRESENT SLIDES AND TRANSPARENCIES PROFESSIONALLY. Use the same principles for preparing slides and transparency masters that you would use for other visual aids.:

5.6.12.1 REVEAL ONE POINT AT A TIME. When people see a whole list of points at once, they have difficulty focusing on any one of them, and they may focus on the one you are NOT discussing. Revealing one point at a time helps you to control the focus of attention and keep your listeners with you. Also, you tend to create a little air of mystery and suspense when they're not sure what's coming next in your talk.

5.6.12.2 FOR COMPUTER SLIDES, such as PowerPoint, select Slide Design. Use the Animation Schemes feature, and select "Fade In One by One" or a similar scheme. You select the next point with the "enter" key or down arrow key.

5.6.12.3 FOR A TRANSPARENCY, cover it with a plain piece of paper or cardboard. Slide the paper down to reveal the first item. Discuss it, giving stories, examples, etc. When you are ready to discuss the next item, slide the paper down to reveal it.

5.6.12.4 IF YOU USE A PROJECTOR, check the focus before you begin discussing information related to your first transparency. Check the picture on the screen to be sure the projector is aligned and focused. When you have finished your talk, be sure to turn the projector so the light doesn't distract people.

5.6.12..5 READ FROM BRIEF NOTES, NEVER FROM THE SCREEN, COMPUTER, OR TRANSPARENCY. Have a printout of the slides or transparencies alongside your notes, so you can easily see what is on each one. Don't just read the slide or transparency. Discuss the points as spontaneously and conversationally as possible, perhaps focusing on an interesting story, striking statistics, or other additional information. Remember, visuals should be aids, not crutches.

5.6.23.6 NEVER TURN YOUR BACK ON YOUR AUDIENCE. A basic principle of giving effective talks is to maintain eye contact at all times with your audience. If necessary, you may glance and gesture briefly toward the screen, body still facing the audience

5.6.13 DO NOT USE HANDOUTS AS VISUAL AIDS. They distract rather than aid. People will bury their noses in handouts and ignore you, missing much of your talk. Meanwhile you lose valuable eye contact.

Handouts are fine if you provide them *after* your talk is completed. Be sure they do not interfere with the next student's talk, however. Note: Handouts are essential for some team meetings where you are leading a work session rather than making a presentation.

5.6.14 TIME THE DISPLAY of each visual to best advantage. Rehearse in front of a mirror, a friend, or both, trying out different patterns. Decide on the best time to expose the visual, the best time(s) to refer to it, and the best time to remove it. Most visuals should remain in view during the entire time you are discussing information related to them—if they help listeners follow your train of thought. However, some visuals should be in view only briefly.

5.6.15 EXPERIMENT WITH PLACEMENT OF VISUALS. You should be able to refer to a visual easily without: (1) standing in front of it and thus blocking it from audience view or (2) turning your back on the audience.

5.6.16 STAND TO ONE SIDE of the visual and point to it, if appropriate, to reinforce certain points of your talk. At all times the audience should be able:

(1) to see the visual fully and clearly

(2) to see your face.

This process can help listeners follow your presentation. The natural movement and gesturing involved will also help dissipate your tension so you can give a more relaxed presentation.

5.6.17 DO NOT GET WRAPPED UP IN THE VISUALS. Remember your audience. Whether your visual is a poster, chalkboard, transparency, or other form, when you display or point to it, your eye contact with the audience should be broken only very briefly and you should not turn your back on even a part of the audience. Quickly look back at your audience and keep speaking to them, not to the visual. Visuals should not be used as crutches for remembering your talk or as escape hatches from interaction with the audience.

5.7 PREPARING TALK NOTES

5.7.1 PREFER NOTE CARDS TO SHEETS OF PAPER. Note cards are tidier than sheets of paper, which tend to drift to the floor, making you appear disorganized. If a lectern is missing and you must hold your notes, cards are much easier to handle than paper. Most people prefer large cards, such as 5x8, so words can be large and spaced out, making it easy to pick up the next major point.

5.7.2 USE BRIEF NOTES. Talk notes should include

(1) the opening sentence of the introduction

(2) the opening sentence of the conclusion

(3) a minimal outline of key points, using very few words for each point

5.7.3 WRITE ENTIRE OPENING SENTENCE. Remember, this is one part of the talk you can memorize. To back up your memory, write out the entire (short) opening sentence on your first note card. The reason: just getting up before a group may distract your thoughts. If you can glance down and see the entire opening sentence of your talk, you will be able to focus in on the presentation you prepared.

5.7.4 WRITE FIRST SENTENCE OF THE CONCLUSION. The principle here is the same as for the opening sentence. The reason: you may get so involved in discussing the key points of the main portion of your talk that you forget exactly how you planned to move into the conclusion. Again, being able to pause, glance down, and see the entire first sentence of the conclusion will guide you into that segment.

5.7.5 KEY POINTS of the main portion of the talk should be outlined briefly. Limit these notes to one-to-five words for each major point and, if necessary, one word for each supporting point.

Greater detail carries the risk of over-dependence on notes. If your introduction or conclusion is fairly long, you may need a brief outline of those segments also.

5.7.6   **PREPARE YOUR NOTES** with lettering, spacing, and breaks designed to implement these goals:

(1) To see the words easily as you stand behind the lectern or podium on which the notes will be placed

(2) To find your place easily as you move from point to point

(3) To use the notes unobtrusively, so the listeners are hardly aware that you have notes

5.7.7   **PLACE YOUR NOTES** in the proper spot on the lectern. Leave them there throughout the talk. Do not pick them up and shuffle them around. If they are on several cards. Simply move a card over as you complete it so that you can see the next one when you need it

5.7.8   **AVOID USING THE LECTERN AS A CRUTCH,** leaning on it, hanging onto it, or staying firmly planted behind it. Stand firmly on your own two feet. Move around to point to your visual aids, to gesture, and to otherwise reinforce your points.

5.7.9   **AVOID USING YOUR NOTES AS A CRUTCH.** The two main principles of delivering an effective talk are (1) don't read and (2) don't memorize. Rehearsing your talk in the right way will enable you to deliver your talk in a conversational, organized way.

5.8 REHEARSING YOUR TALK

CONVERSATIONAL AND ORGANIZED. Keep these two words in mind as you rehearse and actually make your talk. Your classmates must understand your ideas. The more comfortable you are and the more conversational you can make your talk, the more comfortable and responsive they will be. Summon up your enthusiasm, even passion, for the topic—the more you have, the better you'll come across. Making brief notes and rehearsing properly will keep you organized. After that, it's a matter of relaxing enough to talk with classmates as if you were having a one-on-one conversation.

5.8.1   **USE BREATHING AND VISUALIZATION TECHNIQUES DURING REHEARSAL.** Reduce the "nerves and jitters" syndrome by using techniques presented later in this chapter. Work with these techniques long before the talk, and during all rehearsals, to establish the relaxed, spontaneous speaking pattern that you want.

5.8.2   **FOCUS ON COMMUNICATING, NOT IMPRESSING.** Get your ego out of the way as much as possible. Your ego worries too much about such issues as, "Am I good enough? What do they think of me? Am I better than the other speakers? Am I worse than?" A good way to rise above you ego is to imagine yourself as a channel of information or encouragement—then you can focus on your message instead of yourself.

5.8.3   **WHAT'S THE BOTTOM-LINE MESSAGE?** Ask yourself that question. Can you come up with a one-line statement that expresses what you want to get across to people in this talk? Focus on that before and during your presentation. Imagine yourself sending that key message from your mind to their minds. Imagine listeners receiving it, "getting it," accepting it, and responding with the feelings you want to engender. Prepare well; then if your ego becomes concerned about what people are thinking of you personally, replace that concern with a mental image of getting across your bottom-line message. This approach helps alleviate nervousness and helps you to get your message across.

5.8.4 NEVER READ A TALK. "Reading" can be as blatant as reading directly from the report or case analysis that is the basis of the talk. It can be as subtle as using talk notes that are too detailed and then being too dependent on those talk notes.

5.8.4.1 DON'T BORE PEOPLE. Listening to someone read tends to be extremely boring to any audience, at best.

5.8.4.2 DON'T INSULT PEOPLE. At worst, reading a speech is insulting to the audience. They can read the paper for themselves. They deserve the benefit of your special interpretation of your project, your enthusiasm for the topic, and your special selection of high points and illustrations that gives them the main concepts in capsule form.

5.8.4.3 FOCUS ON THE MESSAGE AND THE PEOPLE, NOT THE PAPER. Anyone who reads a talk tends to become more involved with the paper than with the audience. Frequent eye contact of course is impossible. Speaker and listeners tend to become alienated, with the speaker wrapped up with the paper inside his or her "thought-capsule," while the listeners go into their individual thought-capsules with their own thoughts.

5.8.4.4 EXCEPTIONS: 2 KEY SENTENCES. There are two exceptions to the "don't memorize and don't read" principles. These exceptions are the two key sentences where you are most likely to "blank out."

(5.8.4.4.1) THE FIRST SENTENCE OF THE INTRODUCTION. People who don't speak regularly tend to "blank out" during the first few moments that they find themselves facing an audience. Prepare for it and prevent it by memorizing the first sentence of your talk. Back up your memory by writing in your talk notes the entire sentence—rather than the usual "few key words."

(5.8.4.4.2) THE FIRST SENTENCE OF THE CONCLUSION. Speakers tend to get wrapped up in delivering the main points of their talk and forget how to get into the conclusion. This is the other exception to the "don't memorize and don't read" principles. Memorize the first sentence of your conclusions section and back it up by writing in your talk notes the entire sentence—rather than the usual "few key words."

5.8.5 NEVER MEMORIZE A TALK. Although you can maintain eye contact as you give a memorized presentation, you still tend to be wrapped up with a piece of paper—the paper you memorized. Your eyes tend to glaze over, therefore, as you focus on recalling every word just as you wrote it. The thought that you might forget a line, or give it out of sequence, tends to become terrifying. Obviously you cannot be wholly "there" with your listeners, much less be spontaneous, under such conditions. What is most important in delivering a talk is to relax, enjoy the presentation, and behave spontaneously.

5.8.5.1 FORGETTING IS NORMAL. Do not fall into the trap of believing you must give every word and line of the talk in some precise order. Don't worry that you will omit some detail. Risk forgetting minor details of the talk. If they are important, you will probably remember them before the talk is over. Relish the opportunity to say, "Oh, I forgot to tell you that . . . " This is spontaneous conversation and your audience will love it. Relish the opportunity for someone in the audience to ask about a missing piece of information—for the same reasons.

5.8.6 TALK ABOUT THE SUBJECT INFORMALLY AS A MINI-REHEARSAL. Talk about your topic with classmates, friends, or family before and during the preparation period. You become accustomed to spontaneously verbalizing your ideas about your topic. The more times you "give your talk" to friends in normal conversation, the better. This prepares you to speak conversationally to your audience.

5.8.7   **REHEARSE, USING TALK NOTES AND A CLOCK.** Rehearse several times, using brief talk notes, setting a timer, and using your visual aids. Do this until you feel comfortable and confident that you know the organization plan and the key points thoroughly, but you have NOT memorized the talk.

5.8.7.1 VARY EACH REHEARSAL. Each time you rehearse, the presentation of your stories and factual details should vary slightly so that you do not risk memorizing. Leave room for spontaneity in the presentation of your supporting stories, anecdotes, and explanations, but be sure you are generally clear about how you will present these details.

5.8.8   **A REHEARSAL PROCEDURE THAT WORKS** for some people is this:

(1) In the first rehearsal, cover only the introduction.

(2) In the second rehearsal, the introduction and the first major point.

(3) Continue adding major points, then the conclusion, so the last rehearsal includes the entire talk.

Find what works best for you. Be well prepared but not so over-rehearsed that spontaneity is lost. Let the real you shine through. People recognize this type of sincerity, so be your best self, not a pretense of someone you think you "should" be. How do you discuss this topic with friends and family? That's probably the "real you."

5.8.9   **ENCOURAGE ENTHUSIASM AND PASSION FOR THE TOPIC.** Do this as you prepare and rehearse the talk. What interests you about this topic? What difference does it make in the world? What convictions do you have about its truth or importance? Your passion will make the topic interesting to your listeners.

5.8.10   **PRETEND YOU ARE ACTUALLY TALKING TO CLASSMATES.** Make the rehearsal as realistic as you can. Remember to concentrate on your message and the importance of getting it across to your classmates, rather than concentrating on yourself. This practice will help you to concentrate on the message when you actually give the talk—because you have laid down the wiring or programming to do that.

5.8.11   **GET FEEDBACK AS YOU REHEARSE.** You can give the talk to a friend or family member, watch their reaction, and ask for suggestions. You can record the talk on video or audio and play it back. You can look in the mirror. You can combine these methods.

5.8.12   **TIME YOUR TALK.** You can set a timer or alarm clock, or you can ask a friend to time you. Under pressure, are you likely to speak faster or slower than usual? Factor that information into the timing of your talk. Learning to stay within time limits is important so that you do your part in making the schedule work.

5.8.13   **VARY YOUR VOICE TONE.** Make it appropriate to what you're saying and remember to vary it, just as you do when you're talking with a friend about a topic that interests or excites you.

- Is your tone appropriate for the subject matter?

- Does it convey interest and enthusiasm?

- Is it varied enough to avoid a boring monotone effect?

- Do you use both high and low tones? An animated conversational tone?

- Do you vary it according to the feeling or mood that goes with what you are saying?

- Do you let your feelings come through?

5.8.14 VARY YOUR PACE AND TIMING. Listen to whether your pace is generally too slow, too fast, or about right. Then vary it for interest and effect; for example, move rapidly through easy-to-follow detail, pause before important statements or shifts in thought, slow down for more difficult or dramatic ideas.

5.8.15 USE NATURAL GESTURES. Allow yourself to gesture naturally. This helps reinforce your points through non-verbal communication, and the movement helps release your tension.

5.8.16 MAKE EYE CONTACT. When you rehearse, look around at the furniture in the room, pretending that each is a person in your audience. Imagine yourself making eye contact with each person. If you are nervous, focus more on friendly faces than on neutral or unfriendly faces, but remember to include all and to move your glance around the room.

5.8.17 LISTEN FOR SPEECH PATTERNS.

- Is your pronunciation clear and correct?

- Is your grammar correct?

- Are you inserting too many hesitators, such as "uh, um, er, you know"?

- Are you toying with something—your pen, your hair, your notes?

- Are you pacing, shuffling, swaying or using other body movement in a way that might distract your listeners?

- Better yet, get someone to watch and listen as you talk, using the evaluation sheet at the end of this chapter as a guide.

5.8.18 MAKE THE INTRODUCTION COUNT. Never begin with an apology. Never begin with "my name is . . . and my topic is . . ." That puts listeners to sleep. How can you wake them up? Startle them. Excite them. Charm them. Do something !!

5.8.19 DON'T CONCLUDE WITH "THAT'S IT" OR "THANK YOU." Let your conclusion be the conclusion.

5.8.20 AFTER THE TALK, PAUSE. Don't rush to your seat. Take a deep breath, then slowly and deliberately gather up your talk notes and visuals. This gives listeners a few moments to let your message sink in—and it makes you look poised and professional.

5.9 MANAGING NERVOUSNESS

5.9.1 ENERGIZE YOUR TALK. Think of nervous energy as an "energizer" rather than as a "disabler." The key is to channel your nervousness productively. Some nervousness is perfectly normal. In fact, many polls indicate that people fear giving a talk more than just about anything—including dying.

5.9.2 FOCUS ON THE MESSAGE. Your mind is incapable of totally concentrating on two concerns at once. Therefore, if you can focus all your conscious thoughts on getting your main message across, you cannot focus on worries about what people think of you personally. Try thinking of yourself as merely the channel for sending the message.

5.9.3 EXAMINE FEARS AND THEIR SOURCES. An essential step in overcoming fear of speaking before groups is to recognize the fear, face it squarely, and examine it. Just as nocturnal ghosts in the closet disappear when you turn on the light and open the door, fear tends to dissolve when you examine it carefully.

Ask yourself: *What do I fear will happen as a result of giving a talk?*

- A loss of esteem because of giving a poor performance?

- The repetition of a traumatic experience? Maybe you had a bad experience in the past and programmed yourself to connect speeches with disaster.

- Poor response from the audience leading to embarrassment? For example, not coming across the way you want to; people not laughing at the right places; people becoming bored, even going to sleep or leaving the room; people asking embarrassing questions; people not asking questions when they should.

- Amateurish performance because of your inexperience or because you think you are too introverted?

- Mediocre performance because you are not a podium star, dynamic and charismatic?

Now, consider some of the following facts about public speaking.

5.9.4 **EVEN MEDIA STARS GET STAGE FRIGHT.** Their secret: They channel that fear into energy and enthusiasm. If you learn to do that, you can become an effective speaker. That is a valuable skill that corporations will pay for. Because skilled speakers are in high demand in the workplace, they have a leading edge over competitors.

5.9.5 **GOOD SPEAKERS ARE MADE, NOT BORN.** Public speaking is a skill everyone can master reasonably well with a little knowledge and a great deal of practice. Very few people become star speakers; an adequate performance is a worthy goal.

5.9.6 **APPROACH SPEAKING AS A CHALLENGE, NOT A PROBLEM.** Think of it as an exciting experience with many potential rewards and many opportunities to learn how to improve. Then analyze your effectiveness and the results of your talks with the goal of constantly learning and improving. Ineffective behaviors then become learning experiences rather than disasters, defeats, or embarrassments. And you will move ahead professionally far faster than your colleagues who avoid giving presentations.

5.9.7 **LEARN TO CHANNEL YOUR FEAR.** Anxiety can be a positive motivating force: It indicates you are concerned about doing a good job. The key is to find methods of controlling it so it does not become debilitating.

5.9.8 **LEARN EFFECTIVE RELAXATION TECHNIQUES.** Prepare well for your talk by following the suggestions given here and by learning and applying some effective relaxation techniques. The goal is to allow yourself to relax once you are before the group, to set aside ego concerns, and to let your inner self take over. Try thinking of your inner self as consisting of your conscious, subconscious, and super-conscious minds. Your outer self is your body and your ego, which you want to subordinate during the talk. Let the three levels of consciousness work together harmoniously to deliver a message to your audience.

5.9.9 **PROGRAM YOUR SUBCONSCIOUS MIND.** You can do this in the simple three-step process shown at the end of this chapter.

5.9.10 **PLAN FOR RESULTS.** Go through this process frequently in the days preceding your talk, especially just before going to sleep when you are most relaxed.

5.9.11 **DEVELOP A POSITIVE ATTITUDE.** In the days before the talk, develop a positive attitude toward your listeners, the talk, and the situation. Visualize listeners as basically open and friendly. Focus on any warm, supportive feelings you have toward people in the class. Visualize people returning your warmth and supportiveness. View their questions and challenges as indicators that you have aroused their interest in the subject and have moved them toward a desire to probe further. Keep in mind that it is rare for a classmate to carry analysis and debate to the point of rudeness. If one should, it would reflect poorly on him or her, not on you.

5.9.12 PREPARE WELL, REHEARSE WELL, THEN TRUST YOURSELF. If you try to consciously tell yourself how to make gestures, remember every word, regulate your voice tone, and so forth, you merely become self-conscious and tense. A more workable approach is to prepare your subconscious mind beforehand to take care of these matters. Then trust it. Use great conscious effort in preparing the talk, not in delivering it.

5.9.13 BREATHE DEEPLY IMMEDIATELY BEFORE YOUR TALK. This is a sure relaxation device. It cannot fail. You may also want to try some isometric exercises.

5.9.14 AS YOU BEGIN, PAUSE, FIND FRIENDLY FACES. When you get before the group, look for an especially friendly face and focus on it briefly. Even better, find three or four friendly faces around the room. Pause for a moment, look over the group, and begin. This process helps you to master yourself and gain poise and presence.

5.9.15 MAKE EYE CONTACT DURING THE TALK. Be sure you make eye contact with people in all parts of the room. If you feel ill at ease, focus especially on the friendly faces. A high level of eye contact can help you speak conversationally and spontaneously, as well as give you feedback about how your message is getting across. According to research findings, it also increases the likelihood that people will perceive you as credible, well qualified, and honest.

5.9.16 AVOID NERVOUS MANNERISMS. Typical mannerisms are incessantly shuffling your notes, tapping on the lectern with a pencil, pacing, swaying, and overuse of words such as *"you know . . . er . . . uh."*

5.9.17 REWARD YOURSELF. Each talk you make is an achievement—no matter how well you did. Most people will not speak in public at all, so you are already an exception. You decide on the appropriate reward. At the very least, congratulate yourself for having completed the assignment. Go over what you learned in the process. If you gave the talk again, what aspects would you do exactly the same? Expand? Change? Omit? If you reward and evaluate each talk, you will find yourself becoming more adept at speaking with each presentation and better able to channel nervous energy so that it improves your performance.

Relaxation Processes for Channeling Nervous Energy

Process 5.1 The Simple 3-Step Process (Summary)

Purpose   To overcome speaker "nerves and jitters" and deliver a successful talk. To program your subconscious mind. To align your conscious mind with your subconscious and tap into your and super-conscious mind—to get all aspects of your selves working together harmoniously toward a single goal or intention.

(1) BREATHE deeply and slowly. This automatically slows down your body processes and brings on relaxation. Breathing is actually all you need to do in order to relax. However, you may find other techniques increase your relaxation. These may include focusing, centering, grounding, and progressive muscle relaxation.

(2) **VISUALIZE the results you want**. Just imagine, in your mind's eye, the talk ending with exactly the results you want. You may want to see yourself presenting the talk comfortably and spontaneously, giving your introduction, main points, and conclusion clearly and coherently. But the most important point is to focus on the end results you want from your talk—the listener response and the feelings of interest, acceptance, curiosity, and other responses that you want to engender.

(3) **LET GO** of the need to have it happen exactly that way, allowing and trusting that the exact way the talk evolves will happen if you relax enough to allow it to happen. Be willing to consciously let go of any desperate need (as opposed to relaxed intention) to achieve these results.

Process 5.2 Breathing for Deep Relaxation

Purpose: To experiment with various methods of deep relaxation. To turn off "mind chatter" or "ego chatter" in order to connect the conscious mind with the subconscious and super-conscious minds.

Deep relaxation begins with deep breathing. The goal is to slow down your breathing pattern. So start with one of the breathing processes. Then move into one of the focusing devices. If you have trouble moving out of a focus on mind chatter and into a passive attitude, do a process for getting in the here and now.

DEEP BREATHING—FILLING UP WITH AIR AND EMPTYING IT

- Imagine that your body, from seat to shoulders, is a water glass.

- As you breathe in through your nostrils, fill glass from bottom to top with pure white liquid

- As you breathe out through your mouth, imagine that you are emptying the glass from the top down, all the way until it is completely empty

DEEP BREATHING—SLOWING DOWN THE PROCESS

- Breathe in through your nostrils, counting slowly as you do so; hold the breath, starting your counting over again; breathe out through your mouth, lips slightly parted, again counting. The actual process: Breathe in 1-2-3-4-5; Hold it 1-2-3-4-5; Breathe out 1-2-3-4-5.

- Each time you repeat the process, extend the time you take to breathe in, hold it, and breathe out, counting to 6, then to 7, etc. See how long you can extend it.

DEEP BREATHING—WATCHING THE BREATH

Focus all your attention at the tip of your nostrils. Quietly *watch* in your mind's eye the breath flowing in and out past the tip of the nostril. Count from 1 through 10 each time you breathe in and each time you breathe out. Continue counting from 1 through 10 each time you breathe in and out until you're completely relaxed.

DEEP BREATHING—GOING DEEPER

Visualize yourself stepping into the top of an escalator. As you breathe slowly in and out, watch yourself descending on the escalator into a deeper and deeper state of relaxation and count: 10-9-8-7-6-5-4-3-2-1.

DEEP BREATHING—SELF AFFIRMATION

Close your eyes, take a deep breath, and enjoy the pleasure of feeling yourself breathe. As you breathe in, say quietly to yourself, *I am*. As you breathe out, say to yourself *relaxed*. Here are some alternatives:

I am . . . calm.   I am . . . serene.   I am . . . one   I am . . . whole.

Process 5.3 Letting Go of Needs

Purpose: To experiment with processes for letting go of the need to cling to the results you want, to put your purpose out into the universe, trusting that all will work to your benefit.

Remember the simple 3-step process:

STEP 1: Move into a state of deep relaxation (Process 5.2 plus optional 5.5, 5.6. 5.7).

STEP 2: Visualize the end results you want (Process 5.4).

STEP 3: Let go of your pictures of end results by one of the following methods—or devise your own method for putting your goals out into the universe. You have now set the pattern of events in motion. It's time to allow them to happen rather than trying to tightly control what happens. Release the need to control. Relax and trust all levels of consciousness—your own and others—to bring about the results in a way that's best for all.

THE PARADOX of creating the reality you want: You must deeply intend to achieve a specific goal, yet you must let go of the need to make this happen.

VARIATION 1—HOT AIR BALLOON

Picture a beautifully colored hot air balloon with a lovely passenger basket. It's tied to the ground with velvet ropes. Put the picture of your end results into the basket—and the feelings related to the picture. Untie the ropes and watch the balloon float away, up into the sky and away toward the horizon. As it floats out of sight, repeat to yourself, *"Let go . . . let go."*

VARIATION 2—SPACE CAPSULE

Follow the process described in Variation 1, substituting a sleek space capsule for the hot air balloon. Picture all the latest technology and equipment for controlling the capsule; put your end results inside the capsule; lock it; watch it blast off and disappear into space.

VARIATION 3—BOTTLE AT SEA

Follow the process described in Variation 1, substituting a large glass bottle for the hot air balloon. Put your end results inside; place the cork in the bottle top; throw the bottle into the ocean. Watch the tide carry it out to sea; see it disappear toward the horizon.

Process 5.4 Visualization

Purpose: To practice envisioning the end results of an effective talk—or anything else that you want to create in your life.

BASIC VISUALIZATION

1. **CREATE A CLEAR, CONCISE, CONSISTENT PICTURE.** In your mind's eye, develop a clear, concise picture of the desired outcome you want, the end result, the state of being, especially the feeling tone within you and flowing between you and others, in this state of having what you want. Don't get into *how* the result will come about, but stay focused on the end result you want.

2. **CHARGE IT WITH PASSION.** Allow your passion, your strong desire, to charge that picture with energy.

3. **BECOME THE ESSENCE OF THAT PICTURE.** What one word best describes the picture for you? Is it success, abundance, joy, love, peace, elegance, competence, connectedness? *Become* that quality as you focus on your mind's-eye picture.

4. **PERSIST UNTIL IT MATERIALIZES.** Bring up the picture as often as possible, each time seeing the same clear picture—not fuzzy, vague, or changing—each time charging it with passion and desire,

and each time freely letting it go. The more attention and focus you give it, the greater the likelihood of success.

TALK VISUALIZATION

Use this process to overcome the *jitters* that accompany any type of presentation you must make before a group. For best results, practice the visualization several times before your presentation. Just before going to sleep the night before the presentation is an especially good time to visualize positive results. Follow the process described in variation 1, but instead of picturing a problem situation, picture yourself making a successful presentation. See yourself focusing on the major thrust of your message and getting it across in a clear, dynamic, persuasive way. See your audience understanding and accepting it. Get in touch with your positive feelings and theirs. Now let go.

VARIATION #1—PROBLEM RESOLUTION.

Relax deeply. Get in touch with your problem situation. If thinking of it or picturing it causes you to feel anxious, focus again on a relaxation technique. Repeat until you're able to picture your problem situation without feeling anxious.

What do you want the end results of this situation to be? How do you want it to be resolved? Picture that happening—in vivid detail, bringing all your senses into play: colors, patterns, textures you see; sounds you hear; and things you touch, smell, and taste. Picture your interactions with the other person(s) involved, focusing on your specific feelings and feelings flowing between you and others; for example, understanding, acceptance, warmth, good will. Focus on the pictures and feelings until you feel quite comfortable and secure with them. Focus especially on your own positive feelings. Allow yourself to feel passionately. Now use a letting-go technique to release them.

VARIATION #2—GOAL ACHIEVEMENT.

Follow the process described in variation 1, but instead of focusing on a problem situation, focus on a goal you want to achieve. Picture yourself actually achieving the goal. Include all the people involved in helping you reach the goal; focus on the positive feelings flowing between you and them. Focus especially on your own positive feelings. Allow yourself to feel passionately. Now let go.

VARIATION #3—EVALUATING GOALS.

You can carry the process used in variation #2 a step further to help you evaluate possible goals. (For example, if you're not sure whether getting a master's degree should be merely one alternate activity for achieving a career goal or a goal in itself, picture yourself having achieved the career goal without the master's degree.) Picture all the consequences of having achieved the goal. How do you feel about each? Is anything missing? What? Would a different goal have led to better results?

Process 5.5 Focusing Devices for Deepening Relaxation

Purpose: To achieve a state of deep relaxation through various devices for focusing attention internally instead of on ego chatter, or mind chatter.

FOCUSING DEVICE—CANDLE FLAME.

Place a lighted candle about a foot in front of you and focus all your attention on the flame. As thoughts float by, notice them, let them go, and gently bring your attention back to the flame. This form of relaxed concentration can help you notice how your thoughts and senses keep grabbing at your awareness. The goal is to free your awareness from its identification with thoughts. We cling to our senses and thoughts because we're so attached to them. While focusing on the candle flame, you start becoming aware of that clinging and attachment and the process of letting go.

FOCUSING DEVICE 2—CENTERING.

Focus all your consciousness into the center of your head. Visualize a point of light about a foot in front of your eyes. Now focus all your attention on the point of light.

FOCUSING DEVICE 3—GROUNDING.

Visualize the center of the earth as a very dense place of rock or metal. Focus all your attention on the center of the earth, and picture a huge iron bar there. Next bring your attention to your spinal cord. Visualize a large cable or cord running from the base of your spine all the way to the center of the earth. Picture a big hook on the other end of the cord; now hook it into the bar at the center of the earth. Feel a slight pull toward the center of the earth and a slight heaviness of the body.

FOCUSING DEVICE 4—VISUALIZING YOUR PEACEFUL PLACE.

Think of a place where you usually feel especially serene, relaxed, and happy, such as the beach, the forest, a meadow, or the lake. Picture yourself there. Re-experience in your mind's eye all the sights, sounds, smells, and tastes you experience there. Focus on your sense of touch, too—the sun, water, and air on your skin, the sand, earth or grass under your feet. Bring in as much vivid detail as you can. Get in touch with the positive feelings you experience there—your sense of well-being, confidence, serenity.

Process 5.6 Be Here Now Through the Five Senses

Purpose: To prepare for deep relaxation and to deepen the process—by bringing yourself fully into the present moment as an aid to letting go of concerns about the past and the future.

STEP 1: BREATHING. Take a few deep breaths.

STEP 2: SEEING. Become internally aware of what you see around you. Look at it in detail as if you've never seen it before. Pretend you just arrived from another planet. Notice colors, patterns, textures.

STEP 3: HEARING. If the situation permits, close your eyes. What do you hear? Notice every little sound, identify it, and describe it mentally.

STEP 4: TOUCHING. Now focus on your sense of touch—the feel of your clothes against your skin, the air on your skin, the floor under your feet, the chair under your seat if you're sitting. Describe the sensations to yourself.

STEP 5: SMELLING AND TASTING. If there are noticeable odors around you or tastes in your mouth, become aware of them; identify and describe them.

Did you notice that your focus moved away from your mind and its internal chatter about the past or future and into your body and what it was sensing in the present moment?

Now go into your regular deep breathing process, followed by visualization and letting go.

Process 5.7 Progressive Muscle Relaxation

Purpose: To prepare for deep relaxation, to bring consciousness more fully into the present moment, and to deepen the process of relaxing the body—through alternate tensing and relaxing of specific muscle groups.

In this process, you bring your attention into the present moment by focusing on your body, and you also begin the relaxation process. You will alternately tense and then relax all the muscle groups in your body beginning with the toes and moving upward.

STEP 1: TIGHTEN YOUR MUSCLES. Tense up the toes of your right foot and hold the tension for a moment or two.

STEP 2. QUICKLY RELEASE YOUR MUSCLES. Now quickly release these muscles all at once. Notice the resulting feeling of relaxation in this muscle group.

- Continue up your right leg, tensing and relaxing the calf muscles and then the thigh muscles.
- Work the left leg in the same manner.
- Work the hip muscles, then the abdomen, the stomach area, and the chest area.
- Work the right arm, starting by tensing the hand, clutching a fist, then letting go. Move on to the lower arm, then the upper arm, then the shoulder area.
- Work the left arm in the same manner.
- Finally work on your neck and head. Pay special attention to the muscles of the jaw line and between the eyes; both are places where we tend to retain tension.
- Now imagine the crown of your head. Imagine that there is a hole there. Let any tension that is still remaining anywhere in your body to gather and rise up through this imaginary opening in the crown of your head. Experience the total relaxation.

Now go into your regular deep breathing process, followed by visualization and letting go.

EXHIBIT 5.6 TALK EVALUATION CHECKLIST

INTRODUCTION   (BSG reference)

This segment is often evaluated as approximately 20 percent of the talk grade.

Attention-getting, unusual	5.3.1
Effectively sets the stage	5.3.8
Leads into main points	5.3.9

MAIN POINTS   5.4

This segment is often evaluated as approximately 20 percent of the talk grade.

Relevant, credible, rigorous

Backup: use of examples, stories, explanations, other details

Clear, logical progression from point to point

Manageable number of major points

VISUAL AIDS   5.6

This segment is often evaluated as approximately 20 percent of the talk grade.

Aids understanding of topic

Font or letter size large enough to see from back row (at least 16 font)

Contrast—words and figures stand out sharply, make an impact

Key words only—uncluttered, simple, makes an impact

Presenter faces audience at all times, reveals listed items one at a time

CONCLUSION   5.5

This segment is often evaluated as approximately 20 percent of the talk grade.

Effective wrap-up, summary, or persuasive appeal

DELIVERY   5.7

This segment is often evaluated as approximately 20 percent of the talk grade.

Spontaneous, from brief notes	5.7.3
Use of notes not noticeable	
Time management	5.8.11

OTHER DELIVERY   5.8

This segment is often not *evaluated as part of the talk grade, but for student feedback only*

Attitude: sincere, comfortable, enthusiastic	5.8.1
Pace: not too fast or slow	5.8.13
Varied pacing, timing, voice tone	
Use of pauses, emphasis	
Gestures: reinforce points, natural	5.8.14
Eye contact with all listeners	5.8.15
Speech patterns: correct, clear	5.8.16
No distractions: *"um, er, you know,"* toying, shuffling, pacing, weaving	5.8.16

The instructor may evaluate each item on a scale ranging from Excellent to Above Average to Average to Needs Improvement to Inadequate—or a comparable evaluation plan.

Chapter Six
Business Writing:
Style, Grammar, Punctuation

THIS CHAPTER presents suggestions for effective business writing, which applies to both course assignments and to writing in the business world.

6.1 Overview of Business Writing Skills

6.2 Choosing the Right Words

   6.2.1 Make It Readabe

   6.2.2 Be Concise

   6.2.3 Be Accurate

   6.2.4 Use Correct Pronouns

   6.2.5 Use Correct Verbs

6.3 Writing Effective Sentences

   6.3.1 Bones—Subject, predicate, object

   6.3.2 Muscles—Phrases and descriptive clauses

   6.3.3 Skin—Modifying words

   6.3.4 Keep sentences short and clear

   6.3.5 Make sentences give clear messages

   6.3.6 Maintain parallel construction

   6.3.7 Adopt the right tone

6.4 Writing Effective Paragraphs

   6.4.1 Basics

   6.4.2 Select a paragraph pattern and type

   6.4.3 Refine your paragraphs

   6.4.4 Transition: tying ideas together

6.5 Avoiding Violations of Logic

6.6 Punctuating Correctly

6.7 Writing Numbers: Figures or Words?

6.1 OVERVIEW OF BUSINESS WRITING SKILLS

6.1.1   THE MAJOR PURPOSE of business writing is to communicate ideas from your mind to your readers' minds as clearly and accurately as possible. Expressing yourself creatively, subtly, and with a certain style may have its place but is not as important as getting across a clear, concise, accurate, well-focused message.

6.1.2   CLARITY, CORRECTNESS AND COMPLETENESS are important because business readers often must take action on your written words, action that will only be as correct and complete as the message that initiated it.

6.1.3   CORRECTNESS has at least two aspects here. The information you convey must be correct. In addition, correctness includes using the right wording, sentence structure, paragraph organization, transitional devices, logical reasoning, and punctuation. The correctness of your writing affects your credibility and reputation as a business student and as a business professional.

6.1.4   CONCISENESS is important because business readers are virtually always pressed for time and cannot afford to waste it reading rambling, lengthy messages, especially when such messages are not urgently important.

6.1.5   BUSINESS INSTRUCTORS expect students to use business writing style in preparing their course assignments.

6.1.6   INTERESTING, READABLE WRITING is more likely to be fully read and understood. So even though business writing should be concise and convey a clear message, it may also range in tone from quite personal, humorous, or friendly to formal, technical, or assertive.

6.2 CHOOSING THE RIGHT WORDS

KEY FACTORS IN CHOOSING THE WORDS that best convey your message so that it gets the results you want are:

- Make It Readable
- Be Concise
- Be Accurate
- Use Correct Pronouns
- Use Correct Verbs

You'll find more tips on word use in the section on adopting the right tone.

6.2.1 MAKE IT READABLE

6.2.1.1 SHORT, EVERYDAY, FAMILIAR WORDS enhance readability. A common misconception among beginning business writers is that they must use business jargon and obscure, technical, or *fifty-cent* words in order to impress readers. Exhibit 6.1 will give you an idea of how this works. The *avoid* words are perfectly appropriate in some contexts but are often used ineffectively in an effort to sound businesslike or to impress others. Good business writing is usually "talking on paper," so write the words you would use if you were talking directly to the reader.

6.2.1.2 SHORT WORDS are generally easier to read than long ones, and most of our everyday, familiar words are short. Therefore, whenever two or more words would do the job equally well, choose the shorter word if it is also the most familiar, commonly used one.

EXHIBIT 6.1 CHOOSING WORDS

Avoid Saying:	When You Mean:	Avoid Saying:	When You Mean:
Acceded	Agreed	Forward	Send
Advise	Tell or write	Illustrate	Show
Affirmative	Yes	In lieu	Instead
Anticipate	Expect	Indicate	Say
Approximately	About	Initial	First
Ascertain	Find out	Inquire	Ask
Cognizant	Know, aware	Locate	Find
Commence	Start	Numerous	Many
Compel	Make	Obtain	Get
Complete	Fill out	Occurs	Happens
Deem	Think	Operate	Do
Desire	Want	Originated	Began
Determine	Find out	Personnel	People
Effect	Make	Peruse	Read
Endeavor	Try	Precipitated	Caused
Execute	Do, sign	Predicated on	Based on
Expedite	Rush	Prior to	Before
Facilitate	Make easy	Procure	Get, take
Pursuant to	Under	Solicit	Ask
Recapitulate	Sum up	Stated	Said
Remunerate	Pay	Submit	Send
Render	Give, send	Substantial	Large
Represents	Is	Sufficient	Enough
Require	Need	Supply	Send
Retain	Keep	Terminate	End, quit
Review	Check	Thus	So
Said item	The item	Utilize	Use

6.2.1.3 EVERYDAY, FAMILIAR WORDS may not always be the shortest words available. And the most commonly used words may vary from one type of business to another. So you will need to keep developing your vocabulary in order to have a broad range of words to choose from, and to be able to select the right ones for a particular reader.

6.2.1.4 AVOID TRITE, WORN-OUT EXPRESSIONS (see examples below) when simple, straightforward language and original expressions would be more effective.

in this day and age	*plain as day*
it goes without saying	*saving for a rainy day*
to the bitter end	*easy as pie*
dead as a doornail	*sticks out like a sore thumb*

6.2.1.5 USE APPROPRIATE PREPOSITIONS (e.g., *at, by, from, in, on, to, with*). If English is your second language, idiomatic use of prepositions may pose a problem. When in doubt, look up the preposition in the dictionary.

> **Unidiomatic, awkward:** *benefit by, comply to, superior than*

> **Idiomatic, smooth:** *benefit from, comply with, superior to*

6.2.1.6 AVOID OVERUSE OF "PET" WORDS, especially such modifiers as *interesting, impressive, easy, neat, awful*. We all have our pet words and phrases. When you edit your draft, check to see if you've slipped into the habit of over-using certain words.

6.2.1.7 USE THE PROPER ARTICLE WITH NOUNS. You need to use *a, an,* or *the* with most nouns.

> **6.2.1.7.1 THE**. Use *the* to indicate a particular thing(s).
>
> *the book(s) in her lap*

> **6.2.1.7.2 A, AN**. Use *a* or *an* to note one of a class of things.
>
> *a book about dog grooming*

> **6.2.1.7.3 A**. Use *a* before a word that begins with a consonant sound (or a long u sound):
>
> *a computer, a dog, a university, a hat*

> **6.2.1.7.4 AN**. Use *an* before a word that begins with a vowel sound:
>
> *an actor, an egg, an hour (silent h), an unsung hero*

6.2.1.8 EXCEPTIONS: NOUNS WITHOUT ARTICLES. There are some exceptions to the general requirement that every noun must have an article. When certain nouns are preceded by certain pronouns, numbers, prepositions, or adjectives the article is omitted. Most native English speakers automatically select the proper article and know the exceptions. People who have learned English as a second language may have difficulty because there are no all-encompassing guidelines for recognizing the exceptions. They must learn to recognize the exceptions by studying elementary grammar texts, observing how articles are used in standard materials, and listening to the conversations of literate persons. Some examples of exceptions are:

> *your shirt, that boy, two apples, some books, any book, expression of feelings, total concentration*

6.2.2 *BE CONCISE*

Use words carefully and precisely. Edit out unnecessary words for conciseness. People are more likely to read short, clear, to-the-point messages and long, rambling ones.

6.2.2.1 EDIT YOUR PAPERS to see how many needless words you can take out and still retain the meaning and impact you want. Some suggestions follow.

6.2.2.2 CHANGE DESCRIPTIVE PHRASES to adjectives when such changes will sharpen your meaning.

> **Before:** *the houses with the red roofs*
>
> **After:** *the red-roofed houses*
>
> **Before:** *a table made of wood*   *an intersecting of roads*
>
> **After:** *a wooden table*   *intersecting roads*

6.2.2.3 REPLACE PHRASES WITH A WORD OR TWO if they say it as well or better.

> *it will be appreciated if you will*   *please*
>
> *at any time in the future*   *whenever*
>
> *final outcome of the project*   *project outcome*

6.2.2.4 ELIMINATE NEEDLESS WORDS, PHRASES, AND SENTENCES if they are not really necessary to the meaning or impact of the message. Typical phrases that can be eliminated include: *I would like to say . . . , this is to advise that . . . , each and every one of. . . .*

> **Problem:** *She needs to realize that women are capable of doing the same work once believed only to be done by men.*
>
> **Better:** *She needs to realize that women are capable of doing the same work as men.*
>
> **Problem:** *According to my research, all of the information that I've read related fear to be a major problem that each one of us faces each day of our own lives. Different types of fear were discussed, such as the fear of decision-making. In general, all of the authors felt that we as humans make our own fear.*
>
> **Better:** *According to my research, fear is a major problem that everyone faces each day. In general all the authors felt that we make our own fear.*
>
> **Problem:** *It was a common procedure for Acme's sales manager to make early contact with the Best Company's purchasing department as soon as he knew what the tentative production schedule would be.*
>
> **Better:** *When Acme's production schedule was complete, their sales manager routinely contacted the Best Company's purchasing department.*

6.2.3 *BE ACCURATE*

6.2.3.1 USE THE MOST EXACT WORD that conveys your meaning to your reader. This requires that you have some knowledge of your reader's business experience and educational level. It also requires that you know the exact meaning of the words you use; if in doubt, look it up. Think about the feelings and added meanings (connotations) your readers may associate with certain words. For example, words such as *fault, blame, ignorance* may be used correctly and without malice, yet be perceived as threatening or insulting.

6.2.3.2 GIVE COMPLETE INFORMATION. Include everything the reader must know in order to understand what you are saying. If you refer to a law, will the reader know what law? If you mention a theory, will the reader be clear about which theory and its meaning? Read over your paper from the viewpoint of a person who has never seen the material before. If in doubt, before turning in your assignment, have a friend read it to see what questions arise.

6.2.3.3 BE SPECIFIC AND CONCRETE. Consider these techniques:

6.2.4.3.1 GIVE EXACT NAMES, titles, categories, places, times, and dates.

6.2.4.3.2 INCLUDE PRECISE DESCRIPTIONS where appropriate.

6.2.4.3.3 ADD VIVID DESCRIPTIONS such as size, shape, color, attitude, feeling, and other details where necessary to convey a message. Use words that relate to the senses of sight, sound, smell, taste, and touch.

6.2.4.3.4 USE SPECIFIC VERBS (as well as nouns, adjective, adverbs).

6.2.4.3.5 ILLUSTRATE IDEAS by giving concise examples.

6.2.4.3.6 GIVE STEP-BY-STEP SEQUENCES or processes, where appropriate.

6.2.4.3.7 CHECK ALL PRONOUNS—be sure your reader will know who *she, it, they,* or *that* refers to (antecedents).

6.2.3.4 AVOID CONFUSING ABBREVIATIONS, JARGON, and technical terms. If a term or abbreviation is needed, then clearly define the term or spell out the abbreviation the first time you use it.

6.2.3.5 AVOID SLANG, STREET TALK, and other nonstandard English, except when you are quoting someone. If you knowingly use such terms for a particular effect, put them in quotes to indicate that you view them as nonstandard English.

lots of business, a lot of people, ain't going to, hang tough, kind of neat, sort of easy

6.2.3.6 SOME COMMONLY CONFUSED WORDS are listed in Exhibit 6.2. Many writers use one of these pairs of words when the other word should be used. Read these over to see if you know how each word should be used. When in doubt about which word to use, consult a dictionary.

EXHIBIT 6.2 COMMONLY CONFUSED WORDS

a while / awhile	as / like	passed / past
accept / except	cite / site	personal / personnel
advice / advise	farther / further	quiet / quite
affect / effect	fewer / less	real / really
all ready / already	its / it's	set / sit
all right / alright	lay / lie	some time / sometime
among / between	lead / led	to / too
amount / number	moral / morale	who / whom
any time / anytime	number / amount	who's / whose
		your / you're

6.2.3.7 *NUMBER / AMOUNT* **AND** *FEWER / LESS* **SHOULD BE USED PROPERLY**.

Number —refers to discrete (separate, individual) quantities that can be counted.

> *number of gallons, trees, paychecks, dollars, hours, people*

Amount—refers to mass quantities that cannot be counted individually.

> *amount of gasoline, oil, vegetation, income, electricity, time*

Fewer —refers to discrete (separate, individual) quantities that can be counted.

> *fewer gallons, pounds, trees, paychecks, hours, people, potatoes*

Less—refers to mass quantities that cannot be counted individually.

> *less oil, vegetation, income, electricity, time, oxygen, food*

Problem: *The amount of people attending the concert was less than last year.*

Correct: *The number of people attending the concert was fewer than last year.*

6.2.3.8 **SOME WORDS THAT** *SEEM* **PLURAL ARE SINGULAR**. Some words appear to represent numerous items but actually represent a whole concept and so take singular verbs and pronouns.

> *The traffic is worse today; it is more congested than usual.*
>
> *Transportation is a problem for our company.*
>
> *The population of India is finally decreasing.*
>
> *The weather changes every few hours; it never stays the same.*

6.2.3.9 **AVOID** *HIM/HER, AND/OR* **AND SIMILAR BACKSLASH ALTERNATIVES**. This format blocks flow and readability. The use of and/or usually indicates that you are trying to be overly precise. Relax, settle down, and choose one word or the other if at all possible.

Problem: *him/her*   *and/or*

Better: *him or her (or change to plural, use "them")*   *this and that   this or that*

6.2.4 *USE CORRECT PRONOUNS*

6.2.4.1 **PRONOUNS SHOULD CLEARLY REFER TO SOMEONE OR SOMETHING**.

6.2.4.1.1 AVOID UNCLEAR REFERENCES.

Unclear: *Kate phoned Jean every day when she was in Dallas.*

Clear: *When Kate was in Dallas, she phoned Jean every day.*

6.2.4.1.2 USE BROAD REFERENCES ONLY WITH DISCRETION. Pronouns such as *it, this, that, which, such* may refer to a specific word or phrase—or to the general idea of a whole clause, sentence, or paragraph. Be sure the reader will be clear about what each pronoun refers to.

Specific reference: *The coat was a strange mixture of many patterns; it looked like a patchwork quilt draped around the model.*

Unclear broad reference: *Some were religious fundamentalists; some were New Age psychics; some were mainstream Methodists. This had become an important issue for academics.*

Better: *This diversity of belief had become an important issue for academics.*

Clear broad reference: *This was the Brave New World, and Jim had the propaganda pieces to prove it.*

6.2.4.2 PERSONAL PRONOUNS—USE THE RIGHT CASE. Personal pronouns such as *he, she, it, they* should refer to persons mentioned elsewhere in the discussion. The three cases are subjective, objective, and possessive. (Tip on when to use *who* or *whom*: Mentally substitute *he* or *him* in the sentence. *he=who, him=whom*)

6.2.4.2.1 SUBJECTIVE CASE PROUNOUNS are *I, you, he, she, who, it, we, they.* Use a subjective case pronoun in these instances:

(a) for the subject of a sentence: <u>*Who*</u> *is making that noise? (<u>He</u> is making that noise)*

(b) for the complement of a being verb: *This is <u>she</u>.   It is <u>I who</u> wants the map.*

(c) after the infinitive *to be* when this verb has no subject. *It had to be <u>she who</u> broke in.*

6.2.4.2.2 OJBECTIVE CASE PRONOUNS are*: me, you, her, him, whom, it, us, them.* Use the objective case when the pronoun is

    (a) the object of a verb or preposition.

        He will meet <u>me</u> at the airport.   *That is the man from <u>whom</u> I got the facts.*
                                                (from <u>him</u> I got the facts)

    (b) the object of the infinitive *to be* when it has a subject.   *I wanted the winner to be <u>me</u>.*

    (c) the subject or object of any other infinitive.   *We want <u>him</u> to send <u>them</u> at once.*

6.2.4.2.3 POSSESSIVE CASE PRONOUNS are *my, mine, your, yours, his, her, hers, whose, its, our, ours, their, theirs.*

Give me the book; it is mine. Is this your book? Why didn't you tell me it was yours?

He let me borrow his book. Is this their book? That book is theirs. Whose book is this?

The dog loves its master.

6.2.4.3 PRONOUNS SHOULD AGREE IN NUMBER (singular/plural) **AND GENDER** (*he, she, it*) with the nouns they represent (their antecedents) and **BE CONSISTENT** with each other.

Problem: <u>*Women*</u> *continue to be kept out of important positions. I will examine the isolation and the prejudice toward <u>her</u> and how <u>they</u> are responding.*

Correct: *I will examine the isolation and the prejudice toward <u>them</u> and how <u>they</u> are responding.*

Problem: *The <u>outsider</u> risks being ostracized merely because <u>they</u> are different.*

Correct: *The <u>outsider</u> risks being ostracized merely because <u>he or she</u> is different.*

Correct: <u>*Outsiders*</u> *risk being ostracizes merely because <u>they</u> are different.*

Problem: <u>*Everyone*</u> *wanted <u>their</u> project to be noticed.*

Correct: <u>*Everyone*</u> *wanted <u>his</u> project to be noticed.*

Correct: <u>*They*</u> *all wanted <u>their</u> projects to be noticed.*

Problem: <u>*Gap and Nike*</u> *may profess to enforce standards on <u>its</u> manufacturers.*

Correct: <u>*Gap and Nike*</u> *may profess to enforce standards on <u>their</u> manufacturers.*

6.2.4.4 *IT—USE IT* CORRECTLY.

> **6.2.2.4.1 IT USUALLY FOLLOWS AN ANTECEDENT**, just as personal pronouns do.
>
> *The* company *is doing well.* It *showed a good profit this year.*
>
> **6.2.4.4.2 IT MAY BE USED AS A GRAMMATICAL SUBJECT** even though the real subject follows the verb.
>
> > *It is exciting to be here* (real subject).
>
> **6.2.4.4.3 IT CAN BE IMPERSONAL**; for example, to describe a condition.
>
> > *It is raining.   It goes without saying.   It is understood.*

6.2.4.5 *ITS* AND *IT'S*—USE THEM PROPERLY. *Its* shows possession; *it's* means *it is.*

> **Problem:** *Its a lost puppy.* (It is a lost puppy = It's)
>
> **Problem:** *It's fur is matted.* (**Translation**: *It is fur is matted.*)
>
> **Correct:** *It's a lost puppy. Its fur is matted.*
>
> "When is it its? When it's not it is. When is it it's? When it is it is." (Jessica Mitford)

6.2.4.6 *THEIR* AND *THEY'RE*—USE THEM PROPERLY. *Their* shows possession; *they're* means *they are.*

> **Problem:** *Their going to the beach.*
>
> **Correct:** *They're going to the beach.* (They're = they are)
>
> **Problem:** *They're books were stolen.* (**Translation**: *They are books were stolen.*)
>
> **Correct:** *Their books were stolen.*

6.2.4.7 RELATIVE PRONOUNS—*THAT, WHICH, WHO*—SHOW RELATIONSHIPS and have antecedents that should **match. Clauses that start with relative pronouns are always dependent and cannot stand alone.** Use *who* to refer to people. Use *that* when the phrase provides essential information and is integral to the meaning of the sentence. Use *which* when the information in the phrase is "added information."

> *Jones is the* contractor who *built our house. I met* Jean, who *always does the right thing.*
>
> *This is the* computer that *everyone is buying.*
>
> *We painted the room* violet, which *is my favorite color.*

6.2.4.8 DEMONSTRATIVE PRONOUNS DEMONSTRATE or point out. They include *this, that, these, those.*

6.2.4.9 INTERROGATIVE PRONOUNS ASK QUESTIONS. They include *which, what, who, whose, whom.*

> | | | |
> |---|---|---|
> | *Which plate do you want?* | *What is your name?* | *Who is calling?* |
> | *Whose watch is this?* | *The person to whom she spoke is gone.* | |

6.2.4.10 *SELF* **AND** *SELVES* **ARE PRONOUNS** used to

(a) show emphasis (intensive). *He himself took the blame.*

(b) turn action back on the actor (reflective). *I asked myself why.*

Use the *self* and *selves* pronouns only for these two purposes.

Problem: *Judy and <u>myself</u> took the report to the client.*

Correct: *Judy and I took the report to the client.*

Problem: *He brought the supplies to my worker and <u>myself</u>.*

Correct: *He brought the supplies to my worker and <u>me</u>.*

6.2.4.11 **SEXIST USE OF PRONOUNS** should be avoided; for example, using *he, him,* or *his* to mean *one.* Consider using instead

(a) the plural forms *they, them, their.*

(b) *he* or *she* instead of *he.*

(c) neutral terms, such as *worker, manager.*

Problem: *Each <u>employee</u> should prepare <u>his</u> work properly. (sexist language)*

Solution: *All <u>employees</u> should prepare <u>their</u> work properly.*

Solution: *Each <u>employee</u> should prepare <u>his or her</u> work properly.*

6.2.5 USE CORRECT VERBS

6.2.5.1 **VERBS MUST AGREE IN NUMBER** (plural/singular form) with their subjects. A singular subject must have a singular verb form; a plural subject, a plural verb form.

Problem: *The <u>roles</u> a woman plays <u>has</u> changed.*

Correct: *The <u>roles</u> a woman plays <u>have</u> changed.*

6.2.5.1.1 **USE SINGULAR VERBS WITH INDEFINITE PRONOUNS**—*each, one, neither, either, no one, anybody, anyone, anything, nobody, somebody, someone.*

Problem: *<u>Neither</u> of them <u>want</u> to go.*

Correct: *<u>Neither</u> of them <u>wants</u> to go.*

6.2.5.1.2 **USE PLURAL VERBS WITH NUMBERS AND PLURAL PRONOUNS,** such as *all, both, many, several.* Exception: the number <u>one</u> is singular.

Problem: *<u>Both</u> Jim and Mary <u>likes</u> the product.*

Correct: *<u>Both</u> of the clients <u>like</u> the product.*

6.2.5.1.3 **USE SINGULAR VERBS WITH COLLECTIVE NOUNS,** such as group, team, crew, class, audience, family, jury, flock, herd.

Problem: *The <u>group</u> from accounting <u>think</u> we should stop.*

Correct: *The <u>group</u> from accounting <u>thinks</u> we should stop.*

6.2.5.1.4 USE PLURAL VERBS WITH NOUNS OR PRONOUNS JOINED BY *AND*.

Problem: *The lamp <u>and</u> the table <u>is</u> for sale.*   *He <u>and</u> she <u>thinks</u> the plan is a good one.*

Correct: *The lamp <u>and</u> the table <u>are</u> for sale.*   *He <u>and</u> she <u>think</u> the plan is a good one.*

6.2.5.1.5 WHEN SUBJECT NOUNS ARE JOINED BY *OR, NOR*, the verb agrees with the subject noun that is nearest to the verb.

Problem: *Either my uncle or my cousins has the key.*

Correct: *Either my uncle or my cousins have the key.*

Correct: *Either my cousins or my uncle has the key.*

6.2.5.2 USE THE CORRECT VERB TENSE. Refer to a good dictionary. If verb tenses are a problem for you, refer to a good grammar book as well as workbooks that can help you build your skill.

6.2.5.3 USE A VERB TENSE CONSISTENTLY. Select a predominant verb tense (present, future, past perfect, etc.) and use it throughout your paper unless you have a legitimate reason for switching. As a general rule, the present tense is the most forceful and compelling. Chronological discussions and stories are usually written in the past tense.

Problem: *His goal <u>is</u> to be top salesman because he <u>wanted</u> to have more influence with the boss.*

Better: *His goal <u>is</u> to be top salesman because he <u>wants</u> to have more influence with the boss.*

Problem: *Some nonprofits <u>go</u> further and <u>brought</u> a lawsuit against clothing manufacturers.*

Solution: *Some nonprofits <u>went</u> further and <u>brought</u> a lawsuit against the clothing manufacturers.*

6.2.5.4 USE THE CONDITIONAL TENSE CORRECTLY. This is a frequent error:

Problem: *If I was John, I would go home.*

Correct: *If I were John, I would go home.*

The plural form of the verb is used because the statement is conditional ("if").

6.2.5.5 USE CLEAR, SPECIFIC VERBS that bring up the desired image in readers' minds. Vague or abstract verbs to not help to paint vivid pictures:

Abstract: *Those few words of praise affected my self-esteem.*

Better: *Those few words of praise boosted my self-esteem.*

Vague: *As we walked through the forest, we occasionally smelled the pine needles and heard them under our feet.*

Better: *As we tramped through the forest, the pine needles crunched and crackled underfoot. Occasionally their soft perfume teased our senses.*

6.2.5.6 USE ACTIVE VERBS FOR FORCE AND CLARITY and reserve passive verbs for special purposes; for example, to avoid making a direct accusation or to provide a touch of mystery. The active verb form is usually more specific and vivid than the passive form.

Passive: These women were forced to retire early. Early retirements were common.

Active: The management of Fraser Company forced these women to retire early.

6.2.5.7 SELECT STRONG VERBS that convey the most precise meaning with the fewest words. Weak verbs are usually some form of *be*. Other verbs that may weaken your writing are *give, make, provide, serve, use.*

Weak: *The rate of pollution <u>is</u> in excess of EPA standards.*

Better: *The rate of pollution <u>exceeds</u> EPA standards.*

Weak: *Gene <u>gave</u> an explanation of Hanson's path-goal theory.*

Better: *Gene <u>explained</u> Hanson's path-goal theory.*

Weak: *This alarm system <u>provides</u> you with a way to detect any intrusion onto your property.*

Better: *This alarm system <u>alerts</u> you to any intrusion onto your property.*

6.3 WRITING EFFECTIVE SENTENCES:
BONES, MUSCLES, AND SKIN

SENTENCE STRUCTURE is a mystery to many students. Try thinking of sentence structure as similar to body structure. The body is built upon good bone structure, the muscles add power and movement, and the skin is the surface level.

THE BONES ARE THE ESSENTIAL STRUCTURE—SUBJECT AND PREDICATE. In the physical body, bones are, in a sense, the most enduring essentials—they last for thousands of years. The "bones" of your sentence are the most essential parts, the core of what you are saying.

THE MUSCLES ADD POWER—PHRASES AND CLAUSES. They develop around the bones and give the body power and mobility. Adding good phrases and clauses to your sentence can give it powerful meaning and impact, "fleshing it out," giving a more vivid picture of what you have in mind.

THE SKIN IS THE SURFACE LEVEL—WORDS THAT DEFINE AND DESCRIBE. The skin of the physical body encases the muscles. It is the surface aspect of the body. You can think of the "skin" of your sentence as the words you use to further modify the essential meaning.

KEY POINTERS IN WRITING GOOD SENTENCES:

- Rely on the sentence "bones" of subject, predicate, and (sometimes) object.
- Beef up sentences with the "muscles" of phrases and clauses.
- Selectively add the "skin" of modifying words.
- Keep sentences short and clear.
- Make sentences communicate a clear message.
- Maintain parallel construction within sentences.
- Adopt the right tone.

6.3.1 BONES—SUBJECT, PREDICATE, OBJECT

ALL SENTENCES MUST HAVE THE CORE SKELETAL STRUCTURE. Your sentences must always have a subject and a predicate (verb).

SOMEBODY DOING SOMETHING. Typically the subject is somebody (noun) doing something (verb). These bones are the core of the sentence and absolutely necessary to a complete sentence.

SOMEBODY DOING SOMETHING TO SOMEBODY. Often, but not always, the action of the sentence (predicate with verb) requires an object of the action—somebody doing something to someone or something.

MODIFIERS. All other sentence elements serve to modify these "bones" in some way.

6.3.1.1 COMPLETE SENTENCES NEED A SUBJECT AND PREDICATE. All sentences must have a subject and a predicate (verb). This is the "bare bones" of a sentence. In rare instances the subject is implied rather than stated ("Stop!" implying "You stop!").

Someone (something) → doing something

    Subject   Predicate (Verb)

    Examples: *The bird flew*   *I arrived*   *Mary sang*

6.3.1.2 AN OBJECT OF THE VERB is required in many sentences. These sentences could be called "bare bones with object."

Someone (something)→ doing something → to someone (something)

    Subject   Predicate (Verb)   Object

    Examples: *Gene took the invoice.*

                  Love softens the heart.

                  George admires Mary.

                  The fire injured Jim.

6.3.1.3 THE CORE OF YOUR WRITING should consist of bare bones simple sentences. However, if all sentences were simple bones, your writing would become tiresome and boring—even childish. You would limit the complexity of the situations and ideas that you could express. You must also write sentences that add muscle power and skin—but never neglect the bones.

6.3.1.4 SENTENCE TYPES include simple sentence, compound sentence, and complex sentence.

6.3.1.4.1 TYPE #1—SIMPLE SENTENCE: A bare-bones sentence consists of subject and predicate. A simple sentence may also contain muscles (phrases) and skin (modifiers).

She wanted a new dress.

She desperately wanted a new dress for the wedding.

6.3.1.4.2 TYPE #2—COMPOUND SENTENCE: Two sentences (two independent clauses) with closely related meaning that are joined together by ***and, or, nor, but,*** or ***for*** (called coordinating conjunctions) to show relationship. Here is a compound sentence made up of two independent clauses, joined by the word *but*:

She wanted a new dress, but she had no money.

INDEPENDENT CLAUSES can each stand alone as a sentence. We can break apart the previous compound sentence and make it into two simple sentences.

She wanted a new dress.   She had no money.

6.3.1.4.3 TYPE #3—COMPLEX SENTENCE: A complete sentence (an independent clause) plus an incomplete sentence (a dependent clause) that provides further meaning or information.

Before she can buy a dress, she must get some money.

DEPENDENT CLAUSES cannot stand alone as sentences. They have a subject and a predicate, but they begin with a qualifying word—such as *since, because, before, after, that*—which prepares the reader to expect something more. Therefore, they could only stand alone as a sentence if you remove the qualifying word (called a subordinate conjunction)

Before she can buy a dress,

After we leave the theatre,

Because Jane was eager,

Since Gene can't go,

Incomplete sentence: *Before she can buy a dress.*

Complete sentence: *She can buy a dress*   *She cannot yet buy a dress.*

Complete sentence: *Before she can buy a dress, she must get some money.*

6.3.2 MUSCLES—PHRASES AND DESCRIPTIVE CLAUSES

Some sentences need additional phrases or clauses to give them power—by such functions as

- setting a particular time and/or place,
- comparing or contrasting one thing with another
- showing conditions, circumstances, exceptions, or frequency

These phrases and clauses modify the essential "bones" of sentences in some way. They include verb phrases, prepositional phrases, and descriptive clauses.

6.3.2.1 VERB PHRASES—SEVERAL TYPES. Verb phrases begin with a verb form, such as *to push, pushing, pushed.* Three common types of verb phrases are infinitives, gerund, and participial phrases.

6.3.2.1.1 INFINITIVE PHRASES BEGIN WITH "TO" (to push), followed by the object of the action.

We wanted to go all the way with her.

How delightful it is to see again.

6.3.2.1.2 GERUND PHRASES FUNCTION AS NOUNS. They are verb forms that end with "ing" (pushing) and function as a noun.

Pushing people was his favorite pastime. **(gerund phrase as subject)**

We enjoyed seeing good movies. **(gerund phrase as object)**

She believes in going to church every Sunday. **(gerund phrase as object of preposition "in")**

6.3.2.1.3 PARTICIPIAL PHRASES FUNCTION AS ADJECTIVES. They are verb forms that usually end with "ed" (*pushed*—past tense) or "ing" (*pushing*—present tense) and work as adjectives that modify nouns.

The book, having been handled by many students, needed to be replaced. (**modifies "book"**)

Working around the clock, the programmers found all the bugs. (**modifies "programmers"**)

The snow, melted by the March sun, was reduced to small patches. (**modifies "snow"**)

6.3.2.2 VERB PHRASE—SEVERAL FUNCTIONS. You can use verb phrases to set a particular time and place, to compare or contrast things, and to show conditions, circumstances, exceptions, and frequency. Occasionally a verb phrase may be used as the subject or object of a sentence—and even as part of the predicate.

6.3.2.2.1 TO SET TIME AND PLACE. Verb phrases can set a particular time and/or place

To be in Vermont in the fall is our passion.

Being the first holiday of the year, New Year's Day is special.

Pushed back to January, the party occurred in the snow.

6.3.2.2.2 TO COMPARE AND CONTRAST. Verb phrases can compare or contrast one thing with another

To win was the best possible scenario. (**infinitive phrase**)

Remaining optimistic is how she resists their hostile sarcasm. (**gerund phrase**)

Determined to win instead of doomed to fail, she took action. (**participial phrases**)

6.3.2.2.3 TO SHOW CONDITIONS. Verb phrases can show conditions, circumstances, exceptions, or frequency

My main goal is to show up every day. (**infinitive phrase**)

Giving her best performance was her main reward. (**gerund phrase**)

Pressed for time, Joe skipped the introductions. (**participial phrase**)

6.3.2.2.4 TO FURTHER DEFINE. Verb phrases can further define or amplify the word that immediately precedes it.

The favorite activity, shopping for antiques, is also my avocation. (**gerund phrase**)

My goal in life, to become a rock star, may seem ambitious. (**infinitive phrase**)

Miriam, all shopped out, fell onto the sofa. (**participial phrase**)

6.3.2.3 PREPOSITIONAL PHRASES begin with a preposition—such as *at, by, from, in, of, on, through, to, with*—followed by an object. See a more complete list of prepositions in Exhibit 6.3.

with her brother   *in the morning*   *to the beach*

Prepositional phrases that set a particular time and/or place

through August 15   *on July 1*

at 3 o'clock in the evening   *at my home*   *in the park*

Prepositional phrases that compare or contrast one thing with another

from the first moment to the last   *of mice and men*

Prepositional phrases that show conditions, circumstances, exceptions, or frequency.

within five hours   *with a song in my heart*   *through thick and thin*

EXHIBIT 6.3 PREPOSITIONS—THE MOST COMMON

about	below	excepting	onto	toward
above	beneath	excluding	opposite	towards
across	beside	following	outside	under
after	besides	for	over	underneath
against	between	from	past	unlike
along	beyond	in	per	until
amid	but	inside	plus	up
among	by	into	regarding	upon
anti	concerning	like	round	versus
around	considering	minus	save	via
as	despite	near	since	with
at	down	of	than	within
before	during	off	through	without
behind	except	on	to	

6.3.2.4 DESCRIPTIVE CLAUSES BEGINNING WITH *"THAT, WHICH, WHO"* are frequently used to add meaning to sentences. These clauses have a subject and predicate, but they cannot stand alone as a simple sentence because the word "that" or "which" sets up the expectation of another sentence element(s).

We   are studying   all the ways   that children learn and develop.

Subject-→ Predicate---→Object-----→Descriptive clause

He   spoke   a few words, which surprised me, and then he walked away.

Subject---→Predicate→Object-----→Descriptive clause

The President, who came late to the meeting, announced that the meeting would start.

Subject------→Descriptive clause----------→Predicate-→Descriptive clause

6.3.3   SKIN—MODIFYING WORDS

ON THE SURFACE LEVEL, you may use adjectives and adverbs that further define or explain what the sentence is saying. Good writers rely primarily on the "bones and muscle" of their sentences, adding "skin" only as necessary to fine-tune the picture. Typical modifiers are adjectives, adverbs, articles, and possessives. Phrases and clauses also are used to modify the subject or predicate of a sentence. In this section we will focus on modifying words.

ARTICLES (*A, AN, THE*) ARE NEEDED BY SOME NOUNS. See the discussion of use of articles in the section on "Choosing the Right Words."

POSSESSIVES ARE NEEDED BY SOME NOUNS. See the discussion of using the possessive form of nouns, presented in the section on "Choosing the Right Words." In addition to possessive nouns

(*Jane's, the Joneses'*), you will sometimes use possessive pronouns to modify your sentences (*my, mine, your, yours, our, ours, her, hers, his, their, theirs, its, whose*).

6.3.3.1 ADJECTIVES ARE USED TO MODIFY NOUNS.   You may choose from thousands of words that may be used as adjectives to describe the people and things you discuss in your sentences. These modifying words can be most helpful in painting the "word picture" that helps to get what's going on in your mind across to the minds of readers. On the other hand, this is the most superficial level of writing, so learn to rely primarily on the "bones" of your sentences, fortified by the "muscle" of essential phrases and clauses that add meaning.

vivid colors	*somber funeral service*	*spectacular fireworks*
pampered child	*overall plan*	*independent woman*
new idea	*clever joke*	*multicultural workforce*

6.3.3.2 ADVERBS ARE USED TO MODIFY VERBS. You may use adverbs to modify the meaning of the verbs in your sentence. Adverbs are used much more sparingly than adjectives—and they should be used sparingly. Most of them are adjectives with the suffix *"-ly."*

use sparingly	*speak slowly*	*tread softly*
said gleefully	*moved languidly*	*flowed smoothly*
ride long and hard	*try hard*	*come clean*

6.3.3.3 PLACE THE MODIFIER ADJACENT TO THE WORD(S) IT MODIFIES (describes, limits, expands upon).

Problem: *Legislation was introduced in the years following the revolution aimed at helping minorities.*

Correct: *In the years following the revolution, legislation aimed at helping minorities was introduced.*

Correct: *Legislation aimed at helping minorities was introduced in the years following the revolution.*

Problem: *Bangladesh is known as the "best deal" for garment production, where labor cost averages 26 cents an hour.*

Correct: *Bangladesh, where labor cost averages 26 cents an hour, is known as the "best deal" for garment production.*

Problem: *Does this mean we'll run out of dumping space soon for all the old cars?*

Correct: *Does this mean we'll soon run out of dumping space for all the old cars?*

Problem: *Shoppers consider many factors when choosing a product, such as price, style, and safety.*

Correct: *When choosing a product, shoppers consider many factors, such as price, style, and safety.*

Problem: *Crewman is a style pioneer with its classic clothing and hip ads.*

Correct: *Crewman, with its classic clothing and hip ads, is a style pioneer.*

6.3.3.4 AVOID THE DANGLING MODIFIER. A verbal phrase placed at the beginning of a sentence should modify the subject of the sentence. When it does not, it *dangles* in the sentence, unattached to any sentence part, and causes confusion.

Problem: *Coming through the door, the room (subject) looked cozy to him.*

Correct: *Coming through the door, he (subject) noticed how cozy the room was.*

Problem: *As both an alien in the workplace and a threat to those who dominate it, it (subject) may become vitally important for women to gain support.*

Correct: *As both aliens in the workplace and threats to those who dominate it, women must gain support.*

Correct: *Since women are both aliens in the workplace and threats to those who dominate it, they must gain support.*

6.3.3.5 **COMPARATIVE ADJECTIVES** are those that compare one thing to another or to several others.

6.3.3.5.1 REGULAR ONE-SYLLABLE (and sometimes two-syllable) adjectives use the *-er* ending to compare one thing to another and the *-est* ending to compare one thing to all others in a group.

My speech was shorter than his.

My speech was lengthier than his.

My speech was the shortest of all.

My speech was the lengthiest one given that day.

6.3.3.5.2 ALL ADJECTIVES OF THREE SYLLABLES OR MORE (and most two-syllable adjectives) use *more* or *less* to compare two things and *most or least* to compare one thing to all others in a group.

This bag is <u>more</u> ornate than that one.

This is the <u>most</u> ornate bag in the store.

Mr. Dietz is <u>less</u> demanding than our previous manager.

Mr. Dietz is the <u>least</u> demanding manager I've ever had.

6.3.3.5.3 IRREGULAR FORMS FOR ADJECTIVE COMPARISON may be looked up in the dictionary. For instance, if you are unsure how to make a word such as *far* comparative, the dictionary shows that *farther* and *farthest* are used to indicate more/most literal distance *(farther than a mile)*, while *further* and *furthest* indicate more/most figurative distance *(further from the truth and furthest thing from my mind)*. Some other commonly used irregular adjectives are:

Adjective	Comparing Two Things	Comparing All Things
bad, ill	*worse*	*worst*
good, well	*better*	*best*
little	*littler, less*	*littlest, least*
many, much	*more*	*most*

6.3.3.5.4 COMPARISONS OF ONE PERSON OR OBJECT with the other members of a group calls for the word *"other"* or *"else."*

This office gets more calls than any of our other offices.

Jenny has more self-confidence than anyone else in this family.

6.3.3.5.5 ABSOLUTE ADJECTIVES cannot be compared in the regular sense. Use the words *"more nearly"* or *"most nearly"* to show comparison. Some commonly used absolute adjectives are:

alive	*finished*	*round*
complete	*full*	*straight*
dead	*perfect*	*unique*

6.3.3.6 **COMPOUND ADJECTIVES** are two or more words that function as a single adjective and appear before the noun they modify. They are called *temporary compounds* and should be hyphenated. If these words appear after the noun they modify, they are not hyphenated. There are some exceptions; if in doubt, consult a dictionary or grammar manual.

I need an up-to-date schedule.	*This schedule is not up to date.*
This is a well-written analysis.	*This analysis is well written.*
This is a 25-mile-an-hour zone.	*I'm going 25 miles an hour.*

6.3.3.7 **A DOUBLE NEGATIVE** is an error caused by using more than one negative or limiting adverb to express a single idea.

Problem: *I bad not barely begun when he interrupted.*

Correct: *I bad barely begun when he interrupted.*

Problem: *Mamie could not scarcely believe her ears.*

Correct: *Mamie could scarcely believe her ears.*

Problem: *I will not tell this to nobody.*

Correct: *I will not tell this to anyone.*   *I will tell this to no one.*

6.3.4 *KEEP SENTENCES SHORT AND CLEAR*

6.3.4.1 **WATCH AVERAGE SENTENCE LENGTH.** It should be about 17 words for optimal readability, according to research studies. The key words here are "average length." Vary sentence length from one or two words to 30 or 40 words, keeping the 17-word average in mind.

6.3.4.2 **VARY SENTENCE STRUCTURE** as well as sentence length to add interest to your writing. While the simple sentence is powerful for giving a message clearly and directly, also use compound, complex, and compound-complex sentences for variety and for conveying relationships among ideas.

6.3.4.3 **BREAK APART OVERLY LONG SENTENCES.** Any sentence longer than 40 words should be rewritten. Also, check your average sentence length occasionally; if it is significantly longer than 17 words, break up some of the sentences in ways suggested below.

6.3.4.4 **BREAK COMPOUND SENTENCES APART** at the conjunction. Compound sentences are made up of two independent clauses joined by a *coordinating conjunction (*and, or, nor, but, for). Simply remove the conjunction and you have two simple sentences; for example:

Problem: *Supervisors can access the system to get a display of who is on the job at any time, and they can modify the schedule at any time in order to handle emergencies.*

Better: *Supervisors can access the system to get a display of who is on the job. They can also modify the schedule at any time in order to handle emergencies.*

6.3.4.5 **BREAK COMPLEX SENTENCES APART** by making a complete sentence of the independent clause. Complex sentences consist of an independent clause and a dependent clause that begins with a subordinating conjunction (such as *if, because, after*). The independent clause can stand alone as a simple sentence. The dependent clause can be rewritten as a complete sentence, often by merely dropping the subordinating conjunction. Sometimes a transitional word should be added to the independent clause for clarity.

Problem: *Although only the total weekly work hours for each employee will appear on the printout received by top management, each employee's time card will have an accurate record of the hours he or she has worked each day.*

Better: *The printout top management receives will show only the total weekly work hours for each employee. However, each employee's time card will have an accurate record of the hours he or she has worked each day.*

6.3.4.6 MAKE SEPARATE SENTENCES OF CLAUSES, such as *which* clauses. When you use *that* as the beginning of a clause, the information included should be essential to the meaning of the sentence. *Which* clauses, on the other hand, give additional information that is not essential to the basic meaning of the sentence. *Which* clauses may easily be removed and rewritten as separate sentences.

Problem: *Both stores appear to be very progressive, which is indicated by the fact that both have a Clubhouse department where coordinated sportswear separates are grouped together, although they do not display all their sportswear in coordinated groups.*

Better: *Both stores appear to be very progressive. They both have a Clubhouse department where coordinated sportswear separates are grouped together, although they do not display all their sportswear in coordinated groups.*

Note: Stores that are progressive usually display sportswear in coordinated groups. The clause that are progressive is essential to the meaning of the sentence and cannot be broken out.

6.3.4.7 DO NOT CROWD TOO MANY IDEAS INTO A SENTENCE. A good, tight sentence sticks to one idea or, at most, two or three very closely related ideas. When in doubt, make separate sentences.

Problem: *Steiner's, the large German chain store, which Charles Black visited last year, has several outlets in London consisting of budget-priced merchandise, primarily imports from the Orient.*

Better: *Steiner's, the large German chain store, has several outlets in London. When Charles Black visited them last year, he found budget-priced merchandise, primarily imports from the Orient.*

6.3.5 *MAKE SENTENCES COMMUNICATE A CLEAR MESSAGE*

6.3.5.1 USE QUESTIONS JUDICIOUSLY. Readers tend to mentally respond more actively to questions than to statements. Therefore, an occasional question can increase interest and add forcefulness to your writing.

6.3.5.2 DO NOT FUSE TWO SENTENCES; USE PROPER PUNCTUATION. A fused sentence consists of two complete sentences that are run together (fused) with no punctuation or with incorrect punctuation. To correct the problem, first identify the two complete sentences. Then choose one of these two solutions.

6.3.5.2.1 REPLACE THE COMMA WITH A SEMICOLON—if the sentences are fairly short and the ideas are very closely related.

6.3.5.2.2 REPLACE THE COMMA WITH A PERIOD AND CAPITALIZE THE NEXT WORD, creating two sentences—if the sentences are somewhat long or if the ideas are not closely related.

Problem. *Jill went through the same routine every day her pattern never changed.*

Better: *Jill went through the same routine every day; her pattern never changed.*

Problem: *The men who work in those offices with windows tend to sit and stare at us when they're not doing anything we feel we are being judged on nothing more than our movements that they happen to see.*

Better: *The men who work in those offices with windows tend to sit and stare at us when they're not doing anything. We feel we are being judged on nothing more than our movements that they happen to see.*

6.3.5.3 **DO NOT JOIN TWO SENTENCES WITH ONLY A COMMA.** This is called a comma-splice. It consists of two complete sentences joined by a comma, but with no coordinating conjunction (*and, or, nor, but, for*). To correct the problem, first identify the two complete sentences. Then choose one of these solutions:

6.3.5.3.1 REPLACE THE COMMA WITH A SEMI-COLON—if the sentences are short and closely related.

6.3.5.3.2 INSERT A COORDINATING CONJUNCTION (*and, or, nor, but, for*) after the comma, thus creating a compound sentence—if the sentences are short and closely related.

6.3.5.3.3 SUBORDINATE ONE OF THE SENTENCES by beginning it with a subordinate conjunction, such as *since, because, after, even though, still*—creating a complex sentence.

6.3.5.3.4 REPLACE THE COMMA WITH A PERIOD AND CAPITALIZE THE NEXT WORD, creating two sentences—if the sentences are somewhat long or not closely related.

Problem: *They do not intend to promote these men, they are hired on a temporary basis.*

Correct: *They do not intend to promote these men; they are hired on a temporary basis.*

Correct: *They do not intend to promote these men, for they are hired on a temporary basis."*

Correct: *They do not intend to promote these men because they are hired on a temporary basis.*

Correct: *They do not intend to promote those men. To begin with, they are hired on a temporary basis.*

6.3.5.4 **AVOID RAMBLING (RUN-ON) SENTENCES** that string together a number of loosely related ideas expressed in a series of clauses and phrases. To correct the problem, figure out the main ideas and express them in two or more concise sentences.

Problem: *This may have been due to the persistence of traditional notions about women's work, which Stalin's pro-natalist policies of the 1930's, in attempting to foster an image of the dignity of Soviet motherhood, which was none too compatible with heavy physical work, did little to dispel.*

Better: *This may have been due to the persistence of traditional notions about women's work. Stalin's pro-natalist policies of the 1930's, which fostered the dignity of Soviet motherhood, did little to dispel such notions. After all, motherhood is not too compatible with heavy physical work.*

6.3.5.5 **AVOID INCOMPLETE SENTENCES** (fragments) that lack a subject, a predicate (verb), or both. Also, a simple sentence may be fragmentary if it begins with a subordinate conjunction (such as *when, after, if*), which turns it into a dependent clause.

Problem: *Hypertension, ulcers, insomnia—all stress-related illnesses.*

Correct: *Hypertension, ulcers, insomnia—all are stress-related illnesses.*

Problem: *Quite a nice job, I think.*

Correct: *It is quite a nice job, I think.*

Note: *I think* is a parenthetical remark, an aside, not the subject and predicate of the sentence.

Problem: *When they came home from a hard day's work.*

Correct: *They came home from a hard day's work.*

Correct: *When they came home from a hard day's work, they still had home chores to do.*

157

6.3.5.6 EMPHASIZE AND SUBORDINATE IDEAS through sentence structure. Be aware of the power of placement within a paper, a paragraph, or a sentence. When you write and edit your papers, notice if you are emphasizing the ideas and information that you want to highlight—and subordinating those that you want to minimize.

6.3.5.7 EMPHASIZE AN IDEA in one or both of these ways:

6.3.5.7.1 PLACING IT FIRST in the sentence

Problem: *Many women like to travel, and for that type of woman, this is a great opportunity.*

Better: *This is a great opportunity for a woman who likes to travel.*

6.3.5.7.2 STRUCTURING IT AS AN INDEPENDENT CLAUSE that will stand alone

Problem: *This project doesn't pay much, but you'll get a free trip to China.*

Better: *You'll get a free trip to China, even though the stipend is relatively small.*

6.3.5.8 SUBORDINATE AN IDEA (place less emphasis on it) in one or both of these ways:

6.3.5.8.1 PLACING IT LATER in the sentence

Problem: *Sometimes we miss our shipping deadlines, but usually we are on time.*

Better: *We nearly always make our shipping deadlines, and problems rarely occur.*

6.3.5.8.2 STRUCTURING IT AS A DEPENDENT CLAUSE (one that begins with a subordinate conjunction).

Problem: *The company's return on investment decreased last year, and its profits increased.*

Better: *The company's profits increased last year even though its return on investment decreased.*

6.3.5.9 AVOID AWKWARDLY CONSTRUCTED SENTENCES. They confuse readers; their meaning is not clear; they do not flow well. Read your draft with smooth flow and coherence in mind. Mark places where the flow is bumpy or stilted and where meaning is not crystal clear. Ask someone else to read your draft for the same purpose.

You may have to completely rewrite the awkward sentence(s) or find another way of expressing the idea(s) in order to produce clear messages that flow smoothly.

Problem: *Most promotions are determined by seniority and occur within only the company's employees.*

Better: *All upper-level jobs are filled by promoting company employees, who are usually selected according to seniority.*

Problem: *They had that skill in mind when they gave her her second promotion.*

Better: *That skill helped her to get her second promotion.*

Problem: *It left an impressive impression on top management.*

Better: *It left an indelible impression on top management.*

6.3.5.10 MAINTAIN A CONSISTENT POINT OF VIEW (VOICE) unless you have good reason to vary it. You can select from three viewpoints:

6.3.5.10.1 FIRST PERSON (*I, we*)—you, the writer, are speaking as the doer of the action.

When I need information, I go first to the company files.

6.3.5.10.2 SECOND PERSON (*you, your, or your [understood]*)—you are speaking to the reader and the reader is the doer of the action.

When you need information, go first to the company files.

6.3.5.10.3 THIRD PERSON (*she, he, it, they, one*)—you are speaking about someone else being the doer of the action.

When our employees need information, they go first to the company files.

6.3.5.11 USE VOICE TO CONVEY LEVEL OF FORMALITY. When you use the first or second person, your writing is more personal and informal than when you use the third person. The last example below is the most formal.

Problem: *The supervisor may also be expected to help calculate the payroll, but only if you have fewer than ten workers.*

Better: *As supervisor, you may also be expected to help calculate the payroll, but only if you have fewer than ten workers.*

Better: *The supervisor may also be expected to help calculate the payroll but only if he or she has fewer than ten workers.*

6.3.6 MAINTAIN PARALLEL CONSTRUCTION

6.3.6.1 USE PARALLEL CONSTRUCTION FOR PARALLEL THOUGHTS.

Problem: *If a woman's self-esteem is based upon nurturing others, she may associate direct power as something bad, or that she is incapable of achieving it.*

Correct: *. . . she may associate direct power with something bad or with something she is incapable of achieving.*

Correct: *. . . she may decide that direct power is bad or that she is incapable of achieving it.*

6.3.6.2 USE PARALLEL CONSTRUCTION FOR COMPOUND VERBS.

Problem: *She has a sense of <u>being</u> surrounded by men, yet not <u>that</u> she really <u>belongs</u> nor a <u>sense</u> of total acceptance.*

Correct: *She has a sense of <u>being</u> surrounded by men, yet not really <u>belonging</u> to their group nor <u>being</u> totally accepted.*

6.3.6.3 USE PARALLEL CONSTRUCTION FOR A SERIES of words, phrases, or clauses.

Problem: *He is energetic, bright, and takes an interest.*

Correct: *He is energetic, bright, and interested.*

Problem: *They were expected to marry young, being a good wife, and have no career of their own.*

Correct: *They were expected to marry young, to be a good wife, and to have no career of their own.*

Problem: *They want freedom, such as eating in the car, talk on the phone, listen to favorite radio programs, and also could go anywhere they want after work.*

Correct: *They want the freedom to eat in the car, talk on the phone, listen to favorite radio programs, and go anywhere they want after work.*

6.3.6.4 USE PARALLEL CONSTRUCTION FOR LISTS OF ITEMS—OR HEADINGS. You decide to break up a block of solid text by breaking some items apart and turning them into a list that you will set apart by bullets, or (in the case of a sequence or process) you will number. First decide whether to use sentences, phrases, clauses, or single words (with or without modifiers). Then use similar grammatical structure for each item in your list. This rule applies also to all headings of the same level in an outline or report; i.e., all first-level headings (I, II, III) should be parallel, all second level headings should be parallel (A, B, C), etc. See the discussion of outlining and headings in the chapter on Business Research Reports.

Problem:

1. Raising society's expectations.

2. Better career guidance.

3. Children should know more about available occupations.

Note: the first item is a verb phrase; the second is a noun with modifiers; the third is a complete sentence. The solution that follows uses the verb phrase construction.

Better:

1. Raising society's expectations

2. Providing better career guidance

3. Informing children about available occupations

Problem*:*

A regular work week shall be no more than 40 hours

Fair wages, at a minimum wage of $5.15

Workers shall no longer be required to pay recruitment fees

Elimination of forced labor

Safe and healthy working conditions

Note: Some items are complete sentences, but others are nouns with modifiers. To fix the problem, you can make them all nouns with modifiers—or you can make them all complete sentences with subjects and predicates.

Better*:*

A regular work week shall be no more than 40 hours.

Fair wages will be paid, a minimum of $5.15.

Workers shall no longer be required to pay recruitment fees.

Management will eliminate the use of forced labor.

The company will provide safe and healthy working conditions.

6.3.6.5 AVOID OVERUSE OF PARALLELISM in short pieces, where forcing thoughts into parallel structure blocks their natural flow and meaning. Do not use parallel wording for nonparallel thoughts.

Problem: *Monica is intelligent, attractive, and twenty-five.*

Better: *At twenty-five Monica is intelligent and attractive.*

6.3.7 ADOPT THE RIGHT TONE

6.3.7.1 A PERSONAL TONE is established when you speak in the first person and refer to the reader as "you." It is further enhanced by putting the reader into the action being discussed.

6.3.7.2 A FORMAL TONE is established when you avoid referring to yourself at all and also avoid referring to the reader as *you*. Instead you speak of third parties: *he, she, it, they, those, one, people, person*, etc.

6.3.7.3 A CONVERSATIONAL TONE tends to be informal. It is achieved by writing the way you talk. Some devices are:

6.3.7.3.1 USING CONTRACTIONS the way you do in speaking *(I'll, you're, isn't)*.

6.3.7.3.2 OMITTING *THAT* the way you do when you talk

The book you ordered instead of the book that you ordered.

6.3.7.3.3 ENDING SENTENCES WITH PREPOSITIONS, sometimes, the way you do when you talk

John is the only person I work with. rather than ... with whom I work.

6.3.7.3.4 AVOIDING "WRITING TERMS," such as *above, below,* and other reminders of the paper on which the words are written. Substitute such terms as *before, after, mentioned earlier, later,* that refer to the time frame used in speaking.

6.3.7.4 A LIVELY TONE uses human interest to liven up the written message so that it is more readable and interesting and therefore more likely to be understood and to make an impact. Here are some ideas for achieving liveliness:

6.3.7.4.1 USE PEOPLE'S NAMES more frequently—to breathe life into an otherwise dry report about seemingly faceless persons.

6.3.7.4.2 USE PERSONAL PRONOUNS *(you, he, she, they, I)* generously and appropriately, along with people's names, to add liveliness to messages.

6.3.7.4.3 USE CONVERSATIONAL QUOTES. Look for brief, to-the-point, humorous, and/or perceptive statements as you read or interview people for an assignment. Choose statements that add spice and clarity to your write-up.

6.3.7.5 AN EMPATHIC TONE, often called the *You Attitude,* can be especially important in getting a message across. It implies going deeper than merely addressing readers as *you*. It requires writing with the reader's viewpoint in mind, showing how the reader's interests might be affected by the information and how the reader's curiosity, desires, and/or needs might be satisfied.

6.3.7.6 AN ACTIVE TONE that adds liveliness can be achieved—by using active verbs wherever possible because they help you to paint a picture of a person doing something. This makes your message more vivid.

Passive: A report was given on the new computer system.

Active: Nan reported on the new computer system.

6.3.7.7 PASSIVE VERB FORMS are used to avoid placing blame or to maintain a more formal tone, since they avoid using personal pronouns such as *I* and *you*.

6.3.7.8 A POSITIVE TONE can be established in several ways:

6.3.7.8.1 FOCUS ON "CAN DO." Think and write more about what *can* be done than what cannot.

6.3.7.8.2 FOCUS MORE ON POTENTIAL *SOLUTIONS* than on past problems. Focus more on preventing similar problems in the future than on placing blame.

6.3.7.8.3 FOCUS MORE ON WHAT *ACTION* TO TAKE NEXT, what is needed, than on what is wrong or erroneous.

6.3.7.8.4 USE THE PASSIVE VOICE TO AVOID BLAMING. Usually you will focus on the active voice, showing someone doing something, in order to paint the vivid pictures that enliven your writing. However, the passive voice is the best choice when you want to avoid placing blame.

Blaming: *You made a mistake on the report.*

Neutral: *The report contains an error.*

6.3.7.8.5 AVOID NEGATIVE WORDS. See if you can weed out words that have negative connotations, especially in sensitive situations (*blame, claim, complaint, criminal, delinquent, fail, fault, loss, neglect, nonsense, silly, sorry, stupid, wrong*). Sometimes such words may be necessary for accuracy and clarity. Often, though, you can find more positive substitutes that still convey the clarity that you need.

6.3.7.9 A CREDIBLE TONE reflects a businesslike, professional approach that is human but not overly emotional or sensational, that is practical and realistic but also honest and ethical. Consider these suggestions:

6.3.7.9.1 AVOID QUESTIONING OR MALIGNING INTEGRITY AND COMPETENCE of anyone without adequate proof.

6.3.7.9.2 GIVE CREDIT FOR OTHERS' WORK and ideas, and clearly separate your work and ideas from that of other sources.

6.3.7.9.3 AVOID EXAGGERATION and blatant attempts to manipulate others' emotions in order to sell an idea.

6.3.7.9.4 RISE ABOVE PERSONAL BIAS long enough to make an honest effort to explore all sides of controversial issues. Present all sides fairly. Clearly identify personal opinions.

6.3.7.9.5 QUESTION YOUR OWN ASSUMPTIONS about the sources, basis, analysis, and conclusions involved in the writing project, as well as assumptions about what the reader knows and how the reader will interpret the written message.

6.4 WRITING EFFECTIVE PARAGRAPHS

EFFECTIVE PARAGRAPHS are organized to achieve your purposes. They include transitional words and sentences that tie your ideas together and result in a coherent whole. They reflect a logical reasoning process.

6.4.1 PARAGRAPH BASICS

THREE KEY PARTS are essential to most paragraphs:

- a topic sentence
- the body of material
- a conclusion

6.4.1.1 THE TOPIC SENTENCE indicates the main idea and your attitude or stand toward it. Most paragraphs, especially those in reports and articles, need a topic sentence. It should indicate what direction the paragraph will take, its purpose, which might be to show why an opinion is valid, to explain a concept or an attitude, or to describe an event. Before writing a topic sentence, decide:

(1) what the paragraph will include

(2) your attitude or stand regarding this material

If you are writing a research report, you may find it easier to write the topic sentence *after* you have drafted the rest of the paragraph from the material at hand.

6.4.1.2 THE BODY of specific, relevant details that develop the main idea—this is the main material of your paragraph.

6.4.1.3 THE CONCLUSION should clarify the meaning of the materials you've included in this paragraph, or the main point you're trying to make in this paragraph, the "bottom line." Most paragraphs, especially those in reports or articles, need a concluding sentence or two. The conclusion may do any of the following:

(1) Refer to or echo the topic sentence

(2) Pull together or summarize the details

(3) Indicate the main point or meaning of this material and how it relates to other parts of the paper

(4) Lead into the main idea of the next paragraph, although it should *not* introduce a new topic.

6.4.1.4 LIMIT EACH PARAGRAPH TO ONE MAIN IDEA. The *main idea* is often called a *controlling idea* because it should control the amount and type of information you include in the paragraph.

6.4.2 *SELECT A PARAGRAPH ORGANIZATION PATTERN AND TYPE*

6.4.2.1 CHOOSE A PARAGRAPH ORGANIZATION PATTERN. Organizing each paragraph is crucial. Organization plans for paragraphs are similar to those used for an entire paper, as discussed in the chapter on Business Research Reports. You may use any of the following organization patterns as the key organizing format for a paragraph:

(1) Order of Importance

(2) Criteria for Comparison of Choices

(3) Cause & Effect

(4) Chronological Order (time-based)

(5) Logical Order

(6) General to Particular (overview, then details)

(7) Particular to General (details, then overview)

(8) Spatial Order (by location)

6.4.2.2 CHOOSE A PARAGRAPH TYPE. In addition to the organizational approaches, you can choose among several types of paragraphs for developing your main idea. The eight most frequently used approaches are:

(1) DESCRIBING

(2) NARRATING—telling a story

(3) EXPLAINING a process

(4) EXPLAINING with examples

(5) COMPARING OR CONTRASTING

(6) DIVIDING, THEN CLASSIFYING OR CATEGORIZING

(7) DEFINING

(8) PERSUADING

6.4.2.3 DESCRIPTIVE PARAGRAPHS. Use description in any type of paragraph in order to

- communicate a sensory experience—what you see, hear, touch, smell, taste
- help explain technical information
- help develop a narrative (a story)

6.4.2.3.1 OBJECTIVELY DESCRIBING something focuses on the object being described—what it looks like, how it works, etc. You focus on what you see, not what you feel, because the object is more important than your perception of it.

6.4.2.3.2 SUBJECTIVELY DESCRIBING something focuses on how you see something or someone and your feelings about it. You try to make the reader feel what you feel as well as see what you see. Your point of view and your emotional response to the object is as important as the object.

6.4.2.3.3 DECIDE WHAT YOU WANT TO CONVEY. Paragraphs that describe something should help the reader to see and/or feel what you see or feel about an object, person, place, or event. To achieve that purpose, try the following techniques.

6.4.2.3.4 DECIDE ON A WHOLISTIC IMAGE. Make all the details that you observe through your senses and describe to the reader add up to a central impression. What type of person emerges? What atmosphere, mood, or appropriateness of a place are elicited? This central impression is your controlling idea. Work with the details until they convey the holistic impression you want.

6.4.2.3.5 USE THE FIVE SENSES. Base your description on the senses (such as seeing or hearing) that you use to perceive the objects or situations being described. Most descriptions are organized according to spatial arrangement because they are based on things you see. You examine a person from head to toe, a room from left to right or top to bottom, objects as they come into view. Chronological sequence is often the pattern when the other senses are used. When your description is based on things you hear, for example, it's most often in terms of the time sequence in which you hear them.

6.4.2.3.6 LIMIT THE PICTURES TO ONE FOCUS. Limit your descriptions to a particular focus. For example, when describing a place, you may focus on a certain season of the year and time of day. You take a *snapshot* of the place at a particular point in time.

6.4.2.4 NARRATIVE PARAGRAPHS. Paragraphs that tell a story usually consist of

- one story or incident

- told in chronological order, usually, from beginning to end

- that includes highly selective details, the ones that make the story interesting and understandable

- and makes a relevant point, what it all means to you

6.4.2.5 EXPLANATORY PARAGRAPHS—FOR A PROCESS. When you explain a process, you may tell how something is made, how something works, or how to do something.

6.4.2.5.1 HAVE A CLEAR PURPOSE. Why are you explaining the process? What do you want your readers to learn from the process?

6.4.2.5.2 EXPLAIN STEP BY STEP. Use a step-by-step chronological (time) sequence. Explain each step clearly. Include every step; give complete details in precise, accurate language; use transitions to connect steps.

6.4.2.5.3 USE VISUAL AIDS when relevant and feasible.

6.4.2,5,4 EXPLANATORY PARAGRAPHS—WITH EXAMPLES. Use this method of organizing a paragraph when you want to tell the reader what something is, how it works, how it is made, how it is like or unlike something else, or how something is caused. You may explain through either: (a) a series of examples or (b) several extended illustrations or brief anecdotes. The process includes these steps:

6.4.2.5.5 DECIDE ON YOUR PURPOSE. Is it mainly to inform or persuade?

6.4.2.5.6 USE THE TOPIC SENTENCE to tell or imply the kinds of examples that will follow.

6.4.2.5.7 GIVE EXAMPLES. Include in the body of the paper enough representative, specific, relevant examples to clarify the main idea.

6.4.2.5.8 GIVE EXPLANATIONS. Include adequate explanations of how each example ties in with the main idea or conclusion.

6.4.2.6 PARAGRAPHS THAT COMPARE OR CONTRAST. When you compare, you point out similarities between persons, places, things, ideas, or situations. When you contrast, you point out differences between them.

6.4.2.6.1 THE POINT-BY-POINT METHOD. Comparing or contrasting is commonly used for business writing. Every time you say something about *A*, you also say something about *B*. You compare or contrast them point by point as you go. Readers can grasp each similarity or difference immediately.

6.4.2.6.2 THE BLOCK METHOD tells all about *A*, then all about *B*. It is usually simpler to write with the block method, but readers usually have more difficulty grasping the similarities and differences.

6.4.2.6.3 CHOOSE ONE METHOD or the other, and then stick with it.

6.4.1.6.4   A TOPIC SENTENCE normally identifies both subjects to be compared or contrasted, the kind of comparison/contrast you will make, and your attitude toward their relationship. You should have some point to make beyond just a description of the two subjects.

6.4.2.6.5 THE SAME CRITERIA or bases must be used for comparing or contrasting each item. If you discuss *Brand A* in terms of price, style, and endurance, you should discuss the same facets of *Brand B*. Both *A* and *B* should get about the same amount of attention for a fair, balanced appraisal.

6.4.2.6.6 FOCUS ON EITHER DIFFERENCES OR SIMILARITIES within a paragraph. If you want to discuss both, use separate paragraphs.

6.4.2.7 PARAGRAPHS THAT DIVIDE AND CLASSIFY. First you must decide on the type and number of categories you want to have. Then you divide the material according to that plan.

6.4.2.7.1 THE TOPIC SENTENCE of a classification paragraph should indicate the areas and the number of categories into which you are going to classify your topic.

Three types of stones may be used: rubies, garnets, or colored crystal.

6.4.2.7.2 LOGIC AND CONSISTENCY are crucial. Arrange the body of the paragraph in logical order. Explain each part fully so that you produce an even, balanced discussion. Show how each part relates to the whole. End with a conclusion that refers to the whole paragraph, not just to the last part of the paragraph.

6.4.2.8 PARAGRAPHS THAT DEFINE. The purpose of some paragraphs is to define and describe a particular object, process, concept, or idea. Your goal is to give the reader a clear picture of what you have in mind.

6.4.2.8.1 BEGIN BY TELLING THE CLASS OR CATEGORY that you will define.

If you plan to use rubies, try to select the best stones you can afford.

6.4.2.8.2 FOLLOW WITH THE PRINCIPAL CHARACTERISTICS that distinguish or differentiate your idea or subject from others in its class.

The best rubies have the deepest color, the most attractive cut, and are the clearest stones.

6.4.2.8.3 EXTEND THE DEFINITION using any of the following methods: synonyms, examples, origins, comparison and contrast, anecdotes, telling what it is *not,* telling how it works or what it does.

The color tone is also important. It should be as close to a true red as possible, avoiding the brown and grey tones. Some people prefer a slightly bluish cast to the red color, almost a hot pink tone, while others prefer a deeper red.

6.4.2.8.4 AN ABSTRACT IDEA is the most difficult subject to define because its definition depends on the perception of each person and therefore can vary widely. Two approaches are:

6.4.2.8.4.1 SELECT ONE PARTICULAR ASPECT and develop it as fully as possible

Freedom means various things to people, depending on their primary worldview. Libertarians believe we should have the maximum freedom possible, as long as we are not harming anyone through the use of that freedom. Let's look at all the implications of that approach . . . .

6.4.2.8.4.2 LOOK AT IT FROM DIFFERENT VIEWPOINTS, describing each viewpoint and how it looks from there.

Libertarians, Republicans, and Democrats each have quite different viewpoints of freedom. We will explore the beliefs and implications of each worldview. First . . .

6.4.2.9 PERSUASIVE PARAGRAPHS. The purpose of some paragraphs is to persuade the reader to agree to a particular viewpoint and perhaps to take action based on that agreement.

6.4.2.9.1 WRITE A TOPIC SENTENCE THAT CONNECTS with your readers. Think of how you can capture their attention and interest so they will want to read what you have to say. See if you can think of some mutual ground, some way that you can identify with readers, so you can establish some basis for agreement. What do you have in common—what can you agree on to begin with?

6.4.2.9.2 PRESENT STRONG SUPPORT for your idea in the body of the paragraph. Base your appeal on facts or logic that will convince readers to agree with you. Give enough relevant facts to build a case that will convince readers.

6.4.2.9.3 CONCLUDE WITH A STRONG APPEAL. Gear your appeal to the particular situation. Here are some possibilities:

6.4.2.9.3.1 A FINAL APPEAL that is gentle, sensitive, and moving

6.4.2.9.3.2 A DEMAND FOR AGREEMENT, using warnings and even threats

6.4.2.9.3.3 A SUMMARY OF YOUR MAIN REASONS, showing how effectively they support your position. Follow this by restating your position and making an appeal for agreement.

6.4.3 *REFINE YOUR PARAGRAPHS*

6.4.3.1 **DON'T RELY ON HEADINGS** to convey the meaning of your paragraph. Your first sentence should be able to stand alone in communicating its message. Only run-in paragraph headings may become part of the paragraph. Ask yourself, "If I removed all my headings, would my paper still make sense?"

Your section heading is "Time Management Techniques." The first sentence of the paragraph under that heading should not begin, "These are numerous." Instead you should write, "Time management techniques are numerous."

6.4.3.2 **USE THE POWER OF PARAGRAPH POSITIONING.** The first and last sentences of each paragraph are the most important positions within that paragraph. Use them to your advantage. The first sentence should either signal what this paragraph is about (topic sentence) or (more rarely) lure the reader into the paragraph—perhaps by mystifying, giving a clue, providing a startling statistic, etc. The last sentence normally serves a conclusion purpose—highlighting your most important points or purpose. It may also foreshadow what follows, luring the reader into the next paragraphs.

6.4.3.3 **WEED OUT LOOSELY RELATED MATERIAL.** Regardless of the topic or structure of your paragraph, be sure that it is limited to the development of one main idea and that every sentence within it is directly related to the main idea and helps develop it or expand upon it. Sentences that are only loosely related and don't contribute to the main point you want to make should be removed.

6.4.3.4 **SHORT PARAGRAPHS ARE BEST.** They encourage readers to finish reading your paper. Long paragraphs usually appear dry, dreary, and even be intimidating to readers. Effective paragraphs may range from two or three sentences (in a business letter or a summary) to eight or ten sentences. When a paragraph runs much longer, consider the possibility off restructuring it.

6.4.3.5 **BREAK APART LONG PARAGRAPHS** using the following techniques:

6.4.3.5.1 FIND TWO MAIN IDEAS. Look for two or more main ideas (or narrow subjects) within the paragraph. Make separate paragraphs of each main idea and its supporting information.

6.4.3.5.2 FIND TWO SETS OF SUBORDINATE IDEAS. Look for two or more subordinate ideas within the main idea of the paragraph. You may want to state the main idea in a brief paragraph and develop each subordinate idea in separate paragraphs.

6.4.3.5.3 FIND SETS OF DETAILS. See if too many details are lumped together loosely under one main idea. If so, look for commonalities and differences among the details. Try grouping together those details that have the most in common. Next, try to identify a main idea or heading for each group of details and develop each group into a separate paragraph.

6.4.3.5.4 PUT SOME INFORMATION INTO LISTS, TABLES, OR GRAPHS. Look for a block of information that can be listed. See if it would improve comprehension and emphasis of this material to break it out of the body of the paragraph and divide it into bulleted items. For step-by-step processes, number each item. Perhaps certain information would be more effective if presented in a table, chart, or graph. These techniques help to break up long paragraphs or dense blocks of text, making them more inviting to read and easy to grasp.

6.4.4 *TRANSITION: TIE IDEAS TOGETHER*

A PAPER MUST "HANG TOGETHER" in order to make sense to readers. This requires not only a good organization plan, but also good transitional words and paragraphs that show how it all fits together. Transitions can make your paper flow smoothly from one paragraph to the next, and from one section to the next.

6.4.4.1 **SMOOTH FLOW** includes the best sequencing, order, or organization of words within a sentence, sentences within a paragraph, and paragraphs within the paper. It starts, therefore, with a good outline that reflects the overall purpose for the paper and the development of the ideas that support your conclusions, recommendations, solutions, or other purpose.

Poor flow: *In a recent poll subway riders answered "no" to the question, "Is the subway efficient and well run?" 79 percent of the time.*

Better: *In a recent poll, 79 percent of subway riders answered "no" to the question, "Is the subway efficient and well run?"*

6.4.4.2 **CLEAR, SMOOTH TRANSITIONS** from one idea to another are essential for a paper that reads coherently and smoothly.

6.4.4.3 **TRANSITIONAL WORDS AND PHRASES** are used to show relationships between ideas, facts, people, and events.

6.4.4.3.1 SERIES. Transitional words can indicate additional material or a series of things

in addition	*moreover*
first, second, third, etc.	*furthermore*
besides	

6.4.4.3.2 EXPLAIN OR INTERPRET. Transitional words can explain or interpret something

in other words	*to illustrate*
for example	*also*
for instance	*too*

6.4.4.3.3 SIMILARITY. Transitional words can indicate similarity of things

similarly	*likewise*	*in a like manner*

6.4.4.3.4 TIME OR SEQUENCE. Transitional words can show the timing or sequence of things

at the same time	*meanwhile*	*before*
after that	*during*	*while*
afterward	*then*	*since*
earlier	*soon after*	*later*
preceding	*previously*	*as mentioned earlier*
which will be covered later		

6.4.4.3.5 CONTRAST. Transitional words can indicate a contrast between two or more things

however	*in contrast*
in spite of	*on the other hand*
rather	*even though*
but	*contrarily*

6.4.4.3.6 CAUSE-AND-EFFECT. Transitional words can indicate a cause-and-effect relationship.

so	*as*
for	*if*
so that	*because of*
therefore	*consequently*
for this reason	*the reason is that*
since	*as a result*
provided	*assuming*
in case	*unless*

6.4.4.4 TRANSITIONAL SENTENCES are needed when you move from one idea to another within a paragraph that develops a larger main idea. They are also needed when you move from one paragraph to another. They may be needed in the following places.

6.4.4.4.1 BEGINNING OF A PARAGRAPH, where you introduce the main idea of the paragraph and perhaps state your stand or attitude toward it.

The most important approach to motivation involves putting yourself in the other person's place, which will give you some clues about what motivates that person.

6.4.4.4.2 WITHIN A PARAGRAPH, where you are assessing the significance of a previous idea as you move into the next idea, or indicating how the two ideas are related (*similarly, in contrast, the second step,* etc.)

6.4.4.4.3 AT THE END OF A PARAGAPH, where you are forming a conclusion to that paragraph through summarizing the points, focusing on the significance of all the material, and/or making the major point of the paragraph. The transitional sentence should not introduce the next paragraph, but it may lead into it as the topic naturally flows to the next step. For example, the following transitional sentence comes at the end of a paragraph that discusses how managers can influence worker motivation:

The manager's behavior will have a motivating effect on workers to the extent that such behavior (a) makes satisfaction of workers' needs dependent on effective performance and (b) provides a supportive work environment.

The paragraph that follows this concluding transitional sentence begins:

More specifically, managers can increase (a) workers' motivation to perform, (b) their job satisfaction, and (c) their acceptance of the manager by taking the following kinds of action.

The paragraph then discusses (a), (b), and (c) more fully.

6.4.4.5 INTRODUCTORY PARAGRAPHS for each major section of the paper help the reader follow your line of thinking and the pattern of the information. An introductory paragraph should:

(1) Suggest how the following section ties in with other major parts of the paper.

(2) Give a brief overview of the key ideas covered in the section.

6.4.4.6 AVOID TWO HEADINGS NOT SEPARATED BY TEXT. Insert a transitional paragraph between these two headings, even if it's only one or two sentences long. The first heading indicates you are beginning a new section; the second heading indicates that this section is divided into two or more parts and that you are beginning the first part. If the section is long enough to warrant two or more parts, it warrants a brief introductory paragraph.

Example #1: Here is the outline for one major section of a paper:

> *BUILDING A WORK TEAM*
>
> *I. Delegating Effectively*
>
> > *A. Making Plans for Worker Development*
> >
> > *B. When to Delegate*
> >
> > > *1. Why Supervisors Don't Delegate*
> > >
> > > *2. When Supervisors Should Delegate*
> > >
> > > *3. When Supervisors Should Do It Themselves*

Problem of inadequate transition—the student wrote an introduction, then moved on to the body of the paper, based on the outline, as follows:

> *. . . therefore, the manager must first make plans for how to develop workers and then begin the practice of delegating in order to fulfill that plan.*
>
> *DELEGATING EFFECTIVELY*
>
> *MAKING PLANS FOR WORKER DEVELOPMENT*
>
> > *The first step in making plans for worker development is . . .*

This paper needs a transitional paragraph between the major heading "Delegating Effectively" and the lower-level heading "Making Plans for Worker Development."

Solution: Inserting a transitional introductory paragraph between the two headings.

> *. . . therefore, the manager must first make plans for how to develop workers and then begin the practice of delegating in order to fulfill that plan.*
>
> *DELEGATING EFFECTIVELY*
>
> *The first step in delegating effectively is to make plans for the development for each of your workers. You need this plan in order to guide your actions when you actually begin to delegate tasks to employees.*
>
> *MAKING PLANS FOR WORKER DEVELOPMENT*
>
> > *The first step in making plans for worker development is . . .*

Example #2: Transitional paragraph introducing the third major section of the paper.

So far we have examined two major theories of motivation that are based on the assumption that certain needs impel people to behave in certain ways. The theories of Maslow and McClelland deal with innate and learned needs that people bring to the job situation, and they can help the manager understand what people want as well as how people develop patterns of wants. But how does this apply to people on the job? Next we will examine some theories that deal more directly with the job situation itself and the manager's role in enhancing worker motivation.

This transitional paragraph summarizes briefly what has been covered so far and suggests how it fits into the next section.

6.5 AVOIDING VIOLATIONS OF LOGIC

VIOLATIONS OF LOGIC refer to common fallacies (errors in reasoning) that lead to false conclusions because they distort the logical reasoning process.

6.5.1 **PERSONIFICATION—CAN AN ANALYSIS TALK?** A common fallacy is endowing inanimate objects, processes, and ideas with powers enjoyed only by people. In writing papers, students frequently refer to research, surveys, studies, analyses, evaluations, etc. Remember that such instruments and processes cannot talk, decide, judge, manage, or otherwise operate as human beings. They can provide you and your readers with information that will help you do those things. Their authors can do those things.

Problem: *The analysis says laser printers best meet our needs.*

Correct: *The analysis indicates that laser printers best meet our needs.*

Problem: *We think their knowledge will better manage this fund.*

Correct: *We think their knowledge better equips them to manage this fund.*

6.5.2 **HASTY GENERALIZATIONS.** Hasty generalizations result from jumping to conclusions about something. They are blind, sweeping assumptions based on too little evidence.

6.5.3 **NON SEQUITAR (NOT IN SEQUENCE).** A non sequitur is a false conclusion that does not logically follow from the reasoning you have provided. It seems *off the wall* to readers; it doesn't fit. It is usually over-generalized and is often the result of jumping to emotional conclusions.

6.5.4 **FALSE ANALOGY.** A false analogy is an illogical comparison based on trivial similarities that ignores fundamental differences between the two things.

6.5.5 **THE BANDWAGON TECHNIQUE.** When you use the bandwagon technique, you attempt to gain agreement by claiming or implying that everyone who is anyone is thinking or doing a thing. This is usually an emotional appeal that implies that readers will be left out if they don't join the crowd.

6.5.6 **AD HOMINEM (PERSONAL ATTACK).** An ad hominem is an attack against a person instead of attacking an argument, a claimed fact, or other rational aspect is the issue being discussed. It distracts attention away from valid debate to personal attack and emotion. The purpose may be to trick readers into making faulty judgments about the issue. The underlying idea is, "If the person is bad, the issue he defends must be bad."

6.5.7 **POST HOC (CAUSE-EFFECT?).** Post hoc means "after this" or "therefore, because of this." A "post hoc" problem occurs when you create a misplaced connection between cause and effect. Just because there is a *correlation* between the occurrence of one thing and another does not mean that one causes the other. Look for the possibility of other causes or effects. Here is an example:

> *Post hoc statement: I quit eating fruit last week and lost five pounds; eliminating fruit from my diet will cause me to lose weight.*

> *Some unanswered questions: What else did you eat or not eat? Did your activity level go up or down? Could part of the weight loss be a delayed reaction from the previous week's patterns?*

6.5.8 **BEGS THE QUESTION.** Begs the question refers to circular reasoning. Your statement raises a question but you don't answer it. Perhaps you state a conclusion that simply repeats or rephrases your beginning assumption, so nothing is really proved.

> *This brand is better because it is high quality.*

> Note: This statement "begs the question," *What is the specific quality that makes the brand better?*

6.5.9 **POLARIZATION.** Polarization occurs when you present only one viewpoint, usually an extreme one at that, and probably in a highly emotional manner. The discussion offers no alternative action or middle ground and is the opposite of a balanced, fair discussion.

6.5.10 **BIASED OR INCOMPETENT AUTHORITIES.** When you use biased or incompetent authorities as sources of facts or opinions—just because they support your conclusions—you undermine the credibility of your entire presentation. Know something about the experts you quote. See suggestions in the chapter on Business Research Reports on analyzing source materials and objectivity.

6.5.11 **RATIONALIZATION.** Rationalizing is a self-deluding way of explaining away facts or ideas that contradict your position or belief. A rationalization is a *convenient* way of viewing contradicting facts or ideas; it explains away an unwelcome truth.

6.5.12 **SUBJECTIVITY.** Many of the violations of logic outlined here, such as bias and personalization, are forms of subjectivity (as opposed to objectivity). Business and scientific papers, in order to be convincing, need to be as objective as possible. This means they should be based upon information generally accepted as factual and credible by others in the field. In your treatment of this information, you should provide your readers with logical thinking processes that you used in working with that information. Your personal opinion should be clearly identified as separate from other information in the report

> *I believe . . .*   *It is my opinion . . .*   *I concluded that . . .*

6.6 PUNCTUATING CORRECTLY

PROPER PUNCTUATION is essential to clearly convey the meaning of your sentences and paragraph.

6.6.1 *END-OF-SENTENCE PUNCTUATION*

6.6.1.1 A PERIOD is used to end most sentences.

6.6.1.2 A QUESTION MARK is used at the end of a sentence that asks for a reply, such as:

(1) a direct question.

> *Are you ready to leave?*

(2) a direct statement followed by a question.

> *I think we need to leave now, don't you agree?*

(3) a statement that is meant as a question.

> *You really believe she will leave?*

(4) each item of a series of incomplete questions.

> *Do you want milk? tea? coffee?*

6.6.1.3 QUESTION MARKS ARE NOT USED AFTER:

6.6.1.3.1 AN INDIRECT QUESTION.

> *Jerry wants to know when you will arrive.*

6.6.1.3.2 A POLITE REQUEST phrased as a question when the initiator asks for specific action and does not expect a *yes* or *no* answer.

> *Would you please send the catalog by return mail.*

6.6.1.4 AN EXCLAMATION POINT is used to express a high degree of emotion after a word, phrase, clause, or sentence. Avoid overuse of the exclamation point; readers tend to ignore its meaning when it is used more than occasionally.

6.6.2 *COMMAS*

SOME AMATEUR WRITERS seem to keep a bucket of commas nearby. Occasionally they reach in, get a handful, and scatter them randomly here and there in order to break up their sentences. Commas DO often represent pauses, needed for understanding in reading a sentence. However, there are very specific rules about where to use commas. Occasionally, but rarely, you may insert a comma for the "pause that clarifies." Often, though, such sentences would be more effective if you restructured them.

6.6.2.1 IN COMPOUND SENTENCES. When two independent clauses are joined by a coordinating conjunction, (*and, but, or, nor*), place a comma before the conjunction that separates the two clauses. Exception: two very short independent clauses joined by *and*.

Joining two independent clauses: *We would like to take advantage of the discount, but we have no place to store that many cases of merchandise.*

Exception: *I will type the paper and you can proofread it.*

6.6.2.2 AFTER INTRODUCTORY CLAUSES AND PHRASES.

6.6.2.2.1 AFTER INTRODUCTORY CLAUSES: A dependent clause is one that requires more information (that is, it requires an independent clause) in order to make sense. It begins with a subordinating conjunction (***as, by, if, when, because***, **etc.**) that sets up the expectation that something more will follow. When a dependent clause begins the sentence, you must place a comma after the last word of the clause.

> *Although the paper is the right quality, it is the wrong size.*

6.6.2.2.2 AFTER INTRODUCTORY PHRASES, such as gerund, infinitive, participial, and prepositional phrases. These phrases normally must be followed by a comma.

> *To mark the start of the festivities, Mr. Beacon will announce this year's winners.*
> Infinitive phrase Prepositional phrase

> *Pushed beyond endurance, the athletes gave up.*
> Participial phrase

> *This company supports donating time for charity.*
> Gerund phrase

Exceptions:

(1) Very short prepositional phrases:

> *By noon he was on his way home.*

(2) A phrase that represents the subject or is part of the predicate:

> *Helping with the luggage (subject) comes first.*

> *He was helping with the luggage (predicate) all day.*

6.6.2.3 ITEMS IN A SERIES of words, phrases, or short clauses are separated by commas.

SERIES OF WORDS: *He needs information, opinions, and support.*

SERIES OF PHRASES:

He will meet with the clerks, get the necessary information, and ask for support.

SERIES OF SHORT CLAUSES:

He met with the clerks, they gave him the information, and he asked the manager for support.

Exceptions:

(a) COMMAS WITHIN SERIES. When items within a series contain commas, then separate the items with semicolons.

> *Sean is from Dublin, Ireland; Jean is from Nice, France; and Jack is from Oakland, California.*

(b) SERIES OF LONG CLAUSES. A series of long clauses should be separated by semicolons.

6.6.2.4 NONRESTRICTIVE PHRASES AND CLAUSES are set off with commas. They are not essential to the meaning of the sentence, but merely give additional information. Restrictive phrases and clauses are essential to the meaning of the sentence, so they are not set off with commas.

Nonrestrictive:

Helen, who is skilled at delegation, was promoted to department head last week.

Restrictive:

Managers who are skilled at delegation move ahead faster.

Nonrestrictive:

My article on noise pollution, which I co-authored with James, was published.

Restrictive:

The article that I co-authored with James was published.

6.6.2.5 PARENTHETICAL EXPRESSIONS are sometimes called *interrupters* or *asides* and are normally set off with commas.

We will, needless to say, vote against the measure.

Exceptions.

(a) DASHES FOR EMPHASIS. When you want to emphasize the expression, set it off with dashes. To make a dash, use two hyphens with no spaces, or use a hyphen with a space before and after it.

We will—without a doubt—vote against the measure.

(b) PARENTHESES FOR SUBORDINATION. When you want to de-emphasize the expression, enclose it in parentheses. Note: Punctuation rules for the end of a parenthetical phrase or sentence are the same as the rules for the end of a quotation.

We will vote against the measure (needless to say).

6.6.2.6 EXPRESSIONS THAT CONTRAST, LIMIT, OR OPPOSE are set off with commas.

Contrasting:

Let's have pizza, not lasagna, for lunch.

Limiting:

I can talk, but only for moment, and then I must go.

Opposing:

The more you put into the class, the more you'll get out of it.

6.6.2.7 OMITTED WORDS are indicated with commas when the context of the sentence clearly indicates there are omitted word(s).

Last June we sold 325 vases; this June, only 260.

6.6.2.8 NOUNS OF DIRECT ADDRESS, where you are speaking directly to someone, are set off by commas.

> *Boys and girls, please take your seats.*
>
> *I can assure you, Mrs. Glenn, that we will be there on time.*

6.6.2.9 CALENDAR DATES AND TIME ZONES are set off by commas.

> *She will arrive on Monday, December 15, 1989, at 4:30 p.m., CST.*

6.6.2.10 ADDRESSES WITHIN A PARAGRAPH. Each element is separated by a comma.

> *He is now living at 2821 Aster, Fresno, CA 90442, if you care to contact him.*
>
> *I found Paris, Texas, to be quite different from its French counterpart.*

6.6.2.11 TWO OR MORE INDEPENDENT ADJECTIVES are separated by commas. To identify independent adjectives, read them in reverse order putting the word "and" between them; if the sentence has the same meaning and makes sense, the adjectives are independent. If not, the noun and its adjacent adjective must be considered a unit, and the other adjective modifies this unit.

Independent adjectives:

> *You are a loyal, dependable employee. (dependable and loyal employee makes sense)*

Noun/adjective unit:

> *I ordered new business cards. (business and new cards does not make sense)*

6.6.3 SEMICOLONS

6.6.3.1 INDEPENDENT CLAUSES WITHOUT COORDINATING CONJUNCTIONS (*and, or, but, not*) are separated by semicolons, which takes the place of the coordinating conjunction.

> *Jim has called for you at least four or five times today; he won't talk with anyone else.*

6.6.3.2 INDEPENDENT CLAUSES JOINED BY A COORDINATING CONJUNCTION—and one clause contains commas within it—are usually separated by a semicolon for clarity.

> *Barbara, our new sales manager, is in town; but she forgot to bring the catalog you wanted.*

6.6.3.3 INDEPENDENT CLAUSES SEPARATED BY A TRANSITIONAL EXPRESSION (*however, besides, therefore,* etc.) usually require a semicolon before the transitional expression and a comma after it.

> *The needed part arrived today; however, the mechanic cannot make the repairs until Friday.*

Exception: one-syllable transitional expressions (*so, yet, thus, still, then*) do not need to be followed by a comma.

> *The needed part arrived today, so the mechanic can make the repairs.*

6.6.3.4 BEFORE ENUMERATIONS AND EXPLANATIONS. You may frequently want to make a statement, then give examples, explanations, or specifics. Typical transitional words for introducing such explanations are: *such as, for example, for instance, that is.*

> *I can give you many reasons for buying this stock; for instance, . . .*

The introductory statement is followed by a semicolon and the transitional words are followed by a comma.

6.6.4 QUOTATION MARKS

6.6.4.1 **DIRECT QUOTATIONS** are those in which you use the exact words that someone else has used—you quote the person. This section gives suggestions for punctuating direct quotations.

6.6.4.2 **MOST QUOTATIONS ARE PRECEDED BY A COLON.** The colon comes at the end of an introductory sentence or clause. Punctuation varies according to the length of the quotation.

(1) AVERAGE-LENGTH QUOTATIONS of a sentence or two have an introduction followed by a colon or comma. The quote is enclosed in quotation marks.

Arthur Jenson, who is the foremost authority on the subject, says: "At the risk of seeming biased, I must conclude that this type of student is simply not as likely to excel in mathematics."

(2) LONG QUOTATIONS (more than three or four lines of type) are usually blocked in and single-spaced, even in an otherwise double-spaced paper. The introduction is followed by a colon. Quotation marks are not necessary since the change in form indicates quoted material is being used.

Although the Chairman made no comment, President Jonathan Ryker had this to say about the need for assertiveness:

> *You must learn to be assertive with your boss in order to gain respect and to communicate your wants, goals, and requirements. You must be able to assert yourself in every area, from requesting office space to requesting a promotion and raise. You can do this in a tactful, positive way. For example, you can start by asking your boss for an opinion about the goals you should be pursuing. Then you can respond with the goals that you have in mind. This . . .*

(3) SHORT QUOTATIONS of less than one sentence may be incorporated into your own sentences without the introductory comma or colon, and enclosed in quotation marks.

We can just "call on our referent power to see us through," as Dean Surrey would say.

Our economist thinks "the bond market will top out by fall."

6.6.4.3 **END-OF-QUOTATION PUNCTUATION** can be confusing. Does the punctuation mark go inside or outside the quotation mark? Here are the rules:

6.6.4.3.1 PERIODS AND COMMAS always go inside the quotation mark.

John said, "Let's go now," and Bill replied, "I can't leave yet."

6.6.4.3.2 SEMICOLONS AND COLONS always go outside the quotation mark.

John said, "Let's go now"; however, I wanted the following "must-haves":

6.6.4.3.3 QUESTION MARKS AND EXCLAMATION MARKS are placed:

(a) inside the quotation marks if they punctuate only the quotation.

He asked me, "Do you want to go?"

"I can't believe it!" Jean remarked.

(b) outside the quotation marks if they punctuate the entire sentence.

Did you mean it when you said "Let's go home"?

I was shocked when he said "All of you are guilty"!

6.6.4.4 **QUOTATIONS WITHIN QUOTATIONS** call for single quotations marks, typed by using the apostrophe key.

The article went on to state, "There are many managers who, according to Jardim, 'have already worked harder in terms of stress than a 65-year-old man.' "

6.6.4.5 **OMITTED WORDS WITHIN A QUOTE** are shown with an ellipsis, which is a series of three spaced periods. If the omission occurs at the end of a sentence, the ellipsis is followed by a normal punctuation mark.

The new law reads: "No vendors shall be selected until the open bidding process has been completed . . . ."

6.6.4.6 **TITLES OF CHAPTERS, ARTICLES, MOVIES, LECTURES, AND SONGS** are usually placed in quotes.

6.6.4.7 **NAMES OF BOOKS, MAGAZINES, NEWSPAPERS, AND PAMPHLETS** are usually not placed in quotes. Instead they may be italicized, underscored, or placed in all capital letters.

6.6.5 THE APOSTROPHE

6.6.5.1 **FORMING POSSESSIVES AND CONTRACTIONS** are the most common uses of the apostrophe.

6.6.5.2 **FORMING THE POSSESSIVE OF NOUNS, SINGULAR AND PLURAL,** can be confusing.

Here is the question

Do I show possession by adding an apostrophe and *s*? *Joan's book.*

Or do I add only an apostrophe? *The Joneses' book*

Mentally make an *of* phrase using the possessor and the object possessed, as illustrated below. Then follow the rule that applies.

6.6.5.2.1 WORD DOES NOT END IN *S*. When a noun, singular or plural, does *not* end with a pronounced *s,* add an apostrophe *s* to make it possessive.

Bill's opinion is important to me. This is the children's playroom.

of tests: *opinion of Bill; playroom of the children.*

Possessor's name does not end in *s*, so add an apostrophe and *s*.

6.6.5.2.2 WORD ENDS WITH *S*. When a noun, singular or plural, ends with a pronounced *s,* you usually add only an apostrophe to make it possessive.

This is Mr. Jones' wife, Bea.

The Joneses' idea of a good time is to play bridge.

of tests: *wife of Mr. Jones; the idea of the Joneses.*

Possessor's name ends in s, so add only an apostrophe.

6.6.5.2.3 SINGULAR NOUN ENDS WITH *S*. Some singular nouns that end with a pronounced *s* need an additional *s* sound when the possessive is formed in order to make sense; add an apostrophe and *s* in such cases.

> *I will have this class's term papers graded by Monday. Give me your boss's address.*

of tests: *papers of this class; address of your boss*

6.6.5.2.4 INANIMATE OBJECTS generally do not have a possessive case. instead of using the possessive form, use an *of* phrase to show possession.

Incorrect: *The paper's sections.*

Correct: *The sections of the paper.*

6.6.5.2.5 EXCEPTIONS TO THE INANIMATE OBJECTS RULE: time, distance, value, and celestial bodies.

Time: She will be here in one week's time.

Distance: The keys were only an arm's length away.

Value: You have 50 cents' worth of candy.

Celestial bodies: The sun's rays can burn.

6.6.5.3 COMPOUND NOUNS are made possessive by having the last word show possession.

Incorrect: *It is my mother's-in-law birthday.*

Correct: *It is my mother-in-law's birthday.*

6.6.5.4 TWO OR MORE NOUNS may be made possessive as follows:

6.6.5.2.4 TWO PARTIES HAVE JOINT POSSESSION of an item(s). The one mentioned last is the one you make into a possessive.

> *Steven and Linda's new home is beautiful.*

6.6.5.2.5 TWO PARTIES HAVE INDIVIDUAL POSSESSION of separate items. Each party is made into a possessive.

> *The Bryants' and the Joneses' houses have similar entryways.*

6.6.5.5 A NOUN OR PRONOUN BEFORE A GERUND (an " *–ing* " verb used as a noun) should be possessive.

> *Don's <u>typing</u> of the letter started a new work pattern.*

> *Your <u>offering</u> to help me was a thoughtful gesture.*

6.6.5.6 POSSESSIVE PRONOUNS DO NOT NEED APOSTROPHES. Some personal pronouns already show possession: *its, theirs, whose, yours.*

- *It's* means it is.
- *Who's* means who is.
- *Your's* and *their's* are never correct.

6.6.5.7 A CONTRACTION INCLUDES AN APOSTROPHE in place of an omitted letter(s) and space(s) between two words.

For example, in the contraction *she's,* the apostrophe is substituted for the letter *"i"* in *"is,"* as well as for the space between *"she"* and *"is."*

In the phrase *sugar 'n' spice,* the first apostrophe stands for the *a* in *and,* and the second apostrophe stands for the *d.* Two apostrophes are necessary because the deleted letters (and space, in some instances) are not consecutive.

weren't	*were not*
don't	*do not*
we're	*we are*
'95	*1995*

6.6.5.8 OTHER USES OF THE APOSTROPHE include:

6.6.5.8.1 PLURALS OF LETTERS: *a's, b's, c's, D's, E's*

Note: The plurals of numbers do not need the apostrophe: *9s,10s, 1990s*

6.6.5.8.2 SYMBOL FOR FEET in tables and charts: *9' x 12'*

6.6.6 OTHER PUNCTUATION

6.6.6.1 THE HYPHEN is used in these instances:

in numerals   *twenty-one; three-fourths*

with some prefixes   *self-esteem, co-worker*

to replace to or through   *May 1-5; pages 2-15*

to divide a word at the end of a line

in compound adjectives   entry-level course, well-deserved praise

in a series of hyphenated words having the same ending

This class is for first-, second-, and third-year students.

6.6.6.2 THE DASH is used to give an interrupting element greater emphasis than setting it apart with commas or parentheses would do. Use the dash sparingly. There are two acceptable ways to form the dash on the typewriter or computer:

6.6.6.2.1 TWO HYPHENS between words. Leave no space before, between, or after. Your computer program may convert these two hyphens to one long dash.

There was the valley--the most beautiful I had ever seen--lying cool and peaceful below.

I recommend Paradise Valley Tools--they're only two blocks from your office--because they have the best selection of tools.

6.6.6.2.2 SPACE-HYPHEN-SPACE. Type one hyphen for the dash; insert a space before and after the hyphen.

There is only one way to go - up.

Rice, beans, gravy - this was our usual dinner.

6.7 WRITING NUMBERS: FIGURES OR WORDS?

TYPICAL QUESTIONS ABOUT USING NUMBERS in business letters and reports concern how to write them—whether to use figure form or word form. The rules are based on business needs and considerations.

6.7.1   THE BASIC RULES

6.7.1.1   THE BASIC NUMBER RULES ARE SIMPLE. Most of the confusion over use of figures versus words comes from the exceptions to the basic rules. Since there are good reasons for those exceptions, you will need to learn them.

6.7.1.2   USE WORDS FOR THE NUMBERS *ONE* **THROUGH** *TEN*—unless some other rule applies.

> *Here are ten reasons.*

6.7.1.3   USE FIGURES FOR THE NUMBERS ABOVE *TEN*—unless some other rule prevails.

We ordered 11 cases of wine.

6.7.1.4   NUMBERS THAT BEGIN A SENTENCE MUST HAVE WORD FORM. If it's a long number that you cannot write in one or two words, change the sentence structure.

Correct: *Twenty-five girls danced the hula.*

Incorrect: *386 shoppers received free samples.*

Correct: *We gave free samples to 386 shoppers.*

6.7.1.5   USE BOTH FIGURES AND WORDS FOR LARGE ROUND NUMBERS in the millions or billions:

2 million people   5-1/4 billion dollars   3.2 trillion stars

6.7.1.6   SEPARATE BY A COMMA TWO INDEPENDENT FIGURES that appear consecutively in a sentence*:*

> *In 1988, 65 clients filed complaints.*

6.7.1.7   WHEN TWO CONSECUTIVE NUMBERS MODIFY a following noun, use word form for the noun that can be expressed in the fewest words, and use figure form for the other number. If both are the same length, spell out the first one.

> *Let's get twenty 250-watt bulbs.*

> *We have 20 sixty-watt bulbs on hand.*

6.7.1.8   THE PLURAL OF A NUMBER is formed by adding *s*.

> *1800s*   *9s*

6.7.2 *EXCEPTIONS TO THE BASIC NUMBERS RULES*

6.7.2.1 **WEIGHTS AND MEASURES—USE FIGURES** for quick comprehension. Words indicating the units of weight or measure, such as *ounces* or *inches*) are written out, not abbreviated except in visual aids (tables, charts) and business forms.

> *My office measures only 10 feet, 5 inches by 11 feet, 2 inches.*

6.7.2.2 **NUMBERS COMBINED WITH WORDS** to form a unit are written in figures. Page numbers, model numbers, policy numbers, and serial numbers are some common combinations. The word preceding the number is usually capitalized. When the word *number* is a part of the combination, it is abbreviated (except when it starts a sentence).

> *We need repairs on Jetmotor Model No. 17, Serial No. 3382664.*

> *I am enclosing Policy No. 83421098.*

Exceptions to the need for the word No.:   page, paragraph, line, size, verse.

> *Look at page 30, paragraph 2, line 25.*

> *I'm reading from verses 4 through 8.*

6.7.2.3 **PERIODS OF TIME** that can be expressed in one or two words are usually written in word form, while larger numbers are usually written in figure form.

> *The first battle lasted only three days, but this one has been raging for 135 days.*

Exception: time-period data dealing with business contracts call for figures, which are more noticeable within a sentence.

We can give you a 10 percent loan to be repaid in 36 months.

6.7.2.4 **AGES AND ANNIVERSARIES TAKE WORD FORM** if they can be expressed in one or two words.

> *He will be seventy-five on his fiftieth wedding anniversary.*

Exceptions: Figures are used for a person's age when in these instances:

(a) AGE AFTER NAME. The age appears directly after a person's name.

> *Jill Bidwell, 25, is a typical employee.*

(b) AGE IN YEARS, MONTHS. The age is expressed in years, months, and sometimes day

> *I retired when I was 55 years 6 months 9 days old.*

(c) LEGAL OR TECHNICAL AGE. The age is used in a legal or technical sense.

> *This law applies to residents over age 55.*

6.7.2.5 **FRACTIONS ARE USUALLY WRITTEN IN WORD FORM.**

> *Dan completed the work in three fourths of an hour.*

Exceptions. Fractions are written in figure form in these instances:

(a) the fraction is combined with whole numbers.

> *The hole is 6-5/8 inches in diameter.*

(b) the fraction is long and would be awkward to write in words

Less than 1/64 of an inch off center . . .

(c) the fraction is used for technical purposes.

Please send the 3/4-inch dowels by air freight.

6.7.2.6 ORDINAL NUMBERS (FIRST, SECOND, THIRD) ARE WRITTEN IN WORDS if they can be written in one or two words.

a fifteenth-century desk

Exceptions

(a) numbered street names above ten.

25 East First Street   6232 44th Street

(b) dates appearing before the month or standing alone.

the 25tb of December   He will arrive on the 14th.

6.7.2.7 PERCENTAGES ARE WRITTEN IN FIGURES, followed by the word *percent.*

The discount for members is 5 percent.

TEAM PROJECTS can be fun and exciting if handled well, and they can be frustrating for conscientious students when teammates don't carry their load. This chapter includes the following aspects of team projects:

7.1 GENERAL TIPS

7.1.1   **TYPES OF ASSIGNMENTS** given on a team basis vary widely. Informal study groups are often encouraged and occasionally required. Course projects assigned on a group basis include (1) doing business research (2) conducting and reporting on field observation and/or interviews, and (3) analyzing business cases, and (4) developing business plans, marketing plans, advertising campaigns, public relations campaigns, computer programs, wage and salary systems, and similar business projects.

7.1.2   **ENHANCE YOUR LEARNING.** Team projects provide good preparation for productive teamwork in a business career, which invariably involves group effort. Moreover, it can be an immediate help in mastering course work. When you discuss newly-acquired knowledge with others, you are likely to retain it. And when you apply that knowledge to team projects, you develop new skills, including interpersonal skills. In addition, you get to learn from team members about their areas of expertise and to coach others, using your areas of expertise. This experience becomes a part of your set of business skills, readily available to use in career situations that call for similar responses.

7.1.3   **THE FIVE PHASES** of team development that most successful teams move through are as follows:

(1) Getting to know each other better

(2) Deciding on ground rules, goals, and tasks

(3) Competing for power and influence

(4) Cooperating well enough to do an adequate job

(5) Cooperating enthusiastically.

7.1.4   **FOCUS ON END PRODUCT.** To do an adequate job, the group must organize and evaluate individuals' work and integrate it into a quality end product. Frequently the team must solve problems that could block completion of a successful project. Suggestions for moving through these phases and overcoming problems are given in this section.

7.2 FORMING THE GROUP

7.2.1 **GET TO KNOW POTENTIAL MEMBERS** in the class, if you can. It pays to become acquainted with as many class members as possible. Begin this process the first day of class, so you will have time to learn how people might function as team members.

7.2.2 **DETERMINE THE BEST GROUP SIZE.** If the instructor allows class members to form their own groups, the first step is to determine the upper and lower limits, if any, of group size. Groups of four to seven people usually work best. With fewer than four people, it is difficult to get enough input and variety—and the loss of one member might undermine group effort and output. With more than seven people, it becomes difficult to get everyone together, to coordinate the effort, and to have enough time in group discussions for everyone to fully participate. Also, it becomes too easy for shy members to "hide out" within the group and not speak up.

7.2.3 **CONSIDER GROUP COMPOSITION.** Teaming up with social friends may be a mistake unless such friends are committed, dependable, and will make positive contributions to the group. Consider suggesting to a friend that you split up for teamwork in order to get to know some other students.

7.2.4 **AIM FOR A DIVERSE TEAM.** Select members with the goal of having a variety of skills, backgrounds, values, and working styles. This may not be comfortable but it can be interesting and you may learn a great deal from people unlike yourself. Although members must be compatible enough to work well together, diversity can provide members with the opportunity to learn how to resolve group conflict.

A team needs both a leader(s) and followers, but if a leader is so dominant that he or she intimidates followers, then teamwork may suffer. On the other hand, such situations offer a chance to practice tactful confrontation of problems that members are causing, group resolution of problems, and development of a cohesive, productive team.

7.2.5 **CONSIDER MEMBERS' POTENTIAL CONTRIBUTIONS.** Look for members who can contribute something special to the group, such as specific knowledge and skills from work experience or from previous courses, or specific strengths in areas such as math, computer usage, writing, and speaking. The most important contribution is commitment, dependability, and productivity. Getting results, and getting them on time, counts the most.

7.2.6 **CONSIDER HOW MEMBERS WILL COMMUNICATE.** Whether it's by e-mail, telephone, or face-to-face meetings, you must establish whether potential team members will be able to participate.

7.2.7 **THE TIMING OF TEAM FORMATION** can affect its success. If the instructor tells class members to form their own teams, take the initiative early in the course to start organizing a group. That way, you'll have a better chance of enlisting people you think have the most to offer—before they join other teams. Once formed, the group can get a head start on the project.

7.3 AGREEING ON GOALS AND GROUND RULES

7.3.1 **AGREE ON HOW TO COMMUNICATE AND INTERACT.** Your very first task as a team is to exchange information about how, where, and when you can communicate with one another. This may include e-mail addresses, telephone numbers, fax numbers, addresses, and schedules.

7.3.2 **AGREE ON PRELIMINARY GOALS.** These should include (1) time targets, (2) the type of individual assignments to be made, (3) the quality and quantity of work to be done, (4) a specific description of the end product, and (5) how the team will communicate and interact. Goals may be tentative at first and refined later as members' abilities and the instructor's requirements are clarified.

7.3.3 **DETERMINE GROUND RULES** for working together and what will happen to members who violate ground rules. Ground rules are discussed more fully later.

7.3.4 **AGREE ON DATES, TIMES, AND ROUTINES.** Make a tentative schedule of dates that include target dates, or deadline dates for each phase of the project. The group can avoid confusion and absenteeism by establishing set times and routines.

7.3.5 **DECIDE ON GROUP MEETINGS.** Do you need to have some meetings outside of class time? Schedule these meetings as soon as possible. Stick to the starting time to discourage lateness. budget the meeting time by having a written agenda—to discourage digressions and other time-wasters.

7.3.6 **AGREE ON ATTENDANCE REQUIREMENTS.** Attendance at all the team meetings should be required. Legitimate excuses should be designated. The number of absences, legitimate or otherwise, that should trigger removal from the group should be agreed upon in advance.

7.3.7 **DECIDE HOW THE GROUP WILL BE LED** and governed. When the leadership function is not decided in advance, power plays and resentments usually develop. It usually works best to elect one person to chair meetings and oversee the coordination of the work. However, the group may prefer to give each person a different coordination function with the chair monitoring overall coordination. Or, members may want to rotate the chair function meeting-by-meeting or month-by-month; still, someone should have coordination responsibility.

7.3.8 **AGREE ON ASSIGNMENTS PROCEDURES.** Decide when and how individual members will take on assignments. This will depend on the nature of the project(s) to be completed, but make some ground rules in the beginning or as soon as the instructor clarifies the assignment. A key decision is whether the leader will make assignments or whether this will be a group decision.

7.3.9 **PREPARATORY WORK** that each member should complete before each group meeting should be discussed and designated as early in the process and as clearly as possible.

7.3.10 **AGREE ON GROUNDS FOR DISMISSAL** from the group. The most common complaint students make about group assignments is that some group members don't do their share. Early warning signals include absenteeism from class and from group meetings and failure to meet interim target dates for individual assignments. As a result other members may

(1) have to do others' work for them

(2) receive a lowered project grade when the group project suffers

The group needs a "last-resort" procedure for protecting itself from unproductive members. This unpleasant procedure is easier to implement if the ground rules for dismissal are agreed upon early in the process. It is wise to clear such procedures with the instructor. If the group expels a member, the instructor must take action, such as

(a) assigning the member to another group

(b) giving the member an individual assignment

(c) giving the member a failing grade on the project

7.3.11 AGREE ON PARTICIPATING AT MEETINGS. Speaking up should be encouraged. Monopolizing the floor, intimidating others, or failing to speak should be discouraged. The Chair could be instructed to monitor member contributions and behavior but should not squelch innovative ideas, even though they seem weird or illogical to some.

7.3.12 AGREE ON HOW TO ACKNOWLEDGE MEMBER CONTRIBUTIONS. Respecting what people have to say, and giving them credit for their contributions sets the tone for an enthusiastic group atmosphere. For example, the group may decide to let members who make unique contributions present those ideas when the group makes its class presentation.

7.3.13 AGREE TO BE OPEN AND FRANK when discussing important group issues. For example, a group member is digressing or missing the point. The team can decide ahead of time that the Chair or a member will speak up in these instances. Members can agree not to get upset or hold grudges when another speaks up openly and frankly, but with respect, for the group's benefit.

7.3.14 AGREE ON CONFLICT RESOLUTION PROCEDURES. Typical sources of conflict are personality clashes, power or leadership struggles, and differing opinions about what to do or how to do it. Dealing with such conflicts is discussed later.

7.4 ORGANIZING AND EVALUATING THE WORK

7.4.1 REFINE GROUP GOALS, making them specific enough that everyone will know whether they have been met when target dates roll around. Try to incorporate quantity and quality standards (ways of measuring the output) so there will be agreement about how far over or under the stated goals the actual results fall. Decide when and how members will integrate their individual work into a finished end product.

7.4.2 SET INTERIM GOALS AND TARGET DATES. If the instructor's deadline date for submission of the group project is the only target date the group sets, it is almost certain to have problems. The earlier you detect problems, (e.g., a member does not produce or his work is unacceptable) the better chance you have of solving problems in time to complete a successful project.

7.4.3 DETERMINE AREAS OF SPECIALIZATION of each member. Look at special knowledge, skills, background, experience, and talents of members that may apply to the group's work.

7.4.4 AGREE ON PRESENTATION FORMATS, such as documentation style, sequencing, supplementary parts, and exhibits for case analyses or reports. Agree on how members will make a joint oral presentation. Decide who will introduce the project and the team members; the sequencing, format, and length of individual presentations; who will make concluding remarks; and how audience questions will be fielded.

7.4.5 MAKE INDIVIDUAL ASSIGNMENTS. Determine how the work can be divided in order to take advantage of members' abilities and to meet members' needs. Make assignments with similar time and effort requirements so there is a fair division of the work.

7.4.6 DECIDE IF INDIVIDUAL GOALS need to be set - with quality and quantity standards and time targets, using procedures similar to those used in setting group goals. Some projects require such diversified efforts that group goals may be inadequate.

7.4.7 **CONSIDER DUPLICATE OR PAIRED** assignments when:

(1) certain members are more productive working as pairs

(2) the assignment is especially complex or difficult

(3) at least two people in the group need to gain knowledge in the area in order to complete the project

(4) a double-check is needed for a crucial area

(5) a student is weak in a particular area and needs or wants help from a member who is stronger in the area.

7.4.8 **CONSIDER THE NEED TO DEVELOP MEMBERS' WEAK AREAS.** This may be desirable when the group will be working on various projects throughout the semester. Members usually work in their strong areas in the beginning. Later it may be helpful for them to take an assignment in a weak area, perhaps pairing up with someone stronger in that area.

7.4.9 **EVALUATE THE WORK.** The team should evaluate the work of each member, as well as the overall team product. Does a member's contribution fit in properly with the group package? Does it meet quality and quantity standards? If not, what must be done to bring it up to the standards? Does the contributor need help from another member? Should the work be reassigned to another member? Determine what should be done and set new time targets for completion.

When evaluating a member's work, never belittle the person. Focus instead on the work—and take a problem-solving approach. For example, you can ask such questions as

- What is lacking here? What is needed to bring it up to standards?
- How can we make this work better? What needs to be done?
- Does the team member need help? Who can help?

7.4.10 **CONSIDER SELECTING AN EDITOR** or coordinator to oversee the evaluation process. This person could evaluate individuals' work and coordinate the process of editing, refining, and integrating the work into an excellent finished product. If a chair has been selected, he or she might perform this function.

7.4.11 **PEER EVALUATIONS** are sometimes required by the instructor. Most students have difficulty giving written evaluations of their classmates' performances. Try to be as objective as possible by suspending your personal feelings about the person and focusing on the end result, the work itself. Note what works. Be respectful and tactful, but honest in what you think is missing or below standards and what could improve the work.

7.5 MAKING GROUP DECISIONS

7.5.1 **IDENTIFY THE TYPE OF DECISION** that the group needs to make. Most decisions fall into one of four basic types.

7.5.1.1 EXPLORATORY DECISIONS TO FIND WAYS OF MEETING A GOAL. Often a group must find ways and means of reaching an agreed-upon goal. Decide on the criteria (standards) that a good action plan (ways and means) should meet, brainstorm to explore as many alternative methods as possible, then decide which alternative best meets the criteria.

> **Example**. *The goal is to analyze an assigned case. The group must agree on an analytical approach. The criteria might be that the approach chosen must (a) not require gathering data from primary sources and (b) data from secondary sources must be limited to what is available in the campus library.*

7.5.1.2 NEGOTIATED DECISIONS TO RESOLVE CONFLICTS. Sometimes team members don't agree on what the goal should be. Other times they disagree on how to achieve a goal. Sometimes group members take sides. Each side is committed to a different decision, even though the values or logic of both may be generally acceptable to all.

This situation calls for an impartial leader or chair who follows parliamentary procedures. If the number of people in the two factions is unequal, each group should have the right to veto any vote they do not agree with. The goal is to reach a compromise acceptable to both sides. The leader should encourage participants to express their viewpoints frankly and to be open to opposing viewpoints and compromise solutions. Encourage team members to see the conflict as a healthy and natural process for free-thinking individuals, rather than as a disaster. The group may come up with a better decision because alternatives will be explored more rigorously.

7.5.1.3 ROUTINE DECISIONS. When the group has already formulated adequate rules or procedures to provide a framework for making a choice, the decision is considered routine and rarely require much of the group's time or energy.

> **Example**. *One group member wants another member to interview some business executives to gain certain information that might help analyze a case. The group has previously agreed that gathering data from primary sources will not be required.*

7.5.1.4 EMERGENCY DECISIONS TO PREVENT OR HANDLE A CRISIS. Certain problem situations require clear, quick, and precise action to prevent or handle a crisis. The group should try to anticipate the various types of events that could conceivably create a crisis. The types of action to be taken in such situations should be agreed upon in advance, so there will be no complete surprises.

> **Example**. *Setting goals and target dates, agreeing on ground rules, and determining the grounds for removing members from the group are all parts of a crisis-prevention plan. The major crisis in this situation would be failure to have an acceptable completed project on the due date.*

7.5.2 DEVELOP GUIDELINES TO RESOLVE DECISION CONFLICTS. Members may disagree about substance (what to do) or about procedures (how to do it). Develop guidelines at the beginning. Agree on a democratic method for making decisions. Work for a negotiated decision that all can support. If necessary, the group can put it to a vote. Even-numbered groups may have to cope with a tie vote. Decide ahead of time on the way to break ties, such as drawing straws or asking the instructor to vote.

7.6 OVERCOMING SOME COMMON PROBLEMS

7.6.1 THE GROUP BECOMES TOO SMALL OR WEAK. Members may believe that the team cannot produce good results. Talk with the instructor about possible solutions, such as:

(1) merging with another small group

(2) enlisting a member or two from an overly large group

(3) breaking up the group and letting each member join another group.

7.6.2 THE GROUP IS TOO LARGE. Perhaps team member cannot find a mutually agreeable meeting time or place. Perhaps members are not getting enough out of team meetings, or the goals are not being achieved. Consider forming committees or sub-groups. Perhaps most work can be done in small group meetings with less frequent general meetings. Or after a short general meeting, the group breaks into sub-groups.

7.6.3 PERSONALITY CLASHES DEVELOP. Agreeing on ground rules in the beginning helps to keep some clashes from sabotaging group efforts. A frank, honest atmosphere where problems can be openly aired can also help. However, maintaining such an atmosphere is difficult with members who are accustomed to game-playing, manipulating, and running hidden agendas. Such people are often unaware of their motives and resist efforts to uncover them. Other members can be most helpful by

- Dealing with a person's actions or behavior and its effects

- Not attacking a persons' motives or personality

- Basing decisions on the team's needs for productivity

7.6.4   **POWER OR LEADERSHIP STRUGGLES DEVELOP.** This problem can often be prevented by agreeing in the beginning about how the group will be led and governed. If power struggles still develop, consider rotating the role of chair.

7.6.5   **USE CONFLICT RESOLUTION TECHNIQUES.** Regardless of the source of the conflict, it can usually be resolved by following some basic principles:

7.6.5.1 EXPLORE OPPOSING VIEWS. The leader, or members, can help by pointing out what is to be gained by exposing and resolving the conflict rather than letting it fester. Be sure the parties to the conflict are ready to resolve it; otherwise, the time spent may be wasted. Set ground rules to be sure each side has equal time to present its views. See that dominant members do not intimidate timid ones. Encourage openness and willingness to listen to all sides without judgment during the airing phase.

7.6.5.2 ISOLATE THE CAUSE OF THE CONFLICT. Is it faulty communication, resentment of another's past behavior, conflicting goals, conflicting methods, or other conflicting opinions? Sometimes the real cause is hidden under another *reason* that the person thinks is more acceptable.

7.6.5.3 LOOK FOR A SOLUTION. Aim for the solution that will be best for the group, best for both parties, and unlikely to create future conflicts.

Index